A Year with ‘Ā’ishah رضي الله عنها

The Mother of The Believers

ABDUR RAHEEM KIDWAI

A Year with ʿĀ'ishah ﵂: the Mother of the Believers

First published in England by
Kube Publishing Ltd
Markfield Conference Centre Ratby Lane,
Markfield, Leicestershire LE67 9SY
United Kingdom

Tel: +44 (0) 1530 249230
Website: www.kubepublishing.com
Email: info@kubepublishing.com

Cataloguing-in-Publication Data is available from the British Library

ISBN 978-1-84774-227-8 *casebound*
ISBN 978-1-84774-228-5 *ebook*

Editor: Umm Marwan Ibrahim & Mokrane Guezzou
Cover Design and Internal concept Design: Afreen Fazil (Jaryah Studio)
Typesetting: Nasir Cadir
Printed by: Elma Basim, Turkey

Contents

Transliteration Table

Arabic Consonants

Initial, unexpressed medial and final: ء ’

ا	a	د	d	ض	ḍ	ك	k
ب	b	ذ	dh	ط	ṭ	ل	l
ت	t	ر	r	ظ	ẓ	م	m
ث	th	ز	z	ع	‘	ن	n
ج	j	س	s	غ	gh	هـ	h
ح	ḥ	ش	sh	ف	f	و	w
خ	kh	ص	ṣ	ق	q	ي	y

With a *shaddah*, both medial and final consonants are doubled.

Vowels, diphthongs, etc.

Short:	ـَ	a	ـِ	i	ـُ	u
Long:	ـَا	ā	ـِي	ī	ـُو	ū
Diphthongs:			ـَوْ	aw		
			ـَىْ	ay		

Introduction

This Hadith anthology, *A Year with 'Ā'ishah* ﷺ seeks to acquaint readers, with the life-giving message embodied in the Prophet's ﷺ Ahadith, and to pay tribute to the genius of the Prophet's ﷺ beloved wife, 'Ā'ishah ﷺ, who also holds the distinction of being the daughter of the Prophet's most sincere and faithful Companion, Abu Bakr Siddiq ﷺ.

Among the many Companions who have narrated Hadith, 'Ā'ishah ﷺ stands out above others on the following counts:

» On her authority, as many as 2210 Ahadith have been recorded in the authentic Hadith collections. According to some scholars, her juristic opinions account for 25 of the *fiqhi* (juristic) rulings of the day.

» As she observed first-hand and from very close quarters the Prophet Muhammad's ﷺ conduct and way of life, the range of the topics covered in the Ahadith narrated by her is diverse and vast. Her personal account of the Prophet's ﷺ every day domestic life helps us appreciate better, the excellence of the Prophet ﷺ as a perfect human being. Her description of the Prophet's ﷺ way of life presents before us a graphic, comprehensive picture of the Prophet ﷺ as the role model to be emulated by us in all aspects of our life.

» No other Companion of the Prophet ﷺ matches even remotely with her in the quantum of time she spent in the Prophet's ﷺ company.

» Among the Prophet's ﷺ wives too, she stood out above others in terms of her perfect understanding with and service to the Prophet ﷺ, her insights into faith, her transmitting Hadith and her role as a mentor and teacher for the younger Companions and their Successors who being born after the Prophet's ﷺ demise, did not have the good fortune of interacting with the Prophet ﷺ.

» In most of the Ahadith related by her, she has provided some valuable background information or rationale behind the Prophet's ﷺ sayings, which is reflective of her thorough familiarity with the Islamic faith and practices and her own intelligence and discerning ability.

» There are several reports on record, indicating her sound critique on some Hadith reports narrated by others. (For details see Hakim's *Mustadark* and Suyuti's *Ayn Al-Isaba fi Istidrak 'Ā'ishah* رضي الله عنها *'ala Al-Sahaba)*. Since she was well-versed with the Prophet's ﷺ life and actions, she was in the best position to correct occasional discrepancies or half-truths which had crept into some versions of Hadith. In so doing, she accomplished invaluable service in preserving the true spirit of Islam.

» Take the following as an instance in point. When someone told her this Hadith related by Abu Huraira رضي الله عنه: "The Prophet ﷺ said that there is an evil omen in woman, horse and house," she pointed out a serious lacuna in the above report. She explained that the Prophet ﷺ had said that "Jews believe that there is a bad omen in woman, horse and house." Abu Huraira رضي الله عنه had entered the Prophet's ﷺ house in the middle of his above saying and did not, rather could not note the opening part of his saying owing to his late arrival. So he generalised what the Prophet ﷺ had said in particular about the Jews.

» Her close, personal association with the Prophet ﷺ helped her rectify some misperceptions which had gained general currency. When she learnt about this report attributed to the Prophet ﷺ that if a woman, donkey or dog passes in front of a person offering prayer, his/her prayer is rendered null and void, she emphatically rejected the above report on the basis of her everyday life experience. She pointed out that the Prophet ﷺ used to pray at night while she lay asleep right in front of him, as there was no space in the small room which the Prophet ﷺ shared with her. She condemned the misogynistic streak in the above report, degrading women to the level of a donkey or dog. Her assertion, based on her first-hand observation, swiftly busted a negative stereotype about women's alleged impurity. Notwithstanding her overflowing love and adoration for the Prophet ﷺ, she rejected downright any report implying that the Prophet ﷺ had seen Allah ﷻ or that he knew all that which belongs to the realm of *ghayb* (things beyond man's sense perception). In so doing, she cited the Qur'anic verses which rule out the Prophet's ﷺ suprahuman traits.

» Her other major achievement consists in raising and ensuring the issue of gender equality. She forwarded to the Prophet ﷺ cases involving woman's oppression, misery and victimisation. This elicited the Prophet's ﷺ rulings which enforced gender justice and egalitarianism. The following incident illustrates this sharply.

When she noted the shabby appearance of her regular visitor, the wife of 'Uthman b. Maz'un ؓ, she enquired its cause, for he was an affluent person.

'Uthman's wife explained that 'Uthman had taken to the path of monasticism, prayed throughout nights and fasted consecutively, while neglecting her and his children. Immediately she brought it to the Prophet's ﷺ attention who visited 'Uthman and rebuked him thus: "O 'Uthman, we are not asked to lead the life of a hermit. Is my way of life not worth-following for you? Of all of you, I fear Allah most, abide by His commands yet I fulfil my obligations to my wives and family." Accordingly 'Uthman mended his ways (*Musnad Ahmad,* 6, 226).

Likewise, when a lady Companion informed her that her father had married her to someone, without taking her into confidence, 'Ā'ishah رضي الله عنها presented her case before the Prophet ﷺ. He summoned her father and was about to revoke that marriage. However, she requested the Prophet ﷺ not to proceed any further. For she had achieved her purpose of alerting and sensitising people to the importance of securing first the girl's consent for her marriage. This incident went a long way in promoting gender parity. (Nasai, "*Kitab Al-Nikah*").

Abu Sa'id Khudri رضي الله عنه, a Companion, asked for and put on new clothes when he was in the throes of death, remarking: "The Prophet ﷺ said that the dead will be raised alive in the clothes which they had worn while they died." When this report reached 'Ā'ishah رضي الله عنها, she clarified: "May Allah سبحانه وتعالى have mercy on Abu

Sa'id! The Prophet ﷺ had not spoken of clothes. His comment was that the dead will be resurrected with reference to their deeds."

» Apart from being an astute Hadith scholar, she was adept also in oratory, poetry, history, jurisprudence and medicine.

» Her illustrious life provides valuable guidance about how to lead one's life as an excellent wife, a widow and a childless woman in adverse financial circumstances.

» As her father, Abu Bakr ؓ and mother, Umm Ruman ؓ were early Muslims, she had the good fortune of opening her eyes in a devout Muslim family, without any trace of the then rampant idolatry and polytheism in Makkah.

» She regularly listened to the Prophet's ﷺ sayings in his sessions with the Companions held every evening in the Prophet's ﷺ mosque where her apartment too, was located. She clarified her queries when the Prophet ﷺ came home after prayer. At her initiative, the Prophet ﷺ set aside a day in a week for his instructions to and interaction with the Muslim women or lady Companions.

» Her generosity in giving charity was phenomenal. The day she received her annual stipend of 12,000 dirham during the era of the rightly guided Caliphs, she gave the entire amount in charity on the same day and had nothing to eat in the evening.

» When 'Amr b. Al 'Aas asked the Prophet ﷺ: "O Messenger of Allah, who do you like most?" Instantly he named 'Ā'ishah. When he asked about his favourite among men, her replied: "'Ā'ishah's father" (Abu Bakr Siddiq). (*Sahih Bukhari*: "Bab Manqib Abi Bakr").

» The Prophet ﷺ is on record saying: "O Allah I avoid injustice to any of my wives (in social interaction and financial transactions), for these decisions are under my control. However, O Allah, forgive me for what is beyond my control (my fondness for 'Ā'ishah)." (Zurqani)

Equally weighty is the Prophet's ﷺ other compliment for her: "There have been many perfect male servants of Allah. Among women, Maryam, the daughter of 'Imran, and Aasia, the wife of Pharaoh hold the coveted status of perfection. 'Ā'ishah excels all women like the *tharid* dish is superior to all other food items." (Bukhari, 3411).

Her love for the Prophet ﷺ was boundless. Although Hassan b. Thabit had taken part in the slander campaign against her, she forgave him, saying: "He had defended the Prophet's ﷺ honour through his poetry when the Makkan polytheistic poets satirised the Prophet ﷺ. So I have forgiven him."

- Some hypocrites in Madina hurled the ignominious slander of sexual misconduct against her. However, Allah ﷻ exonerated her and proclaimed her chastity and innocence through Qur'anic verses (*Al-Nur* 24: 11-19). This constitutes her great distinction in that Allah paid special attention to bear out her impeccable, chaste character.

- Many eminent Companions consulted her, after the Prophet's ﷺ demise, on various juristic issues. Some of them are on record as having paid glowing tributes to her insightful and profound knowledge of Hadith and Shariah. Abu Musa Ash'ari رضي الله عنه a leading Companion, states: "Whenever we were confronted with a thorny issue, we discussed it with 'Ā'ishah رضي الله عنها and were always enriched by her knowledge." (Hakim, *Mustadarak*) Imam Zuhri, a prominent Successor, acclaims her genius thus: "She was a towering scholar and even the distinguished Companions sought her opinion on a variety of issues." (Ibn Sa'ad, *Tabaqat*, 2, 26).

‘Urwa ibn Zubayr a prominent *tabi’i* (Sahaba’s successor) acclaims: “I did not note anyone excelling ‘Ā’ishah ﵂ in the knowledge of the Qur’an, Hadith, Fiqh, history and Arab genealogy.”

» Among those who narrated Hadith on her authority are such illustrious Companions as Abu Bakr Siddiq ﵁, ‘Umar ibn Al-Khattab ﵁, Abu Huraira ﵁, ‘Abdullah ibn ‘Abbas ﵁, Abdullah ibn Umar ﵁ and ‘Amr ibn Al-‘Aas ﵁.

1

عَنْ عَائِشَةَ قَالَتْ: «مَا ضَرَبَ رَسُولُ اللَّهِ صَلَّى اللهُ عَلَيْهِ وَسَلَّمَ خَادِمًا لَهُ قَطُّ وَلَا امْرَأَةً لَهُ قَطُّ وَلَا ضَرَبَ بِيَدِهِ إِلَّا أَنْ يُجَاهِدَ فِي سَبِيلِ اللَّهِ وَمَا نِيلَ مِنْهُ شَيْءٌ فَانْتَقَمَهُ مِنْ صَاحِبِهِ إِلَّا أَنْ تُنْتَهَكَ مَحَارِمُ اللَّهِ عَزَّ وَجَلَّ فَيَنْتَقِمُ لِلَّهِ عَزَّ وَجَلَّ وَمَا عُرِضَ عَلَيْهِ أَمْرَانِ أَحَدُهُمَا أَيْسَرُ مِنَ الْآخَرِ إِلَّا أَخَذَ بِأَيْسَرِهِمَا إِلَّا أَنْ يَكُونَ مَأْثَمًا، فَإِنْ كَانَ مَأْثَمًا كَانَ أَبْعَدَ النَّاسِ مِنْهُ».

(صحيح مسلم ٢٤٥٣٥، مسند أحمد:٢٣٢٧)

Ā'ishah ﵂ said: "The Messenger of Allah ﷺ never hit a servant or any of his wives. Neither did he strike anyone with his hand unless it be during jihad in the way of Allah. And never did he take revenge from any person who slighted him unless the sanctuaries of Allah had been violated in which case he would take revenge for Allah, glorified and exalted is He. And never was he presented with two alternatives except that he chose the easiest of the two unless it be a sin, in which case he would be the farthest person from it."

(*Ṣaḥīḥ Muslim*: 24535, *Musnad Aḥmad*: 2327)

2

عَنْ عَائِشَةَ قَالَتْ: «كُنَّ - النِّسَاءُ - يُصَلِّينَ مَعَ النَّبِيِّ صَلَّى اللهُ عَلَيْهِ وَسَلَّمَ الْغَدَاةَ ثُمَّ يَخْرُجْنَ مُتَلَفِّعَاتٍ بِمُرُوطِهِنَّ لَا يُعْرَفْنَ».

(صحيح البخاري:٣٧٢، صحيح مسلم:٦٤٥، مسند أحمد:٢٥٥٥٢)

'Āishah ﵂ said: "Women used to pray the *Ṣubḥ* prayer with the Prophet ﷺ then leave wrapped up in their sheets without being recognised by anyone."

(*Ṣaḥīḥ al-Bukhārī*: 372, *Ṣaḥīḥ Muslim*: 645, *Musnad Aḥmad*: 25552)

3

عَنْ عَائِشَةَ بَلَغَهَا أَنَّ نَاسًا يَقُولُونَ إِنَّ الصَّلَاةَ يَقْطَعُهَا الْكَلْبُ وَالْحِمَارُ وَالْمَرْأَةُ. قَالَتْ: «أَلَا أَرَاهُمْ قَدْ عَدَلُونَا بِالْكِلَابِ وَالْحُمُرِ. رُبَّمَا رَأَيْتُ رَسُولَ اللَّهِ صَلَّى اللهُ عَلَيْهِ وَسَلَّمَ يُصَلِّي بِاللَّيْلِ وَأَنَا عَلَى السَّرِيرِ بَيْنَهُ وَبَيْنَ الْقِبْلَةِ فَتَكُونُ لِي الْحَاجَةُ فَأَنْسَلُّ مِنْ قِبَلِ رِجْلِ السَّرِيرِ كَرَاهِيَةَ أَنْ أَسْتَقْبِلَهُ بِوَجْهِي».

(صحيح البخاري:٣٨٢، صحيح مسلم:٥١٢، مسند أحمد:٢٤٦٥٤)

On learning that some people were saying that one's prayer becomes void if a dog, donkey or woman walks in front of one, 'Ā'ishah ﵂ stated: "Are they equating us with dogs or donkeys? It often happened that the Messenger of Allah ﷺ would be praying at night while I was in bed, between him and the direction of prayer, and I would slip out to relieve the call of nature, by the foot of the bed because I disliked facing him directly."

(*Ṣaḥīḥ al-Bukhārī:* 382, *Ṣaḥīḥ Muslim*: 512, *Musnad Aḥmad*: 24654)

4

عَنِ الْأَسْوَدِ قَالَ: «قُلْتُ لِعَائِشَةَ مَا كَانَ رَسُولُ اللَّهِ صَلَّى اللهُ عَلَيْهِ وَسَلَّمَ يَصْنَعُ فِي أَهْلِهِ؟» قَالَتْ: «كَانَ فِي مِهْنَةِ أَهْلِهِ فَإِذَا حَضَرَتْ الصَّلَاةُ خَرَجَ إِلَى الصَّلَاةِ».

(صحيح البخاري:٦٧٦، مسند أحمد:٠٣٧٤٢)

Al-Aswad related that he asked ʿĀ'ishah ﷺ what the the Messenger of Allah ﷺ used to do at home, and so she replied: "He helped with the house chores, but when the time for prayer came, he went out to pray."

(*Ṣaḥīḥ al-Bukhārī*: 676, *Musnad Aḥmad*: 24730)

5

عَنْ عَائِشَةَ، عَنْ النَّبِيِّ صَلَّى اللهُ عَلَيْهِ وَسَلَّمَ قَالَ: «أَبْغَضُ الرِّجَالِ الْأَلَدُّ الْخَصِمُ».

(صحيح البخاري:٢٤٥٧، صحيح مسلم:٢٦٦٨، مسند أحمد:٢٤٧٨١)

ʿĀ'ishah ﵂ reported that the Prophet ﷺ said: "The most loathed of men is the one who is most quarrelsome and argumentative."

(*Ṣaḥīḥ al-Bukhārī* : 2457, *Ṣaḥīḥ Muslim*: 2668, *Musnad Aḥmad*: 24781)

6

عَنْ فَرْوَةَ بْنِ نَوْفَلٍ قَالَ: «سَأَلْتُ عَائِشَةَ عَنْ دُعَاءِ النَّبِيِّ، صَلَّى اللهُ عَلَيْهِ وَسَلَّمَ». قَالَتْ: «كَانَ يَقُولُ اللَّهُمَّ إِنِّي أَعُوذُ بِكَ مِنْ شَرِّ مَا عَمِلَتْهُ نَفْسِي».

(مسند أحمد:٢٤٥٣٤)

Farwah ibn Nawfal related that he asked ʿĀ'ishah ﵂ about the supplications of the Prophet ﷺ so she said: "He used to say: 'O Allah, I seek Your refuge in You from the evil I have committed.'"

(*Musnad Aḥmad*: 24534)

7

عَنْ عَائِشَةَ: «كَانَ أَحَبُّ الشَّرَابِ إِلَى رَسُولِ اللَّهِ صَلَّى اللهُ عَلَيْهِ وَسَلَّمَ الْحُلْوَ الْبَارِدَ».

(سنن الترمذي:١٨٥٩، مستدرك الحاكم:٤/١٣٧، مسند أحمد:٢٤٦٠١)

ʿĀ'ishah ﷺ related: "The favourite drink of the Messenger of Allah ﷺ was that which was sweet and cold."

(*Sunan al-Tirmidhī*: 1859, *Mustadrak al-Ḥākim*: 137/4, *Musnad Aḥmad*: 24601)

8

عَنْ عُرْوَ يَقُولُ: «سَأَلْتُ عَائِشَةَ بِأَيِّ شَيْءٍ طَيَّبْتِ النَّبِيَّ صَلَّى اللهُ عَلَيْهِ وَسَلَّمَ؟» قَالَتْ: «بِأَطْيَبِ الطِّيبِ».

(مسند أحمد:٢٤٦٠٦)

'Urwah related that he asked 'Ā'ishah ﵂: "Which perfume did you apply on the Prophet ﷺ?" She replied: "The best perfumes."

(*Musnad Aḥmad*: 24606)

9

عَنْ عَائِشَةَ قَالَتْ: «سَابَقَنِي النَّبِيُّ صَلَّى اللهُ عَلَيْهِ وَسَلَّمَ فَسَبَقْتُهُ فَلَبِثْنَا حَتَّى إِذَا رَهِقَنِي اللَّحْمُ سَابَقَنِي فَسَبَقَنِي فَقَالَ هَذِهِ بِتِيك».

(مسند أحمد:٢٤٦١٩)

ʿĀ'ishah ﵂ said: "The Prophet ﷺ once raced me and I outpaced him. After a while when I had put on weight, he raced me again and outpaced me, upon which he said: 'This one is for the last one.'"

(*Musnad Aḥmad*: 24619)

10

عَنْ عَائِشَةَ تَبْلُغُ بِهِ النَّبِيَّ صَلَّى اللهُ عَلَيْهِ وَسَلَّمَ: «إِذَا وُضِعَ الْعَشَاءُ وَأُقِيمَتْ الصَّلَاةُ فَابْدَءُوا بِالْعَشَاءِ».

(صحيح البخاري:٥٦٤٥، صحيح مسلم:٨٥٥، مسند أحمد:١٢٦٤٢

ʿĀ'ishah ﷺ relates directly from the Prophet ﷺ: "When food is served and the call to start the prayer is made, you should first start with the food."

11

عَنْ عَائِشَةَ قَبَّلَ رَسُولُ اللَّهِ صَلَّى اللهُ عَلَيْهِ وَسَلَّمَ عُثْمَانَ بْنَ مَظْعُونٍ وَهُوَ مَيِّتٌ حَتَّى رَأَيْتُ الدُّمُوعَ تَسِيلُ عَلَى وَجْهِهِ».

(المستدرك للحاكم:١/١٦٣، سنن الترمذي:٩٨٩، سنن أبي داود:٣٦١٣، مسند أحمد:٢٤٦٦٦)

ʿĀ'ishah ﵂ relates that the Messenger of Allah ﷺ kissed the dead body of ʿUthmān ibn Maẓʿūn and she saw tears trickling down on his face.

(*Mustadrak al-Ḥākim*: 361/1, *Sunan al-Tirmidhī*: 989, *Sunan Abū Dāwūd*: 3163, *Musnad Aḥmad*: 24666)

12

عَنْ عَائِشَةَ أَنَّ رَجُلًا قَالَ لِلنَّبِيِّ صَلَّى اللهُ عَلَيْهِ وَسَلَّمَ إِنَّ أُمِّي افْتُلِتَتْ نَفْسُهَا وَأَظُنُّهَا لَوْ تَكَلَّمَتْ تَصَدَّقَتْ فَهَلْ لَهَا أَجْرٌ إِنْ أَتَصَدَّقْ عَنْهَا؟» قَالَ: «نَعَمْ».

(صحيح البخاري:٢٧٦٠، صحيح مسلم:١٠٠٤، مسند أحمد:٢٤٧٥٥)

ʿĀ'ishah ﵂ related that a man said to the Prophet ﷺ: "My mother has died and, if she could speak before her last breath, I think she would have asked me to give alms on her behaf. So should I give alms on her behalf?" He replied: "Yes, you should do so."

(*Ṣaḥīḥ al-Bukhārī*: 2760, *Ṣaḥīḥ Muslim*: 1004, *Musnad Aḥmad*: 24755)

13

عَنْ عَائِشَةَ أَنَّ أُمَّ حَبِيبَةَ وَأُمَّ سَلَمَةَ ذَكَرَتَا كَنِيسَةً رَأَيْنَهَا بِالْحَبَشَةِ فِيهَا تَصَاوِيرُ فَقَالَ رَسُولُ اللَّهِ صَلَّى اللهُ عَلَيْهِ وَسَلَّمَ: «إِنَّ أُولَئِكَ إِذَا كَانَ فِيهِمُ الرَّجُلُ الصَّالِحُ فَمَاتَ بَنَوْا عَلَى قَبْرِهِ مَسْجِدًا وَصَوَّرُوا فِيهِ تِلْكَ الصُّوَرَ أُولَئِكَ شِرَارُ الْخَلْقِ عِنْدَ اللَّهِ عَزَّ وَجَلَّ يَوْمَ الْقِيَامَةِ»

(صحيح البخاري:٤٢٧، صحيح مسلم:٥٢٨، مسند أحمد:٢٤٧٥٦)

Ā'ishah related that Umm Ḥabībah and Umm Salamah recalled seeing pictures in a church in Abyssinia, so the Messenger of Allah ﷺ said: "When a pious person died amongst them, they built a place of worship on his grave and drew those pictures in it; those are the most evil of people in the sight of Allah on the Day of Judgement."

(*Ṣaḥīḥ al-Bukhārī*: 427, *Ṣaḥīḥ Muslim*: 528, *Musnad Aḥmad*: 24756)

14

عَنْ مَسْرُوقٍ قَالَ: «قُلْتُ لِعَائِشَةَ هَلْ كَانَ رَسُولُ اللَّهِ صَلَّى اللهُ عَلَيْهِ وَسَلَّمَ يَقُولُ شَيْئًا إِذَا دَخَلَ الْبَيْتَ؟» قَالَتْ: «كَانَ إِذَا دَخَلَ الْبَيْتَ تَمَثَّلَ لَوْ كَانَ لِابْنِ آدَمَ وَادِيَانِ مِنْ مَالٍ لَابْتَغَى وَادِيًا ثَالِثًا وَلَا يَمْلَأُ فَمهُ إِلَّا التُّرَابُ وَمَا جَعَلْنَا الْمَالَ إِلَّا لِإِقَامِ الصَّلَا وَإِيتَاءِ الزَّكَا وَيَتُوبُ اللهُ عَلَى مَنْ تَابَ».

(مسند أحمد:٢٤٧٨٠)

Masrūq related that he asked ʿĀ'ishah ﵂ whether the Messenger of Allah ﷺ said anything on entering his house. She said: "Upon entering his house, he used to mention that if the Child of Adam has two valleys full of wealth, he will still want to have a third one but nothing will fill him up completely except dust [when he is buried in his grave]. Wealth is meant only for establishing the prayer and paying the *zakāt* and Allah relents on whoever turns to Him in repentance."

(*Musnad Aḥmad*: 24780)

15

عَنْ عَائِشَةَ قَالَتْ: «مَا غِرْتُ عَلَى امْرَأَةٍ مَا غِرْتُ عَلَى خَدِيجَةَ وَلَقَدْ هَلَكَتْ قَبْلَ أَنْ يَتَزَوَّجَنِي بِثَلَاثِ سِنِينَ لِمَا كُنْتُ أَسْمَعُهُ يَذْكُرُهَا وَلَقَدْ أَمَرَهُ رَبُّهُ عَزَّ وَجَلَّ أَنْ يُبَشِّرَهَا بِبَيْتٍ مِنْ قَصَبٍ فِي الْجَنَّةِ وَإِنْ كَانَ لَيَذْبَحُ الشَّاةَ ثُمَّ يُهْدِي فِي خُلَّتِهَا مِنْهَا».

(صحيح البخاري:٦٠٠٤، صحيح مسلم:٢٤٣٥، مسند أحمد:٢٤٨١٤)

Āʾishah ﷺ states: "Never did I feel jealous of any woman as I did of Khadijah. She had passed away three years before my marriage with the Prophet ﷺ, however the Prophet ﷺ often mentioned her. His Lord, exalted and glorious is He, commanded him to give her the good news of a palace of gold and silver for her in Paradise. And whenever he slaughtered a sheep, he would send of its meat to her friends."

(*Ṣaḥīḥ al-Bukhārī*: 6004, *Ṣaḥīḥ Muslim*: 2435, *Musnad Aḥmad*: 24814)

16

عَنْ عَائِشَةَ قَالَتْ: «قَالَ رَسُولُ اللَّهِ صَلَّى اللهُ عَلَيْهِ وَسَلَّمَ: اللَّهُمَّ مَنْ رَفَقَ بِأُمَّتِي فَارْفُقْ بِهِ وَمَنْ شَقَّ عَلَيْهِمْ فَشُقَّ عَلَيْهِ».

(مسند أحمد:٢٤٨٤١)

ʿĀ'ishah ﵂ related that the Messenger of Allah ﷺ said: "O Allah, be gentle with whoever is gentle with my community and make it difficult for whoever makes it difficult for my community."

(*Musnad Aḥmad*: 24841)

17

عَنْ عَائِشَةَ قَالَتْ: «سَمِعْتُ النَّبِيَّ صَلَّى اللهُ عَلَيْهِ وَسَلَّمَ يَقُولُ: «إِنَّ الْمُؤْمِنَ يُدْرِكُ بِحُسْنِ خُلُقِهِ دَرَجَاتِ قَائِمِ اللَّيْلِ صَائِمِ النَّهَارِ».

(سنن أبي داود:٨٩٧٤، صحيح إبن حبان:٠٨٤، مسند أحمد:٩٥٨٤٢)

'Ā'ishah ﵂ said: "I heard the Prophet ﷺ say: 'The believer attains with his excellent conduct the high ranks held by the one who prays at night and fasts in the daytime.'"

(*Sunan Abū Dāwūd*: 4798, *Ṣaḥīḥ Ibn Ḥibbān*: 480, *Musnad Aḥmad*: 24859)

18

عَنْ عَائِشَةَ، زَوْجِ النَّبِيِّ صَلَّى اللهُ عَلَيْهِ وَسَلَّمَ، أَنَّهَا سَأَلَتْ نَبِيَّ اللَّهِ صَلَّى اللهُ عَلَيْهِ وَسَلَّمَ عَنْ الطَّاعُونِ فَأَخْبَرَهَا نَبِيُّ اللَّهِ صَلَّى اللهُ عَلَيْهِ وَسَلَّمَ أَنَّهُ كَانَ عَذَابًا يَبْعَثُهُ اللهُ عَزَّ وَجَلَّ عَلَى مَنْ يَشَاءُ، فَجَعَلَهُ اللهُ عَزَّ وَجَلَّ رَحْمَةً لِلْمُؤْمِنِينَ فَلَيْسَ مِنْ عَبْدٍ يَقَعُ الطَّاعُونُ فِيهِ فَيَمْكُثُ فِي بَلَدِهِ صَابِرًا مُحْتَسِبًا يَعْلَمُ أَنَّهُ لَمْ يُصِبْهُ إِلَّا مَا كَتَبَ اللهُ عَزَّ وَجَلَّ لَهُ إِلَّا كَانَ لَهُ مِثْلُ أَجْرِ الشَّهِيدِ».

(صحيح البخاري:٣٤٧٤، مسند أحمد:٢٤٨٦٢)

‘Ā’ishah, the wife of the Prophet, related that she asked the Prophet about the plague, and so he informed her that it was a chastisement that Allah sends to whomever He wills. However, Allah, exalted and glorious is He, makes it a mercy for the believers. So when the plague visits a township, and the servant remains there steadfast in expectation of Allah's reward – knowing well that nothing befalls him except that which Allah the Most High has decreed for him – Allah, glorified and exalted is He, will reward him with the reward of the one who dies for the sake of Allah.

(*Ṣaḥīḥ al-Bukhārī*: 3474, *Musnad Aḥmad*: 24862)

19

عَنْ عَائِشَةَ قَالَتْ: «ذُكِرَ رَجُلٌ عِنْدَ رَسُولِ اللَّهِ صَلَّى اللهُ عَلَيْهِ وَسَلَّمَ بِخَيْرٍ، فَقَالَ رَسُولُ اللَّهِ صَلَّى اللهُ عَلَيْهِ وَسَلَّمَ: أَوَلَمْ تَرَوْهُ يَتَعَلَّمُ الْقُرْآنَ».

(مسند أحمد: ٢٤٨٧٨)

ʿĀ'ishah ﷺ said: "A man was praised in the presence of the Messenger of Allah ﷺ, and so the Messenger of Allah ﷺ pointed out: 'Did you not see him learning the Qur'ān?'"

(*Musnad Aḥmad*: 24878)

20

عَنْ عَائِشَةَ قَالَتْ: «إِن الكَافِر يُسَلَّطُ عَلَيْهِ فِي قَبْرِهِ شُجَاعٌ أَقْرَعٌ فَيَأْكُلُ لَحْمَهُ مِنْ رَأْسِهِ إِلَى رِجْلِهِ، ثُمَّ يُكْسَى اللَّحْمُ فَيَأْكُلُ مِنْ رِجْلِهِ إِلَى رَأْسِهِ فَهُوَ كَذَلِكَ».

(كنز العمّال:٣٧٧٩٧)

ʿĀ'ishah ﵂ said: "A venomous snake is assigned for the unbeliever in his grave which eats his flesh from head to toe. Then his flesh is again restored to him and it eats his flesh again from toe to head, and this goes on and on."

(*Kanz al-ʿUmmāl*: 37797)

21

عَنْ عَائِشَةَ قَالَت: «كَانَ رَسُولُ اللهِ صَلَّى اللهُ عَلَيْهِ وَسَلَّمَ يَقُولُ فِي سُجُودِ الْقُرْآن: سَجَدَ وَجْهِي لِمَنْ خَلَقَهُ، وَشَقَّ سَمْعَهُ وَبَصَرَهُ بِحَوْلِهِ وَقُوَّتِه».

(سنن أبي داود:١٤١٤، سنن الترمذي:٥٨٠، مسند أحمد:٢٤٥٢٣)

ʿĀ'ishah ﷺ said: "The Messenger of Allah ﷺ used to say in the prostration of recitation (*sujūd al-tilāwah*): 'I prostrate my face before Him who created it and fashioned its hearing and sight, by His might and power.'"

(*Sunan Abū Dāwūd*: 1414, *Sunan al-Tirmidhī*: 580, *Musnad Aḥmad*: 24523)

22

عَنْ عَائِشَةَ عَنِ النَّبِيِّ صَلَّى اللهُ عَلَيْهِ وَسَلَّمَ أَنَّهُ قَالَ: «إِنَّ أَطْيَبَ مَا أَكَلَ الرَّجُلُ مِنْ كَسْبِهِ، وَإِنَّ وَلَدَهُ مِنْ كَسْبِهِ».

(سنن أبي داود:٨٢٥٣، سنن الترمذي:٨٥٣١، سنن ابن ماجه:٠٩٢٢، مسند أحمد:٣٣٥٤٢)

'Āishah ﵂ relates the Prophet's remark: "The most wholesome thing that a man consumes is that which he acquired through his earnings and his child is from his earnings."

(*Sunan Abū Dāwūd*: 3528, *Sunan al-Tirmidhī*: 1358, *Sunan Ibn Mājah*: 2290, *Musnad Aḥmad*: 24533)

23

عَنْ عَائِشَةَ أَنَّ أَبَا بَكْرٍ دَخَلَ عَلَيْهَا وَعِنْدَهَا جَارِيَتَانِ تَضْرِبَانِ بِدُفَّيْنِ فَانْتَهَرَهُمَا أَبُو بَكْرٍ فَقَالَ لَهُ النَّبِيُّ صَلَّى اللهُ عَلَيْهِ وَسَلَّمَ: «دَعْهُنَّ فَإِنَّ لِكُلِّ قَوْمٍ عِيدًا».

(مسند أحمد:٢٤٥٥٠)

ʿĀ'ishah ﵂ said that Abū Bakr al-Ṣiddīq ﵁ – her father – came to her house on the day of Eid and found two girls beating a tambourine and so he rebuked them, but the Prophet ﷺ said to him: "Leave them be for every community has its own festive day."

(*Musnad Aḥmad*: 24550)

24

عَنْ عَائِشَةَ أَنَّ امْرَأَةً دَخَلَتْ عَلَيْهَا وَمَعَهَا ابْنَتَانِ لَهَا فَأَعْطَيْتُهَا تَمْرَةً فَشَقَّتْهَا بَيْنَهُمَا فَذَكَرْتُ ذَلِكَ لِرَسُولِ اللَّهِ صَلَّى اللهُ عَلَيْهِ وَسَلَّمَ فَقَالَ: «مَنْ ابْتُلِيَ بِشَيْءٍ مِنْ هذِهِ الْبَنَاتِ فَأَحْسَنَ إِلَيْهِنَّ كُنَّ لَهُ سِتْرًا مِنْ النَّارِ».

(صحيح البخاري:١٤١٨، صحيح مسلم:٢٦٢٩، مسند أحمد:٢٤٥٥٦)

ʿĀ'ishah ﵁ related that a woman came to see her along with her two daughters. She said: "I gave her one date which she divided between her daughters" and then mentioned this to the Messenger of Allah ﷺ. He commented: "Whoever is tested on account of their daughters and yet keeps treating them well, they will be a veil for him from the Hellfire."

(*Ṣaḥīḥ al-Bukhārī*: 1418, *Ṣaḥīḥ Muslim*: 2629,
Musnad Aḥmad: 24556)

25

عَنْ عَائِشَةَ أَنَّ نَبِيَّ اللَّهِ صَلَّى اللهُ عَلَيْهِ وَسَلَّمَ كَانَ يَتْرُكُ الْعَمَلَ وَهُو يُحِبُّ أَنْ يَعْمَلَهُ كَرَاهِيَةَ أَنْ يَسْتَنَّ النَّاسُ بِهِ فَيُفْرَضَ عَلَيْهِمْ فَكَانَ يُحِبُّ مَا خُفِّفَ عَلَيْهِمْ مِنْ الْفَرَائِضِ».

(مسند أحمد:٧٥٥٤٢)

ʿĀ'ishah related that the Prophet ﷺ would start a practice but then discontinue it, when he would have rather continued to do it, because he did not want people to emulate him regarding it lest it then be made mandatory on them. He used to like the religious obligations that were made easy for them.

(*Musnad Aḥmad*: 24557)

26

عَنْ عَائِشَةَ أَنَّ النَّبِيَّ صَلَّى اللهُ عَلَيْهِ وَسَلَّمَ صَلَّى فِي خَمِيصَةٍ لَهَا أَعْلَامٌ فَلَمَّا قَضَى صَلَاتَهُ قَالَ: «شَغَلَنِي أَعْلَامُهَا، اذْهَبُوا بِهَا إِلَى أَبِي جَهْمٍ وَأْتُونِي بِأَنْبِجَانِيَّتِهِ».

(صحيح البخاري:٧٥٢، صحيح مسلم:٥٥٦، مسند أحمد:٢٤٥٨٨)

ʿĀ'ishah ﵂ related that once the Prophet ﷺ prayed in a garment which had designs over it. When he finished his prayer, he said: "Its imprints distracted me [in my prayer]. Take it to Abū Jahm and bring me his garment."

(*Ṣaḥīḥ al-Bukhārī*: 752, *Ṣaḥīḥ Muslim*: 556, *Musnad Aḥmad*: 24588)

27

عَنْ عَائِشَةَ أَنَّ النَّبِيَّ صَلَّى اللهُ عَلَيْهِ وَسَلَّمَ قَالَ: «إِنَّ اللَّهَ عَزَّ وَجَلَّ يُحِبُّ الرِّفْقَ فِي الْأَمْرِ كُلِّهِ».

(صحيح البخاري:٦٠٢٤، صحيح مسلم:٥٦٥٦، مسند أحمد:٢٤٥٩٢)

ʿĀ'ishah ﵂ related that the Prophet ﷺ said: "Allah loves gentleness in every matter."

(*Ṣaḥīḥ al-Bukhārī*: 6024, *Ṣaḥīḥ Muslim*: 5656, *Musnad Aḥmad*: 24592)

28

عَنْ عَائِشَةَ أَنَّ النَّبِيَّ صَلَّى اللهُ عَلَيْهِ وَسَلَّمَ قَالَ: «لَا يَحِلُّ لِامْرَأَةٍ تُؤْمِنُ بِاللَّهِ وَالْيَوْمِ الْآخِرِ تُحِدُّ عَلَى مَيِّتٍ فَوْقَ ثَلَاثٍ إِلَّا عَلَى زَوْجٍ».

(صحيح مسلم:١٤٩١، مسند أحمد:٢٤٩٩٣)

ʿĀ’ishah رضي الله عنها related that the Prophet ﷺ said: “A woman who believes in Allah and the Last Day is not allowed to mourn someone’s death for more than three days unless it be her husband.”

(*Ṣaḥīḥ Muslim*: 1491, *Musnad Aḥmad*: 24993)

29

عَنْ عَائِشَةَ قَالَتْ: «رَأَيْتُ رَسُولَ اللهِ صَلَّى اللهُ عَلَيْهِ وَسَلَّمَ وَهُوَ صَائِمٌ يَتَرَصَّدُ غُرُوبَ الشَّمْسِ بِتَمْرَةٍ، فَلَمَّا تَوَارَت أَلْقَاهَا فِي فِيهِ".

(كَنْزُ العُمَّال:٢٤٣٩٧)

'Ā'ishah ﵂ said: "I saw, the Messenger of Allah ﷺ once while he was fasting waiting for the sunset with a date in his hand. When the sun set, he put the date in his mouth."

(*Kanz al-'Ummāl*: 24397)

30

عَنْ عَائِشَةَ أَنَّ هِنْدَ قَالَتْ: «يَا رَسُولَ اللَّهِ إِنَّ أَبَا سُفْيَانَ رَجُلٌ شَحِيحٌ وَلَيْسَ لِي إِلَّا مَا يَدْخُلُ بَيْتِي». قَالَ: «خُذِي مَا يَكْفِيكِ وَوَلَدَكِ بِالْمَعْرُوفِ».

(صحيح البخاري:٥٢٨٣، صحيح مسلم:١٧١٤، مسند أحمد:٢٤٦١٨)

ʿĀ'ishah ﷺ related that Hind [Abū Sufyān's wife] said: "O Messenger of Allah, Abū Sufyān is a miserly man and I don't have anything except that which enters my house." He said in reply: "Take from him what is sufficient for you and your children but in moderation."

(*Ṣaḥīḥ al-Bukhārī*: 3825, *Ṣaḥīḥ Muslim*: 1714,
Musnad Aḥmad: 24618)

31

عَنْ عَائِشَةَ، تَذْكُرُ عَنْ النَّبِيِّ صَلَّى اللهُ عَلَيْهِ وَسَلَّمَ كَانَ إِذَا دَخَلَ الْعَشْرُ أَحْيَا اللَّيْلَ وَأَيْقَظَ أَهْلَهُ وَشَدَّ الْمِئْزَرَ.

(صحيح البخاري:٢٠٢٤، صحيح مسلم:١١٧٤، مسند أحمد:٢٤٦٣٢)

ʿĀ'ishah ﵂ recalled that, upon the arrival of the last ten days of Ramadan, the Prophet ﷺ prayed throughout the night, woke his family up [to do the same] and braced himself for devotional worship.

(*Ṣaḥīḥ al-Bukhārī*: 2024, *Ṣaḥīḥ Muslim*: 1174, *Musnad Aḥmad*: 24632)

32

عَنْ يَحْيَى بْنِ مَعْمَر قَالَ: «سَأَلْتُ عَائِشَةَ: هَلْ كَانَ رَسُولُ اللهِ صَلَّى اللهُ عَلَيْهِ وَسَلَّمَ يَنَامُ وَهُوَ جُنُبٌ؟» قَالَتْ: «رُبَّمَا اغْتَسَلَ قَبْلَ أَنْ يَنَامَ وَرُبَّمَا نَامَ قَبْلَ أَنْ يَغْتَسِلَ وَلَكِنَّهُ يَتَوَضَّأُ».

(كنز العمال: ٤٣٤٧٢)

Yaḥyā ibn Ma'mar asked 'Ā'ishah ﵂: "Did the the Messenger of Allah (peace be uon him) go to sleep while he was in a state of major ritual impurity?" She replied: "At times he took a purificatory bath before sleeping and at others he retired to bed without taking a purificatory bath but, in that case, he performed minor ritual purification (*wuḍū'*)."

(*Kanz al-'Ummāl*: 27434)

33

عَنْ عَائِشَةَ قَالَتْ: «كَانَ رَسُولُ اللَّهِ صَلَّى اللهُ عَلَيْهِ وَسَلَّمَ يُكْثِرُ أَنْ يَقُولَ فِي رُكُوعِهِ وَسُجُودِهِ: سُبْحَانَكَ اللَّهُمَّ رَبَّنَا وَبِحَمْدِكَ اللَّهُمَّ اغْفِرْ لِي يَتَأَوَّلُ الْقُرْآنَ»

(صحيح البخاري:٤٩٦٨، صحيح مسلم:٧٨٤، مسند أحمد:٢٤٦٦٤)

ʿĀ'ishah ﵂ said: "The Messenger of Allah ﷺ used to say in his bowing and prostration: 'Glory be to You, O Allah, our Lord, and praise be to You, O Allah, Forgive me (*Subḥānak Allāhumma Rabbanā wa bi-ḥamdika Allahumma ighfir lī*).' He acted on what the Qur'ān teaches."

(*Ṣaḥīḥ al-Bukhārī*: 4968, *Ṣaḥīḥ Muslim*: 784, *Musnad Aḥmad*: 24664)

34

عَنْ عَائِشَةَ، قَالَتْ: «لَمْ يَكُنْ رَسُولُ اللَّهِ صَلَّى اللهُ عَلَيْهِ وَسَلَّمَ عَلَى شَيْءٍ مِنَ النَّوَافِلِ أَشَدَّ مُعَاهَدَةً مِنَ الرَّكْعَتَيْنِ قَبْلَ الصُّبْحِ».

(صحيح البخاري:١١٦٩، صحيح مسلم:٧٢٤، مسند أحمد:٢٤٦٦٨)

ʿĀ'ishah ﵂ reports that the Messenger of Allah ﷺ did not attach more importance to any supererogatory (*nafl*) prayer than he did to the two cycles of prayers (*rak'ah*) before the *Ṣubḥ* prayer.

(*Ṣaḥīḥ al-Bukhārī*: 1169, *Ṣaḥīḥ Muslim*: 724,
Musnad Aḥmad: 24668)

35

عَنْ عَائِشَةَ، قَالَتْ: «مَا تَرَكَ رَسُولُ اللَّهِ صَلَّى اللهُ عَلَيْهِ وَسَلَّمَ دِينَارًا وَلَا دِرْهَمًا وَلَا شَاةً وَلَا بَعِيرًا وَلَا أَوْصَى بِشَيْءٍ».

(صحيح مسلم:١٦٣٥، مسند أحمد:٢٤٦٧٩)

ʿĀ'ishah ﵂ said: "The Messenger of Allah ﷺ did not leave behind any gold or silver coins, nor any sheep or camels, nor did he leave a final testament."

(*Ṣaḥīḥ Muslim*: 1635, *Musnad Aḥmad*: 24679)

36

عَنْ عَائِشَةَ، قَالَتْ: «قَالَ رَسُولُ اللَّهِ صَلَّى اللهُ عَلَيْهِ وَسَلَّمَ: نَاوِلِينِي الْخُمْرَ مِنَ الْمَسْجِدِ». قَالَتْ: «قُلْتُ: إِنِّي حَائِضٌ». قَالَ: «إِنَّ حَيْضَتَكِ لَيْسَتْ فِي يَدِكِ».

(صحيح مسلم:٢٩٨، سنن والترمذي:١٣٤، مسند أحمد:٢٤٦٨٨)

ʿĀʾishah ﷺ related that the Messenger of Allah ﷺ asked her to bring him a prayer mat from his mosque. She replied: "I am menstruating." He replied: "Your menstruation is not in your hands."'

(*Ṣaḥīḥ Muslim*: 298, *Sunan al-Tirmidhī*: 134, *Musnad Aḥmad*: 24688)

37

عَنْ عَائِشَةَ، قَالَتْ: «كَانَ رَسُولُ اللَّهِ صَلَّى اللهُ عَلَيْهِ وَسَلَّمَ يَقْبَلُ الْهَدِيَّةَ وَيُثِيبُ عَلَيْهَا»..

(صحيح البخاري:٢٥٨٥، مسند أحمد:٢٥٠٩٨)

ʿĀ'ishah ﵂ said: "The Messenger of Allah ﷺ used to accept gifts and reward the givers for them".

38

عَنْ عَائِشَةَ، قَالَتْ: «قَالَ رَسُولُ اللَّهِ صَلَّى اللهُ عَلَيْهِ وَسَلَّمَ: إِنَّ مِنْ أَكْمَلِ الْمُؤْمِنِينَ إِيمَانًا أَحْسَنَهُمْ خُلُقًا وَأَلْطَفُهُمْ بِأَهْلِهِ».

(سنن والترمذي:٢٦١٢، مسند أحمد:٢٤٧٠٨)

'Āishah ﵂ said: "The Messenger of Allah ﷺ said: The most perfect in faith amongst the believers is the one with the most perfect conduct and who is the most gentle with his family members."

(*Sunan al-Tirmidhī*: 2612, *Musnad Aḥmad*: 24708)

39

عَنْ عَائِشَةَ، قَالَتْ: «قَالَ رَسُولُ اللَّهِ صَلَّى اللهُ عَلَيْهِ وَسَلَّمَ: الَّذِي يَقْرَأُ الْقُرْآنَ وَهُو مَاهِرٌ بِهِ مَعَ السَّفَرَ الْكِرَامِ الْبَرَرَ وَالَّذِي يَقْرَؤُهُ وَهُوَ عَلَيْهِ شَاقٌّ فَلَهُ أَجْرَانِ».

(صحيح البخاري:٤٩٣٧، صحيح مسلم:٧٩٨، مسند أحمد:٢٤٧١٥)

ʿĀ'ishah ﵂ said: "The Messenger of Allah ﷺ said: the person who recites the Qur'ān proficiently is in the company of noble and honourable angels and the person who recites it with difficulty will have a double reward."

(*Ṣaḥīḥ al-Bukhārī*: 4937, *Ṣaḥīḥ Muslim*: 798, *Musnad Aḥmad*: 24715)

40

عَنْ عَائِشَةَ، عَنْ النَّبِيِّ صَلَّى اللهُ عَلَيْهِ وَسَلَّمَ: «فُضِّلَتْ الْجَمَاعَةُ عَلَى صَلَاةِ الْفَذِّ خَمْسًا وَعِشْرِينَ».

(سنن النسائي:٨٣٩، مسند أحمد:٢٤٧٢٥)

Āʾishah ﷺ related that the Prophet ﷺ said: "Praying in congregation is twenty-five times better than the prayer of a person by himself."

(*Sunan al-Tirmidhī*: 839, *Musnad Aḥmad*: 24725)

41

أَتَى مَسْرُوقٌ عَائِشَةَ فَقَالَ: «يَا أُمَّ الْمُؤْمِنِينَ: هَلْ رَأَى مُحَمَّدٌ صَلَّى اللهُ عَلَيْهِ وَسَلَّمَ رَبَّهُ؟» قَالَتْ: «سُبْحَانَ اللَّهِ لَقَدْ قَفَّ شَعْرِي لِمَا قُلْتَ. أَيْنَ أَنْتَ مِنْ ثَلَاثٍ مَنْ حَدَّثَكَهُنَّ فَقَدْ كَذَبَ؟ مَنْ حَدَّثَكَ أَنَّ مُحَمَّدًا صَلَّى اللهُ عَلَيْهِ وَسَلَّمَ رَأَى رَبَّهُ فَقَدْ كَذَبَ». ثُمَّ قَرَأَتْ: {لَا تُدْرِكُهُ الْأَبْصَارُ وَهُوَ يُدْرِكُ الْأَبْصَارَ} {وَمَا كَانَ لِبَشَرٍ أَنْ يُكَلِّمَهُ اللهُ إِلَّا وَحْيًا أَوْ مِنْ وَرَاءِ حِجَابٍ}. «وَمَنْ أَخْبَرَكَ بِمَا فِي غَدٍ فَقَدْ كَذَبَ»، ثُمَّ قَرَأَتْ: {إِنَّ اللَّهَ عِنْدَهُ عِلْمُ السَّاعَةِ وَيُنَزِّلُ الْغَيْثَ وَيَعْلَمُ مَا فِي الْأَرْحَامِ} هذِهِ الْآيَةَ. «وَمَنْ أَخْبَرَكَ أَنَّ مُحَمَّدًا صَلَّى اللهُ عَلَيْهِ وَسَلَّمَ كَتَمَ فَقَدْ كَذَبَ». ثُمَّ قَرَأَتْ: {يَا أَيُّهَا الرَّسُولُ بَلِّغْ مَا أُنْزِلَ إِلَيْكَ مِنْ رَبِّكَ}، وَلَكِنَّهُ رَأَى جِبْرِيلَ فِي صُورَتِهِ مَرَّتَيْنِ».

(صحيح البخاري:٥٥٨٤، صحيح مسلم:٧٧١، مسند أحمد:١٣٧٤٢)

Masrūq went to ʿĀ'ishah ﵂ and asked her: "O Mother of the Believers, did the Prophet ﷺ see Allah?" She replied: "Glory be to Allah, I am shocked by what you said. What is your position regarding the saying: 'He lies whoever says anything about three things'. If anyone tells you that the Prophet ﷺ has seen Allah, then he has uttered a lie." Then she recited the Qur'ānic verse: {No sight can encompass Allah. However, He encompasses all sights,} [*al-An'ām* 6: 103] and {It is not given to any human being that Allah should speak to Him. Allah communicates to man by revelation, or from behind a veil, or by the sending of an angel to him who reveals to him by Allah's permission whatever He wills} [*al-Shūrā* 42: 51]. "Moreover, he lies whoever pretends that he knows what will happen in the future." And she recited the words of Allah: {Allah alone has the knowledge of the Last Hour. It is He who sends rain and knows what is in the wombs} [*Luqmān* 31: 34]. "And he also lies whoever relates to you that the Prophet ﷺ has withheld any Divine revelation" and she recited the words of Allah: {O Messenger, convey to people all that has come to you from your Lord} [*al-Mā'idah* 56: 7]. "However, the Prophet ﷺ saw the trustworthy archangel, Jibrīl, twice in his real form."

(*Ṣaḥīḥ al-Bukhārī*: 4855, *Ṣaḥīḥ Muslim*: 177, *Musnad Aḥmad*: 24731)

42

عَنْ عَائِشَةَ، قَالَتْ: «كَانَ رَسُولُ اللَّهِ صَلَّى اللهُ عَلَيْهِ وَسَلَّمَ يَعْتَكِفُ فِي الْعَشْرِ الْأَوَاخِرِ وَيَقُولُ: الْتَمِسُوهَا فِي الْعَشْرِ الْأَوَاخِرِ، يَعْنِي لَيْلَةَ الْقَدْرِ».

(صحيح البخاري:٢٠١٩، صحيح مسلم:١١٧٢، مسند أحمد:٢٤٧٣٧)

ʿĀʾishah رضي الله عنها informs that the Messenger of Allah ﷺ used to practise *iʿtikāf* (devotional retreat) in the last days of Ramadan and exhort Muslims to look for the Night of Power (*Laylat al-Qadr*) in the last ten nights of Ramadan.

(*Ṣaḥīḥ al-Bukhārī*: 2019, *Ṣaḥīḥ Muslim*: 1172, *Musnad Aḥmad*: 24737)

43

عَنْ عَائِشَةَ، عَنْ النَّبِيِّ صَلَّى اللهُ عَلَيْهِ وَسَلَّمَ قَالَ: «مَا زَالَ جِبْرِيلُ عَلَيْهِ السَّلَام يُوصِينِي بِالْجَارِ حَتَّى ظَنَنْتُ أَنَّهُ سَيُوَرِّثُهُ».

(صحيح البخاري:٦٠١٤، صحيح مسلم:٢٦٢٤، مسند أحمد:٢٤٧٦٤)

ʿĀ'ishah ﷺ related that the Prophet ﷺ said: "Jibrīl ﷺ kept reminding me to be kind to my neighbour so much so that I thought he would make him among those who have a right in my inheritance."

(*Ṣaḥīḥ al-Bukhārī*: 6014, *Ṣaḥīḥ Muslim*: 2624, *Musnad Aḥmad*: 24764)

44

عَنْ عَائِشَةَ، أَنَّ الْحَبَشَةَ كَانُوا يَلْعَبُونَ عِنْدَ رَسُولِ اللَّهِ صَلَّى اللهُ عَلَيْهِ وَسَلَّمَ فِي يَوْمِ عِيدٍ قَالَتْ: «فَاطَّلَعْتُ مِنْ فَوْقِ عَاتِقِهِ فَطَأْطَأَ لِي رَسُولُ اللَّهِ صَلَّى اللهُ عَلَيْهِ وَسَلَّمَ مَنْكِبَيْهِ فَجَعَلْتُ أَنْظُرُ إِلَيْهِمْ مِنْ فَوْقِ عَاتِقِهِ حَتَّى شَبِعْتُ ثُمَّ انْصَرَفْتُ».

(سنن النسائي:٥٩٥١، مسند أحمد:٠٠٨٤٢)

ʿĀʾishah ﷺ related that some Abyssinians, on Eid day, were performing tricks in front of the Messenger of Allah ﷺ. She said: "I watched the show over his shoulder and so he lowered his shoulders so that I may have a better view. I watched the show until I had enough and then left."

(*Sunan al-Nasāʾī*: 1595, *Musnad Aḥmad*: 24800)

45

عَنْ عَائِشَةَ أَنَّ رَسُولَ اللَّهِ صَلَّى اللهُ عَلَيْهِ وَسَلَّمَ كَانَ يَدْعُو بِهَؤُلَاءِ الدَّعَوَاتِ: «اللَّهُمَّ فَإِنِّي أَعُوذُ بِكَ مِنْ فِتْنَةِ النَّارِ وَعَذَابِ النَّارِ وَفِتْنَةِ الْقَبْرِ وَعَذَابِ الْقَبْرِ وَمِنْ شَرِّ فِتْنَةِ الْغِنَى وَمِنْ شَرِّ فِتْنَةِ الْفَقْرِ وَأَعُوذُ بِكَ مِنْ فِتْنَةِ الْمَسِيحِ الدَّجَّالِ. اللَّهُمَّ اغْسِلْ خَطَايَايَ بِمَاءِ الثَّلْجِ وَالْبَرَدِ وَنَقِّ قَلْبِي مِنَ الْخَطَايَا كَمَا نَقَّيْتَ الثَّوْبَ الْأَبيضَ مِنْ الدَّنَسِ وَبَاعِدْ بَيْنِي وَبَيْنَ خَطَايَايَ كَمَا بَاعَدْتَ بَيْنَ الْمَشْرِقِ وَالْمَغْرِبِ. اللَّهُمَّ فَإِنِّي أَعُوذُ بِكَ مِنْ الْكَسَلِ وَالْهَرَمِ وَالْمَأْثَمِ وَالْمَغْرَمِ»

(صحيح البخاري:٦٣٦٨، صحيح مسلم:٥٨٩، مسند أحمد:٢٤٨٠٥)

ʿĀ'ishah ﵂ related that the Messenger of Allah ﷺ used to make the following supplications: "O Allah, I indeed seek refuge in You from the trial of Hell, the chastisement of Hell, and from trial and chastisement in the grave, and also from the evil trial of affluence and the evil trial of poverty. And I seek refuge in You from the trial of the Antichrist (*Dajjāl*)."

"O Allah, cleanse my sins with the water of snow and hailstones and purify my heart of sins as a white cloth is cleansed of dirt, and distance me from sins as You distanced the East from the West."

"O Allah, I seek refuge in You from laziness, extreme old age, sins and punishment."

(*Ṣaḥīḥ al-Bukhārī*: 6368, *Ṣaḥīḥ Muslim*: 589, *Musnad Aḥmad*: 24805)

عَنْ عَائِشَةَ، قَالَتْ: «قَالَ لِي رَسُولُ اللَّهِ صَلَّى اللهُ عَلَيْهِ وَسَلَّمَ: إِنِّي لَأَعْلَمُ إِذَا كُنْتِ عَنِّي رَاضِيَةً وَإِذَا كُنْتِ عَلَيَّ غَضْبَى». قَالَتْ: «فَقُلْتُ: مِنْ أَيْنَ تَعْلَمُ ذَاكَ؟» قَالَ: «إِذَا كُنْتِ عَنِّي رَاضِيَةً فَإِنَّكِ تَقُولِينَ: لَا وَرَبِّ مُحَمَّدٍ! وَإِذَا كُنْتِ عَلَيَّ غَضْبَى تَقُولِينَ: لَا وَرَبِّ إِبْرَاهِيمَ عَلَيْهِ السَّلَامُ!» قُلْتُ: «أَجَلْ وَاللهِ مَا أَهْجُرُ إِلَّا اسْمَكَ».

(صحيح البخاري:٨٢٢٥، صحيح مسلم:٩٣٤٢، مسند أحمد:٢٢٨٤٢)

Ā'ishah 🙦 related that the Messenger of Allah 🙥 said to her: "I know when you are angry with me, and when you are happy with me." She asked him: "How do you know?" He said: "When you are happy with me, you say: 'By the Lord of Muḥammad,' and when you are angry with me, you say: 'By the Lord of Ibrāhīm 🙥.'" She admitted: "You are right, I only cease mentioning your name."

(*Ṣaḥīḥ al-Bukhārī*: 5228, *Ṣaḥīḥ Muslim*: 2439, *Musnad Aḥmad*: 24822)

47

عَنْ عَائِشَةَ قَالَتْ: «قَالَ رَسُولُ اللَّهِ صَلَّى اللهُ عَلَيْهِ وَسَلَّمَ: إِنَّمَا جُعِلَ الطَّوَافُ بِالْبَيْتِ وَبِالصَّفَا وَالمَرْوَ وَرَمْيُ الجِمَارِ لِإِقَامَةِ ذِكْرِ اللَّهِ عَزَّ وَجَلَّ».

(سنن أبي داود:٨٨٨١، سنن والترمذي:٢٠٩، مسند أحمد:٥٥٨٤٢)

ʿĀ'ishah ﵂ related that the Messenger of Allah ﷺ said: "Indeed, circumambulating the Kaʿbah (*ṭawāf*), going between al-Ṣafā and Marwah (*saʿy*) and stoning the devil (*ramy āl-jamarāt*) are prescribed for establishing the remembrance of Allah, glorious and exalted is He."

(*Sunan Abī Dāwūd*: 1888, *Sunan al-Tirmidhī*: 902,
Musnad Aḥmad: 24855)

48

عَنْ عَائِشَةَ، قَالَتْ: «كَانَ رَسُولُ اللَّهِ صَلَّى اللهُ عَلَيْهِ وَسَلَّمَ يَقُولُ: اللَّهُمَّ أَحْسَنْتَ خَلْقِي فَأَحْسِنْ خُلُقِي».

(الترغيب والترهيب للمنذري٧٥٣/٣، مسند أحمد:٦٩٨٤٢)

ʿĀ'ishah ﷺ related that the Messenger of Allah ﷺ used to say: "O Allah, just as You have created me in the best of forms, so too make my conduct excellent."

(*Al-Targhīb wa'l-Tarhīb* of al-Mundhirī: 357/3, *Musnad Aḥmad*: 24896)

49

عَنْ عَائِشَةَ، قَالَتْ: «كَانَ رَسُولُ اللَّهِ صَلَّى اللهُ عَلَيْهِ وَسَلَّمَ يَذْكُرُ اللَّهَ عَزَّ وَجَلَّ عَلَى كُلِّ أَحْيَانِهِ».

(صحيح مسلم:٣٧٣، مسند أحمد:٤١٩٤٢)

ʿĀ’ishah رضي الله عنها said: “The Messenger of Allah ﷺ used to remember Allah, glorified and exalted is He, all the time.”

(*Ṣaḥīḥ Muslim*: 373, *Musnad Aḥmad*: 24914)

50

عَنْ عَائِشَةَ، قَالَتْ: «قَالَ رَسُولُ اللَّهِ صَلَّى اللهُ عَلَيْهِ وَسَلَّمَ: مَنْ صَنَعَ أَمْرًا مِنْ غَيْرِ أَمْرِنَا فَهُو مَرْدُودٌ».

(صحيح البخاري:٧٩٦٢، صحيح مسلم:٨١٧١، مسند أحمد:٤٥٩٤٢)

ʿĀ'ishah ﵂ related that the Messenger of Allah ﷺ said: "Any matter that is initiated contrary to our command is rejected."

(*Ṣaḥīḥ al-Bukhārī*: 2697, *Ṣaḥīḥ Muslim*: 1718, *Musnad Aḥmad*: 24954)

51

عَنْ عَائِشَةَ أَنَّهَا سَأَلَتْ النَّبِيَّ صَلَّى اللهُ عَلَيْهِ وَسَلَّمَ فَقَالَتْ: «يَا رَسُولَ اللَّهِ، أَعَلَى النِّسَاءِ جِهَادٌ؟» قَالَ: «الْحَجُّ وَالْعُمْرَةُ هُوَ جِهَادُ النِّسَاءِ».

(صحيح البخاري:٢٨٧٦، سنن النسائي:٢٦٢٨، مسند أحمد:٢٤٩٦٧)

ʿĀʾishah ﵁ related that she asked the Prophet ﷺ: "O Messenger of Allah, is jihad obligatory on women?" He replied: "The Greater and Lesser Pilgrimage (*ḥajj* and *ʿumrah*) are the jihad of women."

(*Ṣaḥīḥ al-Bukhārī*: 2876, *Sunan al-Nasāʾī*: 2628, *Musnad Aḥmad*: 24967)

52

عَنْ عَائِشَةَ أَنَّ رَسُولَ اللَّهِ صَلَّى اللهُ عَلَيْهِ وَسَلَّمَ دَعَا فَاطِمَةَ ابْنَتَهُ فَسَارَّهَا فَبَكَتْ ثُمَّ سَارَّهَا فَضَحِكَتْ، فَقَالَتْ عَائِشَةُ: «فَقُلْتُ لِفَاطِمَةَ: مَا هَذَا الَّذِي سَارَّكِ بِهِ رَسُولُ اللَّهِ صَلَّى اللهُ عَلَيْهِ وَسَلَّمَ فَبَكَيْتِ ثُمَّ سَارَّكِ فَضَحِكْتِ؟» قَالَتْ: «سَارَّنِي فَأَخْبَرَنِي بِمَوْتِهِ فَبَكَيْتُ ثُمَّ سَارَّنِي فَأَخْبَرَنِي أَنِّي أَوَّلُ مَنْ أَتْبَعُهُ مِنْ أَهْلِهِ فَضَحِكْتُ».

(صحيح البخاري:٣٦٢٥، صحيح مسلم:٢٤٥٠، مسند أحمد:٢٤٩٨٨)

ʿĀ'ishah related that the Messenger of Allah called his daughter, Fāṭimah, and whispered something to her, which made her cry and then he whispered something to her again, and she laughed. Later [after the Prophet's demise] I asked Fāṭimah why she had first cried and then laughed when the Messenger of Allah had whispered to her. She said: "He told me first about his impending death, which made me cry and then he informed me that I will be the first among his family to join him, and this made me laugh."

(*Ṣaḥīḥ al-Bukhārī*: 3625, *Ṣaḥīḥ Muslim*: 2450, *Musnad Aḥmad*: 24988)

53

عَنْ عَائِشَةَ، قَالَتْ: «كُنْتُ أَشْرَبُ وَأَنَا حَائِضٌ، ثُمَّ أُنَاوِلُهُ النَّبِيَّ صَلَّى اللهُ عَلَيْهِ وَسَلَّمَ فَيَضَعُ فَاهُ عَلَى مَوْضِعِ فِيَّ فَيَشْرَبُ، وَأَتَعَرَّقُ الْعَرْقَ وَأَنَا حَائِضٌ ثُمَّ أُنَاوِلُهُ النَّبِيَّ صَلَّى اللهُ عَلَيْهِ وَسَلَّمَ فَيَضَعُ فَاهُ عَلَى مَوْضِعِ فِيَّ».

(صحيح مسلم:٦٩٢)

ʿĀ'ishah ﵂ said: "It often happened, when I was menstruating, that I would drink from a container and then hand it to the Prophet ﷺ and he would drink from the same spot that my lips had touched; and it often happened, while I was menstruating, that I would eat from a boney piece of meat and then hand it to him and he would eat from the same spot that my teeth had touched."

(*Ṣaḥīḥ Muslim*: 692)

54

عَنْ عَائِشَةَ، قَالَتْ: «عَطَسَ رَجُلٌ عِنْدَ رَسُولِ اللَّهِ صَلَّى اللهُ عَلَيْهِ وَسَلَّمَ، قَالَ: مَا أَقُولُ يَا رَسُولَ اللَّهِ؟ قَالَ: قُلْ الْحَمْدُ لِلَّهِ. قَالَ الْقَوْمُ: مَا نَقُولُ لَهُ يَا رَسُولَ اللَّهِ؟ قَالَ: قُولُوا لَهُ: يَرْحَمُكَ اللهُ. قَالَ: مَا أَقُولُ لَهُمْ يَا رَسُولَ اللَّهِ؟ قَالَ: قُلْ لَهُمْ يَهْدِيكُمُ اللهُ وَيُصْلِحُ بَالَكُمْ».

(سنن والترمذي:١٤٧٢، مسند أحمد:١٠٠٥٢)

ʿĀ'ishah ﷺ said: "A man sneezed in the presence of the Messenger of Allah ﷺ and then exclaimed: 'What should I say, O Messenger of Allah?'. He said: 'Say: Praise be to Allah (*al-ḥamdu Lillāh*).' Those present asked: 'What should we say?' He said: 'Say: May Allah have mercy on you (*Yarḥamuka Llāh*).' The person who had sneezed asked: 'O Messenger of Allah, what should I say to them in response?' He said: "Say to them: May Allah guide and improve your condition (*Yahdīkum Llāhu wa yuṣliḥu bālakum*).'"

(*Sunan al-Tirmidhī*: 2741, *Musnad Aḥmad*: 25001)

55

قَالَ مُحَمَّدُ بْنُ إِبْرَاهِيمَ أَنَّ أَبَا سَلَمَةَ حَدَّثَهُ وَكَانَتْ بَيْنَهُ وَبَيْنَ أُنَاسٍ خُصُومَةٌ فِي أَرْضٍ وَأَنَّهُ دَخَلَ عَلَى عَائِشَةَ فَذَكَرَ ذَلِكَ لَهَا فَقَالَتْ: «يَا أَبَا سَلَمَةَ اجْتَنِبْ الْأَرْضَ فَإِنَّ رَسُولَ اللَّهِ صَلَّى اللهُ عَلَيْهِ وَسَلَّمَ قَالَ: مَنْ ظَلَمَ قِيدَ شِبْرٍ مِنْ الْأَرْضِ طُوِّقَهُ مِنْ سَبْعِ أَرَضِينَ».

(صحيح البخاري:٣٥٤٢، صحيح مسلم:٢١٦١، مسند أحمد:٩٠٠٥٢)

Abū Salamah related that one day he visited ʿĀ'ishah ﵂ to speak with her about a land dispute. When he explained to her the matter, she said to him: "O Abū Salamah, stay away from that plot of land for the Messenger of Allah ﷺ said: 'If one usurps even a foot of ground, Allah will place a fetter around his neck equal to seven earths.'"

(*Ṣaḥīḥ al-Bukhārī*: 2453, *Ṣaḥīḥ Muslim*: 1612, *Musnad Aḥmad*: 25009)

56

عَنْ عَائِشَةَ، قَالَتْ: «مَا كَانَ رَسُولُ اللَّهِ صَلَّى اللهُ عَلَيْهِ وَسَلَّمَ يَصُومُ مِنْ شَهْرٍ مِنْ السَّنَةِ أَكْثَرَ مِنْ صِيَامِهِ مِنْ شَعْبَانَ كَانَ يَصُومُهُ كُلَّهُ».

(صحيح البخاري:٩٦٩١، صحيح مسلم:٢٨٧، مسند أحمد:٩٤٠٥٢)

ʿĀ'ishah ﵂ said: "The Messenger of Allah ﷺ did not fast in any of the months of the year as much as he did in Shaʿbān: he fasted the whole month."

(*Ṣaḥıḥ al-Bukhārī*: 1969, *Ṣaḥīḥ Muslim*: 782, *Musnad Aḥmad*: 25049)

57

عَنْ عَائِشَةَ زَوْجِ النَّبِيِّ صَلَّى اللهُ عَلَيْهِ وَسَلَّمَ أَخْبَرَتْهُ أَنَّ رَسُولَ اللَّهِ صَلَّى اللهُ عَلَيْهِ وَسَلَّمَ كَانَ يَدْعُو فِي الصَّلَاةِ: «اللَّهُمَّ إِنِّي أَعُوذُ بِكَ مِنَ الْمَأْثَمِ وَالْمَغْرَمِ». فَقَلْتُ: «مَا أَكْثَرَ مَا تَسْتَعِيذُ مِنَ الْمَغْرَمِ؟» فَقَالَ: «إِنَّ الرَّجُلَ إِذَا غَرِمَ حَدَّثَ فَكَذَبَ، وَوَعَدَ فَأَخْلَفَ».

(صحيح البخاري:٢٣٨، صحيح مسلم:٩٨٥، مسند أحمد:٥٨٠٥٢)

‘Ā’ishah رضي الله عنها, the wife of the Prophet ﷺ informed that the Messenger of Allah ﷺ used to supplicate in his prayer: “O Allah, I seek refuge in You from sinning and from debt” and so I remarked: “You do seek refuge from debt quite a lot!” So he said: “A man burdened by debt lies when he speaks and makes promises but breaks them.”

(*Ṣaḥīḥ al-Bukhārī*: 832, *Ṣaḥīḥ Muslim*: 589, *Musnad Aḥmad*: 25085)

58

عَنْ عَائِشَةَ أَنَّ رَسُولَ اللَّهِ صَلَّى اللهُ عَلَيْهِ وَسَلَّمَ لَمْ يَكُنْ يَدَعُ فِي بَيْتِهِ ثَوْبًا فِيهِ تَصْلِيبٌ إِلَّا قَضَبَهُ.

(مسند أحمد:٢٦١٤٢)

ʿĀ'ishah ﵂ related that the Messenger of Allah ﷺ did not leave any item of clothing in the house that had a cross on it except that he cut it off from it.

(*Musnad Aḥmad*: 26142)

59

عَنْ عَائِشَةَ، قَالَتْ: «قَالَ رَسُولُ اللَّهِ صَلَّى اللهُ عَلَيْهِ وَسَلَّمَ: إِنَّ اللَّهَ عَزَّ وَجَلَّ وَمَلَائِكَتَهُ عَلَيْهِمْ السَّلَام يُصَلُّونَ عَلَى الَّذِينَ يَصِلُونَ الصُّفُوفَ وَمَنْ سَدَّ فُرْجَةً رَفَعَهُ اللهُ بِهَا دَرَجَةً».

(صحيح الجامع الصغير:١٨٤٣، مسند أحمد:٢٥٠٩٤)

ʿĀ'ishah ﵂ related that the Messenger of Allah ﷺ said: "Allah and His angels send mercy upon those who maintain proper rows in congregational prayer, and whoever fills a gap in a row of prayer, Allah raises him one rank."

(*Ṣaḥīḥ al-Jāmiʿ al-Ṣaghīr*: 1843, *Musnad Aḥmad*: 25094)

60

عَنْ عَائِشَةَ أَنّ النَّبِيَّ صَلَّى اللهُ عَلَيْهِ وَسَلَّمَ قَالَ: «لَا يَدْخُلُ الدَّجَّالُ مَكَّةَ وَلَا الْمَدِينَةَ».

(مسند أحمد:٢٦٠٤٧)

ʿĀ’ishah (may Allah be pleased with her) related that the Prophet ﷺ said: “The Antichrist (*al-Dajjāl*) will not be able to enter Makkah and Madinah.”

(*Musnad Aḥmad*: 26047)

61

عَنْ سَعْدِ بْنِ هِشَامِ بْنِ عَامِرٍ، قَالَ: «أَتَيْتُ عَائِشَةَ فَقُلْتُ: يَا أُمَّ الْمُؤْمِنِينَ أَخْبِرِينِي بِخُلُقِ رَسُولِ اللَّهِ صَلَّى اللهُ عَلَيْهِ وَسَلَّمَ. قَالَتْ: كَانَ خُلُقُهُ الْقُرْآنَ. أَمَا تَقْرَأُ الْقُرْآنَ، قَوْلَ اللَّهِ عَزَّ وَجَلَّ، {وَإِنَّكَ لَعَلَى خُلُقٍ عَظِيمٍ}؟ قُلْتُ: فَإِنِّي أُرِيدُ أَنْ أَتَبَتَّلَ. قَالَتْ: لَا تَفْعَلْ. أَمَا تَقْرَأُ {لَقَدْ كَانَ لَكُمْ فِي رَسُولِ اللَّهِ أُسْوَةٌ حَسَنَةٌ}؟ فَقَدْ تَزَوَّجَ رَسُولُ اللَّهِ صَلَّى اللهُ عَلَيْهِ وَسَلَّمَ وَقَدْ وُلِدَ لَهُ».

(مسند أحمد:٢٥١٠٨، مسند أبي يعلى:٤٨٦٢)

Sa'd ibn Hishām ibn 'Āmir related that he went to see 'Ā'ishah ﵂ and he asked her: "O Mother of the Believers, tell me about the character of the Messenger of Allah ﷺ." She replied: "His character was an embodiment of the Qur'ān. Have you not pondered over the words of Allah the Most High: "You [Prophet Muḥammad] are of a high and noble character [*al-Qalam* 68: 4]." Sa'd asked her again: "I want to retreat completely from life." She responded: "Do not do so; do you not find written in the Qur'ān: {Indeed, in the Messenger of Allah you have an excellent example}? The Messenger of Allah ﷺ did marry and had children."

(*Musnad Aḥmad*: 25108; *Musnad Abū Ya'lā*: 4862)

62

عَنْ عَائِشَةَ، قَالَتْ: «دَعَوَاتٌ كَانَ رَسُولُ اللَّهِ صَلَّى اللهُ عَلَيْهِ وَسَلَّمَ يُكْثِرُ أَنْ يَدْعُوَ بِهَا: يَا مُقَلِّبَ الْقُلُوبِ ثَبِّتْ قَلْبِي عَلَى دِينِكَ. قَالَتْ: فَقُلْتُ يَا رَسُولَ اللَّهِ، إِنَّكَ تُكْثِرُ تَدْعُو بِهَذَا الدُّعَاءِ؟ فَقَالَ: إِنَّ قَلْبَ الْآدَمِيِّ بَيْنَ أُصْبُعَيْنِ مِنْ أَصَابِعِ اللَّهِ عَزَّ وَجَلَّ فَإِذَا شَاءَ أَزَاغَهُ وَإِذَا شَاءَ أَقَامَهُ».

(السنن الكبرى للنسائي:٧٣٧٧، مسند أحمد:١١١٥٢)

‘Ā’ishah ﵂ related: “The Messenger of Allah ﷺ often made this supplication: ‘O You who changes hearts, make my heart firm on Your religion.’ I asked him: ‘O Messenger of Allah, why do you make this supplication so often?’ He replied: ‘A person’s heart is between Allah’s two fingers; if He wills, He makes him go astray and, if He wills, He keeps him on the straight path.’”

(*Al-Sunan al-Kubrā* of al-Nasā’ī: 7737,
Musnad Aḥmad: 25111)

63

عَنْ عَائِشَةَ، قَالَتْ: «كَانَ رَسُولُ اللَّهِ صَلَّى اللهُ عَلَيْهِ وَسَلَّمَ يَقُولُ: اللَّهُمَّ اجْعَلْنِي مِنَ الَّذِينَ إِذَا أَحْسَنُوا اسْتَبْشَرُوا وَإِذَا أَسَاءُوا اسْتَغْفَرُوا».

(مسند أحمد:١٢٠٦٢)

ʿĀ'ishah ﵂ said: "The Messenger of Allah ﷺ used to say: "O Allah, make me among those who are hopeful when they do something good and of those who seek forgiveness when they lapse."

(*Musnad Aḥmad*: 26021)

64

عَنْ عَائِشَةَ، أَنَّهَا قَالَتْ: «كَانَ رَسُولُ اللَّهِ صَلَّى اللهُ عَلَيْهِ وَسَلَّمَ يُحِبُّ التَّيَمُّنَ فِي شَأْنِهِ كُلِّهِ مَا اسْتَطَاعَ فِي طُهُورِهِ وَتَرَجُّلِهِ وَتَنَعُّلِهِ».

(صحيح البخاري:٨٦١، صحيح مسلم:٨٦٢، مسند أحمد:٤٣١٥٢)

ʿĀ'ishah ﵂ said: "The Messenger of Allah ﷺ loved to start from the right-hand side in all his matters: upon performing ritual ablution, combing his hair and putting on his shoes."

(*Ṣaḥīḥ al-Bukhārī*: 168, *Ṣaḥīḥ Muslim*: 268, *Musnad Aḥmad*: 25134)

65

عَنْ عَائِشَةَ أَنَّ رَسُولَ اللَّهِ صَلَّى اللهُ عَلَيْهِ وَسَلَّمَ بَالَ فَقَامَ عُمَرُ خَلْفَهُ بِكُوزٍ، فَقَالَ: «مَا هَذَا يَا عُمَرُ؟» قَالَ: «مَاءٌ تَوَضَّأُ بِهِ يَا رَسُولَ اللَّهِ». قَالَ: «مَا أُمِرْتُ كُلَّمَا بُلْتُ أَنْ أَتَوَضَّأَ وَلَوْ فَعَلْتُ ذَلِكَ كَانَتْ سُنَّةً».

(سنن أبي داود:٤٢، سنن ابن ماجه:٣٧٢، مسند أحمد:٢٥١٥٠)

ʿĀ'ishah ﷺ related that the Messenger of Allah ﷺ went out to urinate and ʿUmar Ibn al-Khaṭṭāb] followed him with a water pot. After he finished, he asked: "What is this, O ʿUmar?" He said: "Water, O Messenger of Allah, for you to perform minor ritual ablution (*wuḍū'*)." He replied: "I have not been commanded to perform *wuḍū'* whenever I go to the lavatory, otherwise it will be affirmed as a sunnah."

(*Sunan Abū Dāwūd*: 42, *Sunan Ibn Mājah*: 372, *Musnad Aḥmad*: 25150)

66

عَنْ عَائِشَةَ أَنَّ رَسُولَ اللَّهِ صَلَّى اللهُ عَلَيْهِ وَسَلَّمَ أُهْدِيَتْ لَهُ هَدِيَّةٌ فِيهَا قِلَادَةٌ مِنْ جَزْعٍ فَقَالَ: «لَأَدْفَعَنَّهَا إِلَى أَحَبِّ أَهْلِي إِلَيَّ»، فَقَالَتِ النِّسَاءُ: «ذَهَبَتْ بِهَا ابْنَةُ أَبِي قُحَافَةَ». فَدَعَا النَّبِيُّ صَلَّى اللهُ عَلَيْهِ وَسَلَّمَ أُمَامَةَ بِنْتَ زَيْنَبَ فَعَلَّقَهَا فِي عُنُقِهَا.

(مسند أحمد:٢٥٢١١، مسند أبي يعلى:٤٤٧١)

ʿĀ'ishah ﵁ related that the Messenger of Allah ﷺ received some gifts which included an onyx necklace and he said: "I shall give it to the most beloved member of my family." So the women present there said: "The daughter of Ibn Abi Quhafah [i.e. ʿĀ'ishah] will certainly get it." However, the Prophet ﷺ called Umāmah, the daughter of his daughter Zaynab, and put it around her neck.

(*Musnad Aḥmad*: 25211, *Musnad Abū Yaʿlā*: 4471)

67

عَنْ هِشَامٍ عَنْ أبيهِ قَالَ: «قِيلَ لِعَائِشَةَ: مَا كَانَ النَّبِيُّ صَلَّى اللهُ عَلَيْهِ وَسَلَّمَ يَصْنَعُ فِي بَيْتِهِ؟» قَالَتْ: «كَمَا يَصْنَعُ أَحَدُكُمْ يَخْصِفُ نَعْلَهُ وَيُرَقِّعُ ثَوْبَهُ».

(صحيح ابن حبّان:٥٦٧٦، مسند أحمد:٢٥٢٥٦)

Hishām narrated from his father, 'Urwah, that 'Ā'ishah ﷺ was asked: "What the Prophet (peace be upon) used to do at home." She said: "He used to do as any of you would do: he mended his shoes and patched his clothes."

(*Ṣaḥīḥ Ibn Ḥibbān*: 5676, *Musnad Aḥmad*: 25256)

68

عَنْ عَائِشَةَ قَالَتْ: «كَانَتْ امْرَأَ عُثْمَانَ بْنِ مَظْعُونٍ تَخْتَضِبُ وَتَتَطَيَّبُ فَتَرَكَتْهُ فَدَخَلَتْ عَلَيَّ فَقُلْتُ لَهَا: أَمُشْهِدٌ أَمْ مُغِيبٌ؟ فَقَالَتْ: مُشْهِدٌ كَمُغِيبٍ. قُلْتُ لَهَا: مَا لَكِ؟ قَالَتْ: عُثْمَانُ لَا يُرِيدُ الدُّنْيَا وَلَا يُرِيدُ النِّسَاءَ. قَالَتْ عَائِشَةُ: فَدَخَلَ عَلَيَّ رَسُولُ اللَّهِ صَلَّى اللهُ عَلَيْهِ وَسَلَّمَ فَأَخْبَرْتُهُ بِذَلِكَ فَلَقِيَ عُثْمَانَ فَقَالَ: يَا عُثْمَانُ أَتُؤْمِنُ بِمَا نُؤْمِنُ بِهِ؟ قَالَ: نَعَمْ يَا رَسُولَ اللَّهِ. قَالَ: فَأُسْوَةٌ مَا لَكَ بِنَا».

(سنن أبي داود:١٣٦٩، مسند أحمد:٢٥٢٦٠)

Ā'ishah ﵂ related that the wife of ʿUthmān ibn Maẓʿūn used to apply henna and perfume but she then abandoned all this. One day when she visited me, I asked her: "Is he [i.e., her husband] present or absent?" She replied: "He is present but it is the same as if he was absent." When I requested her to elaborate, she replied: "He is no longer interested in this world or women." "Then the Messenger of Allah ﷺ came home and I informed him of what she said to me. So he asked him: "O ʿUthmān, do you believe in what we believe?" ʿUthmān replied: "Yes, O Messenger of Allah." Upon this the Prophet ﷺ said to him: "Then why are you not following my example?"

(*Sunan Abū Dāwūd*: 1369, *Musnad Aḥmad*: 25260)

69

عَنْ عَائِشَةَ أَنَّ رَسُولَ اللَّهِ صَلَّى اللهُ عَلَيْهِ وَسَلَّمَ كَانَ إِذَا عَادَ مَرِيضًا قَالَ: «أَذْهِبْ الْبَاسَ رَبَّ النَّاس وَاشْفِ إِنَّكَ أَنْتَ الشَّافِي وَلَا شِفَاءَ إِلَّا شِفَاؤُكَ شِفَاءً لَا يُغَادِرُ سَقَمًا».

(صحيح البخاري:٥٦٧٥، صحيح مسلم:٢١٩١، مسند أحمد:٢٥٢٨٥)

ʿĀ'ishah رضي الله عنها related that the Messenger of Allah ﷺ used to say whenever he visited an ill person: "O Lord of People, remove his illness and heal him, You alone are the Healer, there is no cure other than Your cure, a cure that leaves no trace of illness whatsoever."

(*Ṣaḥīḥ al-Bukhārī*: 5675, *Ṣaḥīḥ* Muslim: 2191, *Musnad Aḥmad*: 25285)

70

عَنْ عَائِشَةَ قَالَتْ: «كَانَ رَسُولُ اللَّهِ صَلَّى اللهُ عَلَيْهِ وَسَلَّمَ إِذَا صَلَّى قَامَ حَتَّى تَتَفَطَّرَ رِجْلَاهُ». قَالَتْ عَائِشَةُ: «يَا رَسُولَ اللَّهِ صَلَّى اللهُ عَلَيْهِ وَسَلَّمَ: أَتَصْنَعُ هَذَا وَقَدْ غُفِرَ لَكَ مَا تَقَدَّمَ مِنْ ذَنْبِكَ وَمَا تَأَخَّرَ؟» فَقَالَ: «يَا عَائِشَةُ، أَفَلَا أَكُونُ عَبْدًا شَكُورًا؟»

(صحيح البخاري:٤٨٣٧، صحيح مسلم:٢٨٢٠، مسند أحمد:٢٥٣٥٦)

ʿĀ'ishah ﷺ said: "The Messenger of Allah ﷺ used to stand in prayer until his feet would swell." She asked him: "O Messenger of Allah ﷺ why would you do this when Allah has already forgiven your past and future lapses?" He replied: "O ʿĀ'ishah, should I not be a grateful servant?"

(*Ṣaḥīḥ al-Bukhārī*: 4837, *Ṣaḥīḥ Muslim*: 2820, *Musnad Aḥmad*: 25356)

71

عَنْ عَائِشَةَ رَضِيَ اللهُ عَنْهَا أَنّ النَّبِيَّ صَلَّى اللهُ عَلَيْهِ وَسَلَّمَ كَانَ يُحَدِّثُ حَدِيثًا لَوْ عَدَّهُ الْعَادُّ لَأَحْصَاهُ.

(صحيح البخاري:٧٦٥٣)

ʿĀʾishah رضي الله عنها related that the Prophet ﷺ used to speak so clearly and with such adequate pauses that one could count the words spoken by him.

(*Ṣaḥīḥ al-Bukhārī*: 3567)

72

عَنْ عَائِشَةَ رَضِيَ اللهُ عَنْهَا، قَالَت: «حَشَوْتُ لِلنَّبِيِّ صَلَّى اللهُ عَلَيْهِ وَسَلَّمَ وِسَادَةً فِيهَا تَمَاثِيلُ كَأَنَّهَا نُمْرُقَةٌ، فَجَاءَ فَقَامَ بَيْنَ الْبَابَيْنِ وَجَعَلَ يَتَغَيَّرُ وَجْهُهُ، فَقُلْتُ: مَا لَنَا يَا رَسُولَ اللَّهِ؟ قَالَ: مَا بَالُ هَذِهِ الْوِسَادَةِ؟ قَالَتْ: وِسَادَةٌ جَعَلْتُهَا لَكَ لِتَضْطَجِعَ عَلَيْهَا. قَالَ: أَمَا عَلِمْتِ أَنَّ الْمَلَائِكَةَ لَا تَدْخُلُ بَيْتًا فِيهِ صُورَةٌ وَأَنَّ مَنْ صَنَعَ الصُّورَةَ يُعَذَّبُ يَوْمَ الْقِيَامَةِ، يَقُولُ: أَحْيُوا مَا خَلَقْتُمْ».

(صحيح البخاري:٣٢٢٤، صحيح مسلم:٥٥١١)

‘Ā’ishah رضي الله عنها said: “I prepared a pillow for the Prophet ﷺ that had some pictures imprinted on it. When he arrived, he paused at the door, and I noted a change in his facial expression. So I asked him: ‘Is anything the matter, O Messenger of Allah?’ He said: “What’s with this pillow?” I said: ‘I prepared it for you so that you can lie down on it.’ Upon this he said: “Do you not know that the angels do not enter a house in which there are pictures? Whoever draws a picture will be punished on the Day of Judgement. It will be said to him: ‘Bring to life what you have created!’”

(*Ṣaḥīḥ al-Bukhārī*: 3224, *Ṣaḥīḥ Muslim*: 5511)

73

وَقَالَتْ عَائِشَةُ رَضِيَ اللهُ عَنْهَا عَنِ النَّبِيِّ صَلَّى اللهُ عَلَيْهِ وَسَلَّمَ: «يُبْعَثُونَ عَلَى نِيَّاتِهِمْ».

(صحيح البخاري)

ʿĀ'ishah ﷺ related that the Prophet ﷺ said: "People shall be resurrected on the Day of Judgement in accordance with their intentions."

(*Ṣaḥīḥ al-Bukhārī*, The Book of Fasting)

74

عَنْ عَائِشَةَ رَضِيَ اللهُ عَنْهَا، زَوْجِ النَّبِيِّ صَلَّى اللهُ عَلَيْهِ وَسَلَّمَ، أَنَّ حَمْزَ بْنَ عَمْرٍو الْأَسْلَمِيَّ قَالَ لِلنَّبِيِّ صَلَّى اللهُ عَلَيْهِ وَسَلَّمَ: «أَأَصُومُ فِي السَّفَرِ (وَكَانَ كَثِيرَ الصِّيَامِ)؟» فَقَالَ: «إِنْ شِئْتَ فَصُمْ، وَإِنْ شِئْتَ فَأَفْطِرْ».

(صحيح البخاري:١٩٤٣، صحيح مسلم:٢٦٢٥)

Ā'ishah ﷺ related that Ḥamzah ibn ʿAmr al-Aslamī, who was in the habit of fasting often, asked the Prophet ﷺ: "Should I fast while travelling?" The Prophet ﷺ replied: 'You are free to fast or not."

(*Ṣaḥīḥ al-Bukhārī*: 1943, *Ṣaḥīḥ Muslim*: 2625)

75

عَنْ عائِشَةَ أَنَّ رَسُولَ اللَّهِ صَلَّى اللهُ عَلَيْهِ وَسَلَّمَ قَالَ: «مَا نَفَعَنَا مَالٌ قَطُّ مَا نَفَعَنَا مَالُ أبي بَكْرٍ».

(مسند الحميدي:٢٥٢)

ʿĀ'ishah ﵂ related that the Messenger of Allah ﷺ said: "No wealth has benefitted us more than Abū Bakr's wealth."

(*Musnad al-Ḥumaydī*: 252)

76

عَنْ عَائِشَةَ أَنّ رَسُولَ اللَّهِ صَلَّى اللهُ عَلَيْهِ وَسَلَّمَ كَانَ إِذَا رَأَى الْمَطَرَ قَال: «اللَّهُمَّ صَيِّبًا نَافِعًا».

(صحيح البخاري:١٠٣٢، صحيح مسلم:٢٠٨٥)

ʿĀ'ishah ﵁ related that the Messenger of Allah ﷺ used to say whenever he saw rain: "O Allah, let it be a beneficial rain."

(*Ṣaḥīḥ al-Bukhārī*: 1032, *Ṣaḥīḥ Muslim*: 2085)

77

عَنْ عَائِشَةَ رَضِيَ اللهُ عَنْهَا قَالَت: «كَانَتْ عِنْدِي امْرَأَةٌ مِنْ بَنِي أَسَدٍ فَدَخَلَ عَلَيَّ رَسُولُ اللَّهِ صَلَّى اللهُ عَلَيْهِ وَسَلَّمَ فَقَالَ: «مَنْ هذِهِ؟» قُلْتُ: «فُلَانَةُ لَا تَنَامُ بِاللَّيْلِ فَذُكِرَ مِنْ صَلَاتِهَا». فَقَالَ: «مَهْ! عَلَيْكُمْ مَا تُطِيقُونَ مِنَ الْأَعْمَالِ فَإِنَّ اللَّهَ لَا يَمَلُّ حَتَّى تَمَلُّوا».

(صحيح البخاري:١٥١١، صحيح مسلم:٧٢٨١)

Ā’ishah ﵂ said: “A woman from the Banū Asad tribe was with me when the Messenger of Allah ﷺ came home, and so he asked me who she was. I said she was so-and-so and that she does not sleep at night [i.e., standing in prayer] and I mentioned her extensive prayers. Upon hearing this, he said: ‘Desist! Confine yourselves to what you are able to do, for Allah shall not give up rewarding you until you give up yourselves your works due to excessiveness.’”

(*Ṣaḥīḥ al-Bukhārī*: 1151, *Ṣaḥīḥ Muslim*: 1827)

78

عَنْ عَائِشَةَ رَضِيَ اللهُ عَنْهَا قَالَتْ: «قَالَ النَّبِيُّ صَلَّى اللهُ عَلَيْهِ وَسَلَّمَ: لَا تَسُبُّوا الْأَمْوَاتَ فَإِنَّهُمْ قَدْ أَفْضَوْا إِلَى مَا قَدَّمُوا».

(صحيح البخاري:١٣٩٣)

‘Ā’ishah ﵂ related that the Prophet ﷺ said: “Do not insult the dead, for they have proceeded to face the consequences of the actions they had sent forth.”

(*Ṣaḥīḥ al-Bukhārī*: 1393)

79

عَنْ عَائِشَةَ رَضِيَ اللهُ عَنْهَا قَالَتْ: «قَالَ رَسُولُ اللَّهِ صَلَّى اللهُ عَلَيْهِ وَسَلَّمَ: إِذَا أَنْفَقَتِ الْمَرْأَةُ مِنْ طَعَامِ بَيْتِهَا غَيْرَ مُفْسِدٍ كَانَ لَهَا أَجْرُهَا بِمَا أَنْفَقَتْ، وَلِزَوْجِهَا أَجْرُهُ بِمَا كَسَبَ، وَلِلْخَازِنِ مِثْلُ ذَلِكَ لَا يَنْقُصُ بَعْضُهُمْ أَجْرَ بَعْضٍ شَيْئًا».

(صحيح البخاري:٥٢٤١، صحيح مسلم:٤٦٣٢)

Āʾishah (رضي الله عنها) related that the Messenger of Allah (ﷺ) said: "If a woman spends something out of her husband's belongings, without any intention of wasting it, she will be rewarded for her spending and her husband will also be rewarded because he earned it and the keeper will earn the same reward – all of them will be rewarded without diminishing each other's reward."

(*Ṣaḥīḥ al-Bukhārī*: 1425, *Ṣaḥīḥ Muslim*: 2364)

80

عَنْ عَائِشَةَ رَضِيَ اللهُ عَنْهَا قَالَتْ: «كَانَ النَّبِيُّ صَلَّى اللهُ عَلَيْهِ وَسَلَّمَ إِذَا خَرَجَ مِنَ الْخَلَاءِ قَالَ: غُفْرَانَكَ».

(سنن الترمذي:٧٠، سنن أبي داود:٠٣)

ʿĀ'ishah related that the Prophet ﷺ used to say after coming out from the lavatory: "O Allah, I seek Your forgiveness."

(*Sunan al-Tirmidhī*: 7, *Sunan Abū Dāwūd*: 30)

81

عَنْ عَائِشَةَ عَنِ النَّبِيِّ صَلَّى اللهُ عَلَيْهِ وَسَلَّمَ أَنَّهُ قَالَ: «لَا يَقْبَلُ اللهُ صَلَاةَ حَائِضٍ إِلَّا بِخِمَارٍ».

(سنن أبي داود:١٤٦، سنن والترمذي:٧٧٣)

ʿĀ'ishah related that the Prophet said: "The prayer of a woman who has reached the age of puberty is not accepted unless she wears something that covers her hair and chest (*khimār*)."

(*Sunan Abū Dāwūd*: 641, *Sunan al-Tirmidhī*: 377)

82

عَنْ أَبِي سَلَمَةَ قَالَ: «سَأَلْتُ عَائِشَةَ أُمَّ الْمُؤْمِنِينَ بِأَيِّ شَيْءٍ كَانَ نَبِيُّ اللَّهِ صَلَّى اللهُ عَلَيْهِ وَسَلَّمَ يَفْتَتِحُ صَلَاتَهُ، إِذَا قَامَ مِنَ اللَّيْلِ؟ قَالَتْ: كَانَ إِذَا قَامَ مِنَ اللَّيْلِ افْتَتَحَ صَلَاتَه: اللَهُمَّ رَبَّ جَبْرَائِيلَ وَمِيكَائِيلَ وَإِسْرَافِيلَ فَاطِرَ السَّمَاوَاتِ وَالأَرْضِ عَالِمَ الْغَيْبِ وَالشَّهَادَةِ، أَنْتَ تَحْكُمُ بَيْنَ عِبَادِكَ فِيمَا كَانُوا فِيهِ يَخْتَلِفُونَ، اهْدِنِي لِمَا اخْتُلِفَ فِيهِ مِنَ الْحَقِّ بِإِذْنِكَ، إِنَّكَ تَهْدِى مَنْ تَشَاءُ إِلَى صِرَاطٍ مُسْتَقِيمٍ».

(صحيح مسلم:١٨١١)

Abū Salamah said: "I asked 'Ā'ishah ﵂ about the supplication with which the Prophet ﷺ opened his prayer when he got up to pray at night. So she said: 'Whenever he got up to pray at night, he started his prayer with: O Allah, Lord of Jibrā'īl, Mīkā'īl and Isrāfīl, Originator of the heavens and the Earth, Knower of the unseen and the manifest, You judge between Your servants about that which they used to differ; guide me to the Straight Path, by Your leave, You guide whom You will to the straight path.'"

(*Ṣaḥīḥ Muslim*: 1181)

83

عَنْ عَائِشَةَ قَالتْ: «كُلُّ ذٰلكَ قَدْ فَعلَ رَسُولُ اللهِ صَلَّى اللهُ عَلَيْهِ وَسَلَّم قَصَّرَ الصَّلاةَ وَأتمَّ».

(كتاب الأمّ للشافعي ٦٥٣/٢، معرفة السنن والآثار البيهقي.٤٦٠٦)

Ā'ishah ﷺ said: "The Messenger of Allah ﷺ sometimes shortened his prayers and sometimes prayed them in full [when he was travelling]."

(*Kitāb al-Umm* of al-Shāfi'ī: 356/2,
Ma'rifat al-Sunan wa'l-Āthār of al-Bayhāqī: 6064)

84

عَنْ عَائِشَةَ قَالَتْ إِنَّ رَسُولَ اللَّهِ صَلَّى اللهُ عَلَيْهِ وَسَلَّمَ، قَالَ: «إِنَّهُ خُلِقَ كُلُّ إِنْسَانٍ مِنْ بَنِي آدَمَ عَلَى سِتِّينَ وَثَلَاثِمِائَةِ مَفْصِلٍ، فَمَنْ كَبَّرَ اللَّهَ، وَحَمِدَ اللَّهَ، وهَلَّلَ اللَّهَ، وَسَبَّحَ اللَّهَ، وَاسْتَغْفَرَ اللَّهَ، وَعَزَلَ حَجَرًا عَنْ طَرِيقِ النَّاسِ، أَوْ شَوْكَةً، أَوْ عَظْمًا عَنْ طَرِيقِ النَّاسِ، وَأَمَرَ بِمَعْرُوفٍ، أَوْ نَهَى عَنْ مُنْكَرٍ عَدَدَ تِلْكَ السِّتِّينَ وَالثَّلَاثِمِائَةِ السُّلَامَى، فَإِنَّهُ يَمْشِي يَوْمَئِذٍ وَقَدْ زَحْزَحَ نَفْسَهُ عَنِ النَّارِ».

(صحيح مسلم:٧٠٠١)

ʿĀ'ishah ﷺ said that the Messenger of Allah ﷺ said: "Every person amongst the Children of Adam has 360 joints [in his body], so whoever says 'Allah is the greatest' or praises Allah or says 'there is no God except Allah' or says 'glory be to Allah', or seeks forgiveness from Allah, or removes a stone, thorn or bone from the path of people, or enjoins good and forbids evil, by the number of these 360 joints of his body, has removed himself on that day from Hellfire."

(*Ṣaḥīḥ Muslim*: 1007)

85

عَنْ عَائِشَةَ عَنِ النَّبِيِّ ﷺ قَالَ: «تَهادُوا فَإِنَّ الهَدِيَّةَ تُذْهِبُ الضَغَائِنَ».

(مسند الشهاب القضاعي:٦٦٠)

ʿĀ'ishah ﵂ reported that the Prophet ﷺ said: "Exchange gifts among yourselves, for the act of exchanging gifts does away with grudges."

(*Musnad al-Shihāb* of al-Qaḍāʿī: 660)

86

عَنْ عَائِشَةَ قَالَت: قَالَ رَسُولُ اللَّهِ صَلَّى اللهُ عَلَيْهِ وَسَلَّمَ: «أَعْلِنُوا هَذَا النِّكَاحَ وَاجْعَلُوهُ فِي الْمَسَاجِدِ وَاضْرِبُوا عَلَيْهِ بِالدُّفُوفِ».

(سنن الترمذي:١٠٨٩)

ʿĀ'ishah رضي الله عنها related that the Messenger of Allah ﷺ said: "Announce this wedding [of yours], let it take place in a mosque and celebrate it by playing the tambourine."

(*Sunan al-Tirmidhī*: 1089)

87

عَنْ عَائِشَةَ رَضِيَ اللهُ عَنْهَا أَنَّ قُرَيْشًا أَهَمَّهُمْ شَأْنُ الْمَرْأَةِ الْمَخْزُومِيَّةِ الَّتِي سَرَقَتْ فَقَالُوا: «وَمَنْ يُكَلِّمُ فِيهَا رَسُولَ اللَّهِ صَلَّى اللهُ عَلَيْهِ وَسَلَّمَ؟» فَقَالُوا: «وَمَنْ يَجْتَرِءُ عَلَيْهِ إِلَّا أُسَامَةُ بْنُ زَيْدٍ حِبُّ رَسُولِ اللَّهِ صَلَّى اللهُ عَلَيْهِ وَسَلَّمَ؟» فَكَلَّمَهُ أُسَامَةُ. فَقَالَ رَسُولُ اللَّهِ صَلَّى اللهُ عَلَيْهِ وَسَلَّمَ: «أَتَشْفَعُ فِي حَدٍّ مِنْ حُدُودِ اللَّهِ». ثُمَّ قَامَ فَاخْتَطَبَ ثُمَّ قَالَ: «إِنَّمَا أَهْلَكَ الَّذِينَ قَبْلَكُمْ أَنَّهُمْ كَانُوا إِذَا سَرَقَ فِيهِمُ الشَّرِيفُ تَرَكُوهُ وَإِذَا سَرَقَ فِيهِمُ الضَّعِيفُ أَقَامُوا عَلَيْهِ الْحَدَّ. وَأَيْمُ اللَّهِ، لَوْ أَنَّ فَاطِمَةَ بِنْتَ مُحَمَّدٍ سَرَقَتْ لَقَطَعْتُ يَدَهَا».

(صحيح البخاري:٥٧٤٣، صحيح مسلم:١١٤٤)

ʿĀ'ishah related that people were very concerned about a woman from the Banū Makhzum [Fāṭimah bint al-Aswad] who had committed a theft [on the eve of the conquest of Makkah], and so they said: "Who will approach the Messenger of Allah ﷺ about interceding for her?" They said among themselves: "There is no one else who can dare to approach him except Usāmah ibn Zayd, the beloved of the Messenger of Allah ﷺ". When Usāmah spoke on her behalf, the Messenger of Allah ﷺ said: "O Usāmah, do you intercede with me regarding a set punishment prescribed by Allah?" Then he got up and addressed everyone: “Indeed, what destroyed communities before you was that when a noble person committed a theft, they would let him get away with it, but when a weak person committed a theft, they applied the relevant punishment on him. By Allah, if Fāṭimah the daughter of Muḥammad were to commit a theft, I would cut off her hand.”

(*Ṣaḥīḥ al-Bukhārī*: 3475, *Ṣaḥīḥ Muslim*: 4411)

88

عَنْ عَائِشَةَ قَالَ رَسُولُ اللهِ صلَّى اللهُ عَلَيْهِ وَسَلَّمَ: «أتَدْرُونَ مَنِ السَّابِقونَ إلى ظِلِّ اللهِ عزَّ وجلَّ يومَ القيامةِ؟» قالوا: «اللهُ عزَّ وجلَّ وَرَسُولُهُ أعْلَمُ». قال: «الّذِينَ إِذَا أُعْطُوا الحَقَّ قَبِلُوهُ وَإِذَا سُئِلُوهُ بَذَلُوهُ وَحَكَمُوا للنَّاسِ حُكْمَهَمْ لأَنْفُسِهِمْ».

(مسند أحمد:٨٩٣٤٢)

ʿĀ'ishah ﷺ related that the Messenger of Allah ﷺ said: "Do you know who will be the first to be shaded under the shade of Allah, glorified and exalted is He, on the Day of Judgement?" The Companions responded: "Allah and His Messenger know best." He said: "It will be those who accept the truth when they are presented with it, and those who expend it when it is demanded of them, and those who decide for others as they would decide for themselves."

(*Musnad Aḥmad*: 24398)

89

عَنْ عَائِشَةَ رَضِيَ اللهُ عَنْهَا، قَالَت: «كَانَ رَسُولُ اللَّهِ صَلَّى اللهُ عَلَيْهِ وَسَلَّمَ يُحِبُّ الْحَلْوَاءَ وَالْعَسَلَ.»

(صحيح البخاري:١٣٤٥، صحيح مسلم:٩٧٦٣)

ʿĀ'ishah said: "The Messenger of Allah ﷺ used to like sweet dishes and honey."

(*Ṣaḥīḥ al-Bukhārī*: 5431, *Ṣaḥīḥ Muslim*: 3679)

90

عَنْ عَائِشَةَ أَنَّ رَسُولَ اللَّهِ صَلَّى اللهُ عَلَيْهِ وَسَلَّمَ أَوْلَمَ عَلَى بَعْضِ نِسَائِهِ بِشَعِيرٍ»

(مسند الحميدي:٨٢٢)

‘Ā’ishah ﵂ reported that the Messenger of Allah ﷺ served barley upon getting married to one of his wives.

(*Musnad al-Ḥumaydī*: 228)

91

عَنْ عَائِشَةَ رَضِيَ اللهُ عَنْهَا أَنَّ أَسْمَاءَ بِنْتَ أَبِي بَكْرٍ دَخَلَتْ عَلَى رَسُولِ اللَّهِ صَلَّى اللهُ عَلَيْهِ وَسَلَّمَ وَعَلَيْهَا ثِيَابٌ رِقَاقٌ، فَأَعْرَضَ عَنْهَا رَسُولُ اللَّهِ صَلَّى اللهُ عَلَيْهِ وَسَلَّمَ، وَقَالَ: «يَا أَسْمَاءُ إِنَّ الْمَرْأَةَ إِذَا بَلَغَتِ الْمَحِيضَ لَمْ تَصْلُحْ أَنْ يُرَى مِنْهَا إِلَّا هَذَا وَهَذَا، وَأَشَارَ إِلَى وَجْهِهِ وَكَفَّيْهِ».

(سنن أبي داود:٤٠١٤)

‘Ā’ishah رضي الله عنها related that Asmā’, daughter of Abū Bakr رضي الله عنهما, entered in on the Messenger of Allah ﷺ wearing thin clothes and so he turned his face away from her and said: “O Asmā’, it is not lawful that any part of the body of a female who has reached the age puberty be seen, except this and this - pointing to his face and hands.”

(*Sunan Abī Dāwūd*: 4104)

92

عَنْ أُمِّ الْمُؤْمِنِينَ عَائِشَةَ رَضِيَ اللهُ عَنْهَا أَنّهَا قَالَت: «مَا رَأَيْتُ أَحَدًا كَانَ أَشْبَهَ سَمْتًا وهَدْيًا وَدَلًّا بِرَسُولِ اللَّهِ صَلَّى اللهُ عَلَيْهِ وَسَلَّمَ مِنْ فَاطِمَةَ كَرَّمَ اللهُ وَجْهَهَا. كَانَتْ إِذَا دَخَلَتْ عَلَيْهِ قَامَ إِلَيْهَا فَأَخَذَ بِيَدِهَا وَقَبَّلَهَا وَأَجْلَسَهَا فِي مَجْلِسِه. وَكَانَ إِذَا دَخَلَ عَلَيْهَا قَامَتْ إِلَيْه فَأَخَذَتْ بِيَدِهِ فَقَبَّلَتْهُ وَأَجْلَسَتْهُ فِي مَجْلِسِهَا».

(سنن أبي داود:٥٢١٧)

The Mother of the Believers ʿĀ'ishah ﷺ said: "I have not seen anyone who resembled the Messenger of Allah ﷺ in his gait, composure and gravity more than Fāṭimah, may Allah ennoble her face. Whenever she visited him, he would stand for her, hold her by the hand, kiss her and make her sit where he was sitting; and when he visited her, she would stand for him, hold him by the hand, kiss him and make him sit where she was sitting."

(*Sunan Abī Dāwūd*: 5217)

93

عَنْ عَائِشَةَ قَالَتْ: «مرَّ النَّبِيُّ صَلَّى اللهُ عَلَيْهِ وَسَلَّمَ بِأَبِي بَكْرٍ وَهُوَ يَلْعَنُ بَعْض رَقِيقِهِ فَقَالَ: لَعَّانِينَ وَصِدِّيقِينَ، كَلَّا وَرَبِّ الكَعْبَةِ! فَعَتَقَ أَبُو بَكْرٍ رَضِيَ اللهُ عَنْهُ يَوْمَئِذٍ بَعْضَ رَقِيقِهِ ثُمَّ جَاءَ إِلَى النَّبِيِّ صَلَّى اللهُ عَلَيْهِ وَسَلَّمَ فقال: لَا أَعُودُ».

(الترغيب والترهيب للمنذري:٣/٣٩٧، مشكا المصابيح:٤٧٩٦)

ʿĀ'ishah ﵂ said: "The Prophet ﷺ passed by Abū Bakr ﵁ and saw him cursing one of his slaves. Upon hearing this, he said to him: 'A curser and a most truthful one, at one and the same time, never so by the Lord of the Ka'bah?' On that day, Abū Bakr ﵁ freed some of his slaves and then went to see the Prophet ﷺ and said to him: 'I will never do that again.'"

(*Al-Targhīb wa'-Tarhīb* of al-Mundhirī: 397/3,
Mishkāt al-Maṣābīḥ: 4796)

94

عَنْ عَائِشَةَ أَنَّ رَسُولَ اللَّهِ صَلَّى اللهُ عَلَيْهِ وَسَلَّمَ، قَالَ: «يَا عَائِشَةُ، إِنَّ اللَّهَ رَفِيقٌ يُحِبُّ الرِّفْقَ وَيُعْطِي عَلَى الرِّفْقِ مَا لَا يُعْطِي عَلَى الْعُنْفِ وَمَا لَا يُعْطِي عَلَى مَا سِوَاهُ».

(صحيح مسلم:٦٦٠١)

'Ā'ishah ﵂ related that the Messenger of Allah ﷺ said to her: "O 'Ā'ishah, Allah is gentle and He loves gentleness; and He grants those who act gently that which He does not grant those who act harshly nor, in fact, those who act in any other way."

(*Ṣaḥīḥ Muslim*: 6601)

95

عَنْ عَائِشَةَ قالت: «قَالَ النَّبِيُّ صَلَّى اللهُ عَلَيْهِ وَسَلَّمَ: «مَنْ أُعْطِيَ حَظَّهُ مِنَ الرِّفقِ أُعْطِيَ حَظَّهُ مِنْ خَيْرِ الدُّنْيَا وَالآخِرَ، ومَنْ حُرِمَ حَظَّهُ مِنَ الرِّفْقِ حُرِمَ حَظَّهُ مِنْ خَيْرِ الدُّنْيَا وَالآخِرَ».

(شرح السنّة للبغوي: ٦/٢٧٤)

'Āishah ﷺ related that the Messenger of Allah ﷺ said: "Whoever is given his share of gentleness has been given his share of the good of this world and the Hereafter; and whoever has been deprived of his share of gentleness has been deprived of his share of the good of this world and the Hereafter."

(*Sharḥ al-Sunnah* of al-Baghawī: 472/6)

96

عَنْ عَائِشَةَ قَالَتْ: «قَالَ لِي رَسُولُ اللَّهِ صَلَّى اللهُ عَلَيْهِ وَسَلَّم: يَاعَائِشَةُ، إِيَّاكِ وَمُحَقَّرَاتِ الْأَعْمَال فَإِنَّ لَهَا مِنَ اللَّهِ طَالِبًا».

(سنن ابن ماجه:٣٤٢٤)

ʿĀ'ishah رضي الله عنها said: "The Messenger of Allah ﷺ said to me: 'O ʿĀ'ishah, beware of what looks like insignificant deeds, for Allah will take you to account for them.'"

(*Sunan Ibn Mājah*: 4243)

97

عَنْ عَائِشَةَ أَنّهَا ذَكَرَتِ النَّارَ فَبَكَتْ، فَقَالَ رَسُولُ اللَّهِ صَلَّى اللهُ عَلَيْهِ وَسَلَّمَ: «مَا يُبْكِيكِ؟» قَالَتْ: «ذَكَرْتُ النَّارَ فَبَكَيْتُ، فَهَلْ تَذْكُرُونَ أَهْلِيكُمْ يَوْمَ الْقِيَامَةِ؟» فَقَالَ رَسُولُ اللَّهِ صَلَّى اللهُ عَلَيْهِ وَسَلَّمَ: «أَمَّا فِي ثَلَاثَةِ مَوَاطِنَ فَلَا يَذْكُرُ أَحَدٌ أَحَدًا: عِنْدَ الْمِيزَانِ حَتَّى يَعْلَمَ أَيَخِفُّ مِيزَانُهُ أَوْ يَثْقُلُ، وَعِنْدَ الْكِتَابِ حِينَ يُقَالُ: {هَاؤُمُ اقْرَءُوا كِتَابِيَهْ} حَتَّى يَعْلَمَ أَيْنَ يَقَعُ كِتَابُهُ أَفِي يَمِينِهِ أَمْ فِي شِمَالِهِ أَمْ مِنْ وَرَاءِ ظَهْرِهِ، وَعِنْدَ الصِّرَاطِ إِذَا وُضِعَ بَيْنَ ظَهْرَيْ جَهَنَّمَ».

(سنن أبي داود:٥٥٧٤)

ʿĀ'ishah ﵁ related that one day she cried upon remembring Hellfire and so the Messenger of Allah ﷺ asked her: "Why are you crying?" She said: "I cried because I remembered Hell; will you remember your family members on the Day of Judgement?" The Messenger of Allah ﷺ replied: "No one will remember anyone else at three places: At the Scale until one knows whether one's scale is heavy or light; upon being presented with one's record of deeds when it is said {Here, take and read my book!} [*al-Ḥāqqah*: 19] until one knows whether it is given in his right hand or left hand or from behind his back; and at the Bridge over Hell (*al-Ṣirāṭ*) when one is placed by the side of Hell."

(*Sunan Abī Dāwūd*: 4755)

98

عَنْ عَائِشَةَ قَالَت: «قَالَ رَسُولُ اللَّهِ صَلَّى اللهُ عَلَيْهِ وَسَلَّمَ : مَنْ قَرَأَ بَعْدَ صَلَا الْجُمُعَةِ (قُلْ هُوَ اللهُ أَحَدٌ) وَ(قُلْ أَعُوذُ بِرَبِّ الفَلَقِ) [سُورَةِ الفَلَقِ] وَ(قُلْ أَعُوذُ بِرَبِّ النَّاسِ) [سُورَةِ النَّاسِ] سَبْعَ مَرَّاتٍ أَعَاذَهُ اللهُ بِهَا مِنَ السُّوءِ إِلَى الْجُمُعَةِ الْأُخْرَى».

(الدُرُّالمَنْثُورُ للسُيُوطِي:٦/٢١٤)

‘Ā’ishah related that the Messenger of Allah ﷺ said: “Whoever recites *Sūrah al-Ikhlāṣ*, *Sūrah al-Falaq* and *Sūrah al-Nās* seven times after Friday prayer, Allah will protect him from misfortune until the following Friday.”

(*Al-Durr al- Manthūr* of al-Suyūṭī, 2:412)

99

عَنْ ابْنُ أَبِي مُلَيْكَةَ أَنَّ عَائِشَةَ زَوْجَ النَّبِيِّ صَلَّى اللهُ عَلَيْهِ وَسَلَّمَ كَانَتْ لَا تَسْمَعُ شَيئًا لَا تَعْرِفُهُ إِلَّا رَاجَعَتْ فِيهِ حَتَّى تَعْرِفَهُ، وَأَنَّ النَّبِيَّ صَلَّى اللهُ عَلَيْهِ وَسَلَّمَ، قَالَ: «مَنْ حُوسِبَ عُذِّبَ». قَالَتْ عَائِشَةُ: «فَقُلْتُ أَوَلَيْسَ يَقُولُ اللهُ تَعَالَى: {فَسَوْفَ يُحَاسَبُ حِسَابًا يَسِيرًا} [سور الانشقاق آية 8]؟» قَالَتْ: «فَقَالَ: إِنَّمَا ذَلِكِ الْعَرْضُ، وَلَكِنْ مَنْ نُوقِشَ الْحِسَابَ يَهْلِكْ».

(صحيح البخاري: ٩٣٩٤)

Ibn Abī Mulaykah related that ʿĀ'ishah ﵂ never heard anything that she did not understand except that she asked the Prophet ﷺ about it. So, when the Prophet ﷺ said: "Whoever is taken to account is by force chastised," ʿĀ'ishah ﵂ is related to have said: "Has Allah Most High not declared: {He who is given his record in his right hand (on the Day of Judgement), his account taking will be easy} [*al-Inshiqāq* 84: 7–8]?" The Prophet ﷺ replied: "That refers only to the presentation of accounts, but he is doomed whoever is probed about his deeds."

(*Ṣaḥīḥ al-Bukhārī*: 4939)

100

عَنْ عَائِشَةَ رَضِيَ اللهُ عَنْهَا قَالَت: «إِنَّ يَوْمَ الْجُمُعَةِ مِثْلُ يَوْمِ عَرَفَةَ وَإِنَّ فِيهِ لَسَاعَةٌ تُفْتَحُ أَبْوَابُ الرَّحْمَةِ». فَقيل: «أَيُّ سَاعَةٍ؟» قَالَت: «حِين يُنَادَى بِالصَّلَا».

(الدُّرُّ المَنْثُورُ للسُّيُوطي:٦/٢١٧)

ʿĀʾishah ﷺ said: "Friday is like the Day of Arafah; there is a time in it when the gates of mercy are opened." When asked about this exact time, she said: "It is when the *adhān* is called for the Friday prayer."

(*Al-Durr al-Manthūr of al-Suyūṭī*, 6: 217)

101

عَنْ عَائِشَةَ أَنَّ رَسُولَ اللَّهِ صَلَّى اللهُ عَلَيْهِ وَسَلَّمَ، قَالَ: «إِذَا نَعَسَ أَحَدُكُمْ وَهُو يُصَلِّي فَلْيَرْقُدْ حَتَّى يَذْهَبَ عَنْهُ النَّوْمُ، فَإِنَّ أَحَدَكُمْ إِذَا صَلَّى وَهُو نَاعِسٌ لَا يَدْرِي لَعَلَّهُ يَسْتَغْفِرُ فَيَسُبُّ نَفْسَهُ».

(صحيح البخاري:٢١٢)

ʿĀ'ishah ﵂ related that the Messenger of Allah ﷺ said: "When one of you feels sleepy while praying, let him sleep until he is refreshed, for if he prays while sleepy, he might vituperate himself when he wants to seek forgiveness from Allah."

(*Ṣāḥīḥ al-Bukhārī*: 212)

102

عَنْ عَائِشَةَ - رَضِيَ اللهُ تَعَالَى عَنْهَا - قَالَتْ: «قَالَ رَسُولُ اللَّهِ - صَلَّى اللهُ عَلَيْهِ وَسَلَّمَ: أَتَدْرُونَ مَنِ السَّابِقُونَ إِلَى ظِلِّ اللَّهِ عَزَّ وَجَلَّ؟» قَالُوا: «اللهُ وَرَسُولُهُ أَعْلَمُ». قَالَ: «الَّذِينَ إِذَا أُعْطُوا الْحَقَّ قَبِلُوهُ، وَإِذَا سُئِلُوهُ بَذَلُوهُ، وَحَكَمُوا لِلنَّاسِ كَحُكْمِهِمْ لِأَنْفُسِهِمْ».

(حِلْيَةُ الأَوْلِيَاءِ لِأَبِي نُعَيْمٍ: ٢/١٨٧)

ʿĀ'ishah ﷺ related that Messenger of Allah ﷺ said: "Do you know who will be the first to enjoy shade under Almighty Allah's throne?" Those present replied: "Allah and His Messenger know better." He explained: "They are the ones who accepted what was due to them, who spent in Allah's way when asked to do so and who preferred the same standard of justice and equity for themselves and for others."

(*Ḥilyat al-Awliyā'*, Abū Nuʿaym, 2:187)

103

عَنْ عَائِشَةَ، قَالَتْ: «كَانَ النَّبِيُّ صَلَّى اللهُ عَلَيْهِ وَسَلَّمَ إِذَا أَرَادَ أَنْ يَنَامَ وَهُوَ جُنُبٌ غَسَلَ فَرْجَهُ وَتَوَضَّأَ لِلصَّلَاةِ».

(صحيح البخاري:٢٨٨)

ʿĀ'ishah ﵂ said: "When the Prophet ﷺ wanted to go to sleep while in a state of major ritual impurity (*janābah*), he washed his private parts and performed *wuḍū'*."

(*Ṣaḥīḥ al-Bukhārī*: 288)

104

عَنْ عَائِشَةَ زَوْجِ النَّبِيِّ صَلَّى اللهُ عَلَيْهِ وَسَلَّمَ، أَنَّهَا قَالَتْ: «كُنْتُ أَنَامُ بَيْنَ يَدَيْ رَسُولِ اللَّهِ صَلَّى اللهُ عَلَيْهِ وَسَلَّمَ وَرِجْلَايَ فِي قِبْلَتِهِ، فَإِذَا سَجَدَ غَمَزَنِي فَقَبَضْتُ رِجْلَيَّ، فَإِذَا قَامَ بَسَطْتُهُمَا». قَالَتْ: «وَالْبُيُوتُ يَوْمَئِذٍ لَيْسَ فِيهَا مَصَابِيحُ».

(صحيح البخاري: ٣٨٢)

ʿĀ'ishah ﵂ said: "I used to sleep in front of the Messenger of Allah ﷺ with my feet facing the direction of his prayer and, when he wanted to prostrate, he nudged my feet and I withdrew them and, when he stood up, I stretched them again; the houses at that time did not have lamps."

(*Ṣaḥīḥ al-Bukhārī*: 382)

105

عَنْ عَائِشَةَ زَوْجَ النَّبِيِّ صَلَّى اللهُ عَلَيْهِ وَسَلَّمَ، قَالَتْ: «لَمْ أَعْقِلْ أَبَوَيَّ إِلَّا وَهُمَا يَدِينَانِ الدِّينَ، وَلَمْ يَمُرَّ عَلَيْنَا يَوْمٌ إِلَّا يَأْتِينَا فِيهِ رَسُولُ اللَّهِ صَلَّى اللهُ عَلَيْهِ وَسَلَّمَ طَرَفَيِ النَّهَارِ بُكْرَةً وَعَشِيَّةً، ثُمَّ بَدَا لِأَبِي بَكْرٍ فَابْتَنَى مَسْجِدًا بِفِنَاءِ دَارِهِ، فَكَانَ يُصَلِّي فِيهِ وَيَقْرَأُ الْقُرْآنَ، فَيَقِفُ عَلَيْهِ نِسَاءُ الْمُشْرِكِينَ وَأَبْنَاؤُهُمْ يَعْجَبُونَ مِنْهُ وَيَنْظُرُونَ إِلَيْهِ، وَكَانَ أَبُو بَكْرٍ رَجُلًا بَكَّاءً لَا يَمْلِكُ عَيْنَيْهِ إِذَا قَرَأَ الْقُرْآنَ، فَأَفْزَعَ ذَلِكَ أَشْرَافَ قُرَيْشٍ مِنَ الْمُشْرِكِينَ».

(صحيح البخاري: ٤٧٦)

ʿĀ'ishah ﵂ said: "I have never seen my parents practising any other religion except Islam and no day did pass without the Messenger of Allah ﷺ visiting us, either in the morning or the evening. Then it occurred to Abū Bakr to build a mosque in his house's courtyard. He used to pray and recite the Qur'ān there. The wives and children of the polytheists often stopped to listen to him in astonishment. Abū Bakr was a very tender-hearted person who could not control his tears when he recited the Qur'ān and this fact made the Quraysh nobility panic."

(*Ṣaḥīḥ al-Bukhārī*: 476)

106

عَنْ عَائِشَةَ رَضِيَ اللهُ عَنْهَا عَنِ النَّبِيِّ صَلَّى اللهُ عَلَيْهِ وَسَلَّمَ قَالَ: «يُورِثُ الْقَسْوَ فِي الْقلب ثَلَاثُ خِصَالٍ: حُبُّ الطَّعَامِ وَحُبُّ النَّوْمِ وَحُبُّ الرَّاحَةِ».

(الدُّرُّالمَنْثُورُ للسُّيُوطي:٥/٥٢٣)

ʿĀ'ishah ﷺ related that the Prophet ﷺ said: "Three traits harden the heart: love of food, love of sleep and love of ease."

(*Al-Durr al-Manthūr of al-Suyūṭī*, 5: 325)

107

عَنْ عَائِشَةَ رَضِيَ اللهُ عَنْهَا قَالَت: «زَيِّنُوا مَجَالِسَكُمْ بِالصَّلَاةِ عَلَى النَّبِيِّ صَلَّى اللهُ عَلَيْهِ وَسَلَّمَ».

(الدُّرُّ المَنْثُورُ للسُّيُوطي: ٥/٢١٩)

ʿĀ'ishah ﷺ said: "Adorn your assemblies with invoking blessings upon the Prophet ﷺ."

(*Al-Durr al-Manthūr of al-Suyūṭī*, 5: 219)

108

عَنْ عَائِشَةَ زَوْجِ النَّبِيِّ صَلَّى اللهُ عَلَيْهِ وَسَلَّمَ، قَالَتْ: «كَانَ النَّاسُ يَنْتَابُونَ يَوْمَ الْجُمُعَةِ مِنْ مَنَازِلِهِمْ وَالْعَوَالِيِّ، فَيَأْتُونَ فِي الْغُبَارِ يُصِيبُهُمُ الْغُبَارُ وَالْعَرَقُ فَيَخْرُجُ مِنْهُمُ الْعَرَقُ، فَأَتَى رَسُولَ اللَّهِ صَلَّى اللهُ عَلَيْهِ وَسَلَّمَ إِنْسَانٌ مِنْهُمْ وَهُوَ عِنْدِي، فَقَالَ النَّبِيُّ صَلَّى اللهُ عَلَيْهِ وَسَلَّمَ: لَوْ أَنَّكُمْ تَطَهَّرْتُمْ لِيَوْمِكُمْ هَذَا»

(صحيح البخاري:٩٠٢)

ʿĀʾishah ﷺ said: "People used to come from their homes and from al-ʿAwālī[1] on Friday (for the Friday prayer). They came covered with dust and soaked in sweat, and so, sweat used to trickle from them. When one of them came to the Prophet ﷺ who was with me, the Prophet ﷺ said to him: 'It is better that you clean yourself (i.e., take a bath) on this day of yours.'"

(*Ṣaḥīḥ al-Bukhārī*: 902)

1 A place in the outskirts of Madinah, up to a distance of four miles or more from Madinah.

109

عَنِ ابْنِ شِهَابٍ، قَالَ: أَخْبَرَنِي عُرْوَةُ، أَنَّ عَائِشَةَ أَخْبَرَتْهُ أَنّ رَسُولَ اللَّهِ صَلَّى اللهُ عَلَيْهِ وَسَلَّمَ خَرَجَ ذَاتَ لَيْلَةٍ مِنْ جَوْفِ اللَّيْلِ فَصَلَّى فِي الْمَسْجِدِ فَصَلَّى رِجَالٌ بِصَلَاتِهِ، فَأَصْبَحَ النَّاسُ فَتَحَدَّثُوا فَاجْتَمَعَ أَكْثَرُ مِنْهُمْ فَصَلَّوْا مَعَهُ، فَأَصْبَحَ النَّاسُ فَتَحَدَّثُوا فَكَثُرَ أَهْلُ الْمَسْجِدِ مِنَ اللَّيْلَةِ الثَّالِثَةِ، فَخَرَجَ رَسُولُ اللَّهِ صَلَّى اللهُ عَلَيْهِ وَسَلَّمَ فَصَلَّوْا بِصَلَاتِهِ، فَلَمَّا كَانَتِ اللَّيْلَةُ الرَّابِعَةُ عَجَزَ الْمَسْجِدُ عَنْ أَهْلِهِ حَتَّى خَرَجَ لِصَلَا الصُّبْحِ، فَلَمَّا قَضَى الْفَجْرَ أَقْبَلَ عَلَى النَّاسِ فَتَشَهَّدَ، ثُمَّ قَالَ: «أَمَّا بَعْدُ، فَإِنَّهُ لَمْ يَخْفَ عَلَيَّ مَكَانُكُمْ لَكِنِّي خَشِيتُ أَنْ تُفْرَضَ عَلَيْكُمْ فَتَعْجِزُوا عَنْهَا».

(صحيح البخاري:٤٢٩)

ʿUrwah was informed by ʿĀ'ishah ﵂ that one day the Messenger of Allah ﷺ came out in the hollow of the night and prayed in his mosque. Some Companions prayed behind him. The next morning, they told other Companions about it. So, the following night more Companions turned up to pray behind the Prophet ﷺ. The next day this news spread far and wide, and on the third night, many more Companions joined the prayer behind the Prophet ﷺ. On the fourth night, the mosque was full of Companions, however the Prophet ﷺ did not come out to lead the prayer. The next day, after Fajr prayer, he addressed the people. He first recited the creedal statement of Islam and then said: "I am aware that you were here [last night]. However, I feared that this prayer would be made obligatory for you and you would be unable to perform it."

(*Ṣaḥīḥ al-Bukhārī*: 924)

110

عَنْ عَائِشَةَ قَالَتْ: «كَانَ يُوضَعُ لِرَسُولِ اللهِ صَلَّى اللهُ عَلَيْهِ وَسَلَّمَ ثَلَاثَةُ آنِيَةٍ تُخَمَّرُ مِنَ اللَّيْلِ: إِنَاءٌ لِطُهُورِهِ وَإِنَاءٌ لِشَرَابِهِ وَإِنَاءٌ لِسِوَاكِهِ».

(كَنْزُ العُمَّالِ:٢٣٤٢٨)

'Ā'ishah ﵂ said: "Three covered pots of water were kept at night for the Messenger of Allah ﷺ: one for *wuḍū'*, one for drinking, and one for his *siwāk* (toothbrush)."

(*Kanz al-'Ummāl*: 23428)

111

عَنْ عَائِشَةَ رَضِيَ اللهُ عَنْهَا قَالَتْ: «إِنْ كَانَ رَسُولُ اللَّهِ صَلَّى اللهُ عَلَيْهِ وَسَلَّمَ لَيَدَعُ الْعَمَلَ وَهُو يُحِبُّ أَنْ يَعْمَلَ بِهِ خَشْيَةَ أَنْ يَعْمَلَ بِهِ النَّاسُ فَيُفْرَضَ عَلَيْهِمْ، وَمَا سَبَّحَ رَسُولُ اللَّهِ صَلَّى اللهُ عَلَيْهِ وَسَلَّمَ سُبْحَةَ الضُّحَى قَطُّ وَإِنِّي لَأُسَبِّحُهَا».

(صحيح البخاري:١١٢٨)

ʿĀ'ishah ﵂ said: "The Messenger of Allah ﷺ would stop a practice even though he liked doing it for fear that people might act on it and then it is made compulsory for them. The Prophet ﷺ never offered the midmorning prayer (*ḍuḥā*), though I do perform it."

(*Ṣaḥīḥ al-Bukhārī*: 1128)

112

قَالَ مَسْرُوْقٌ سَأَلْتُ عَائِشَةَ رَضِيَ اللهُ عَنْهَا: «أَيُّ الْعَمَلِ كَانَ أَحَبَّ إِلَى النَّبِيِّ صَلَّى اللهُ عَلَيْهِ وَسَلَّمَ؟»،قَالَتْ: «الدَّائِمُ».

(صحيح البخاري:١١٣٢)

Masrūq related that he asked ʿĀ'ishah ﷺ: "Which deed was liked most by the Prophet ﷺ?" She replied: "That which was continuous."

(*Ṣaḥīḥ al-Bukhārī*: 1132)

113

عَنْ أَبِي سَلَمَةَ بْنِ عَبْدِ الرَّحْمَنِ أَنَّهُ سَأَلَ عَائِشَةَ رَضِيَ اللهُ عَنْهَا: «كَيْفَ كَانَتْ صَلَاةُ رَسُولِ اللَّهِ صَلَّى اللهُ عَلَيْهِ وَسَلَّمَ فِي رَمَضَانَ؟» فَقَالَتْ: «مَا كَانَ يَزِيدُ فِي رَمَضَانَ وَلَا فِي غَيْرِهِ عَلَى إِحْدَى عَشْرَ رَكْعَةً، يُصَلِّي أَرْبَعًا، فَلَا تَسَلْ عَنْ حُسْنِهِنَّ وَطُولِهِنَّ، ثُمَّ يُصَلِّي أَرْبَعًا، فَلَا تَسَلْ عَنْ حُسْنِهِنَّ وَطُولِهِنَّ، ثُمَّ يُصَلِّي ثَلَاثًا، فَقُلْتُ: يَا رَسُولَ اللَّهِ، أَتَنَامُ قَبْلَ أَنْ تُوتِرَ؟» قَالَ: «يَاعَائِشَةُ، إِنَّ عَيْنَيَّ تَنَامَانِ وَلَا يَنَامُ قَلْبِي».

(صحيح البخاري:٢٠١٣)

Abū Salamah ibn ʿAbd al-Raḥmān related that he asked ʿĀ'ishah ﵂: "How was the prayer of the Prophet ﷺ during Ramadan?" She replied: "He did not offer more than eleven units of prayer (*rakʿah*) in his prayer in Ramadan or in other than Ramdan. He first prayed four units, and don't ask about their perfection and length; and then he prayed four units, and don't ask about their perfection and length. Finally, he prayed three units. I once asked him: 'O Messenger of Allah, do you sleep before performing the *witr* prayer?' He replied: 'O ʿĀ'ishah, my eyes sleep but my heart does not.'"

(*Ṣaḥīḥ al-Bukhārī*: 2013)

114

قَالَ ابْنُ عَبَّاسٍ رَضِيَ اللهُ عَنْهُمَا: «فَلَمَّا مَاتَ عُمَرُ رَضِيَ اللهُ عَنْهُ ذَكَرْتُ ذَلِكَ لِعَائِشَةَ رَضِيَ اللهُ عَنْهَا فَقَالَتْ: رَحِمَ اللهُ عُمَرَ، وَاللَّهِ مَا حَدَّثَ رَسُولُ اللَّهِ صَلَّى اللهُ عَلَيْهِ وَسَلَّمَ إِنَّ اللَّهَ لَيُعَذِّبُ الْمُؤْمِنَ بِبُكَاءِ أَهْلِهِ عَلَيْهِ وَلَكِنَّ رَسُولَ اللَّهِ صلَّى اللهُ عَلَيْهِ وَسَلَّمَ قَالَ: إِنَّ اللَّهَ لَيَزِيدُ الْكَافِرَ عَذَابًا بِبُكَاءِ أَهْلِهِ عَلَيْهِ». وَقَالَتْ: «حَسْبُكُمُ الْقُرْآنُ {وَلَا تَزِرُ وَازِرَةٌ وِزْرَ أُخْرَى} [سور الأنعام آية: ١٦٤]» .

(صحيح البخاري:١٢٨٨)

Ibn ʿAbbās ﷺ said: "When ʿUmar [ibn al-Khaṭṭāb] ﷺ died, I mentioned that [i.e., a certain *ḥadīth*] to ʿĀ'ishah ﷺ [that the deceased person is punished when his family members cry over his death]. So she commented: 'May Allah's mercy be upon ʿUmar, the Messenger of Allah ﷺ did not say that a deceased believer faces punishment on account of the crying of his family members, what he said is that the deceased unbeliever suffers from when he sees his family members cry over him.'" She added: "Let this Qur'ānic verse be sufficient for you: {No one will bear another's burden} [*al-Anʿām* 6: 164]."

(*Ṣaḥīḥ al-Bukhārī*: 1288)

115

عَنْ عَائِشَةَ رَضِيَ اللهُ عَنْهَا عَنِ النَّبِيِّ صَلَّى اللهُ عَلَيْهِ وَسَلَّمَ قَالَ فِي مَرَضِهِ الَّذِي مَاتَ فِيهِ: «لَعَنَ اللهُ الْيَهُودَ وَالنَّصَارَى اتَّخَذُوا قُبُورَ أَنْبِيَائِهِمْ مَسْجِدًا»، قَالَتْ: «وَلَوْلَا ذَلِكَ لَأَبْرَزُوا قَبْرَهُ غَيْرَ أَنِّي أَخْشَى أَنْ يُتَّخَذَ مَسْجِدًا».

(صحيح البخاري:١٣٣٠)

ʿĀ’ishah ﵂ related that the Prophet ﷺ said on his death bed: “May the Jews and Christians be cursed! They turned the graves of their Prophets into places of worship.” She added: “Had it not been for this, the Prophet’s grave would have been made prominent, except that I fear that his grave would have been turned into a place of worship.”

(*Ṣaḥīḥ al-Bukhārī*: 1330)

116

عَنْ عَائِشَةَ رَضِيَ اللهُ عَنْهَا قَالَت: «يَرْحَمِ اللهُ زَيْنَبَ بِنْتَ جَحْشٍ لَقَدْ نَالَتْ فِي هَذِهِ الدُّنْيَا الشَّرَفَ الَّذِي لَا يَبْلُغُهُ شَرِيفٌ إِنَّ اللهَ زَوَّجَهَا نَبِيَّهُ صَلَّى اللهُ عَلَيْهِ وَسَلَّمَ فِي الدُّنْيَا وَنَطَقَ بِهِ الْقُرْآنُ».

(الدُّرُّ الْمَنْثُورُ للسُّيُوطِي: ٥/٢٠٢)

ʿĀ'ishah ﵂ said: "May Allah have mercy on Zaynab bint Jaḥsh; she has obtained an honour in this world that no noble person can attain: Allah got her married to His Messenger in this world and the Qur'ān spoke of it."

(*Al-Durr al-Manthūr of al-Suyūṭī*, 5: 202)

117

عَنْ عَائِشَةَ أُمِّ الْمُؤْمِنِينَ رَضِيَ اللهُ عَنْهَا أَنَّهَا قَالَتْ: «يَا رَسُولَ اللَّهِ، نَرَى الْجِهَادَ أَفْضَلَ الْعَمَلِ، أَفَلَا نُجَاهِدُ؟»، قَالَ: «لَا، لَكِنَّ أَفْضَلَ الْجِهَادِ حَجٌّ مَبْرُورٌ».

(صحيح البخاري:١٥٢٠)

ʿĀ'ishah ﵂ asked: "O Messenger of Allah, we note that jihad is the best of deeds, so shall we (women) not participate in jihad?" He replied: "No, rather the best jihad (for women) is an accepted *Ḥajj*."

(*Ṣaḥīḥ al-Bukhārī*: 1520)

118

عَنْ عَائِشَةَ رَضِيَ اللهُ عَنْهَا قَالَتْ: «سَأَلْتُ النَّبِيَّ صَلَّى اللهُ عَلَيْهِ وَسَلَّمَ عَنِ الْجَدْرِ أَمِنَ الْبَيْتِ هُوَ؟». قَالَ: «نَعَمْ»، قُلْتُ: «فَمَا لَهُ لَمْ يُدْخِلُوهُ فِي الْبَيْتِ؟» قَالَ: «إِنَّ قَوْمَكِ قَصَّرَتْ بِهِمُ النَّفَقَةُ». قُلْتُ: «فَمَا شَأْنُ بَابِهِ مُرْتَفِعًا؟» قَالَ: «فَعَلَ ذَلِكَ قَوْمُكِ لِيُدْخِلُوا مَنْ شَاءُوا وَيَمْنَعُوا مَنْ شَاءُوا، وَلَوْلَا أَنَّ قَوْمَكِ حَدِيثٌ عَهْدُهُمْ بِالْجَاهِلِيَّةِ فَأَخَافُ أَنْ تُنْكِرَ قُلُوبُهُمْ أَنْ أُدْخِلَ الْجَدْرَ فِي الْبَيْتِ وَأَنْ أُلْصِقَ بَابَهُ بِالْأَرْضِ».

(صحيح البخاري:١٥٨٤)

Ā'ishah ﷺ said: I asked the Prophet ﷺ if the Ḥaṭīm was part of the House of Allah and he replied in the affirmative. I then asked him: "Why is it not included in the House of Allah?" He said: "Your people had run short of money." Then I asked him: "Why is the Ka'bah door above the ground level?" He said: "Your people did it so that they could allow whoever they wanted in and prevent whoever they wanted from getting in the Ka'bah. Had they not been close to their time of paganism, and did I not fear their objection, I would have included the Ḥaṭīm inside the House of Allah and levelled the Ka'bah door to the ground level."

(*Ṣaḥīḥ al-Bukhārī*: 1584)

119

عَنْ عَائِشَةَ رَضِيَ اللهُ عَنْهَا، قَالَتْ: «كَانُوا يَصُومُونَ عَاشُورَاءَ قَبْلَ أَنْ يُفْرَضَ رَمَضَانُ، وَكَانَ يَوْمًا تُسْتَرُ فِيهِ الْكَعْبَةُ، فَلَمَّا فَرَضَ اللهُ رَمَضَانَ، قَالَ رَسُولُ اللَّهِ صَلَّى اللهُ عَلَيْهِ وَسَلَّمَ: مَنْ شَاءَ أَنْ يَصُومَهُ فَلْيَصُمْهُ، وَمَنْ شَاءَ أَنْ يَتْرُكَهُ فَلْيَتْرُكْهُ».

(صحيح البخاري:٢٩٥١)

‘Ā’ishah رضي الله عنها said: “Before the fast of Ramadan was made obligatory, the Muslims used to fast on ‘Āshūrā’ (10th of Muḥarram), and on that particular day the Ka‘bah used to be covered. When Allah made the fasting of Ramadan compulsory, the Messenger of Allah ﷺ said: ‘Whoever wishes to fast (on ‘Āshūrā’) may do so, and whoever wishes not to fast, can do so too.’”

(*Ṣaḥīḥ al-Bukhārī*: 1592)

120

عَنْ عَائِشَةَ رَضِيَ اللهُ عَنْهَا، قَالَتْ: «نَزَلْنَا الْمُزْدَلِفَةَ، فَاسْتَأْذَنَتِ النَّبِيَّ صَلَّى اللهُ عَلَيْهِ وَسَلَّمَ سَوْدَةُ أَنْ تَدْفَعَ قَبْلَ حَطْمَةِ النَّاسِ، وَكَانَتِ امْرَأَةً بَطِيئَةً فَأَذِنَ لَهَا فَدَفَعَتْ قَبْلَ حَطْمَةِ النَّاسِ، وَأَقَمْنَا حَتَّى أَصْبَحْنَا نَحْنُ، ثُمَّ دَفَعْنَا بِدَفْعِهِ فَلَأَنْ أَكُونَ اسْتَأْذَنْتُ رَسُولَ اللهِ صَلَّى اللهُ عَلَيْهِ وَسَلَّمَ كَمَا اسْتَأْذَنَتْ سَوْدَةُ أَحَبُّ إِلَيَّ مِنْ مَفْرُوحٍ بِهِ».

(صحيح البخاري:١٦٨١)

'Āishah ﵂ said: "When we arrived at Muzdalifah [as part of the rituals of *Ḥajj*], Sawdah asked permission from the Prophet ﷺ to leave before other people make a move because she was slow-footed and he allowed her to do so, and she proceeded before the crowd of people. We on the other hand spent the night there and in the morning we made a move along with the Prophet ﷺ. Had I asked permission from the Messenger of Allah ﷺ to leave ahead of people, as Sawdah did, it would have made me as happy as I could possibly ever be."

(*Ṣaḥīḥ al-Bukhārī*: 1681)

121

عَنْ عَائِشَةَ رَضِيَ اللهُ عَنْهَا قَالَت: «قَالَ رَسُول الله صَلَّى اللهُ عَلَيْهِ وَسَلَّمَ: من قَرَأَ فِي لَيْلَةٍ (الم تَنْزِيل) السَّجْدَ و (يٰسٓ) و(اقْتَرَبَتِ السَّاعَةُ) وَ(تبَارَكَ الَّذِي بِيَدِهِ الْمُلْكُ) كُنَّ لَهُ نورًا وَحِرْزًا مِنَ الشَّيْطَانِ وَرُفِعَ فِي الدَّرَجَات إِلَى يَوْم الْقِيَامَة».

(الدُّرُّالمَنْثُورُ للسُّيُوطي:٥/١٧٠)

ʿĀ'ishah ﵂ related that the Messenger of Allah ﷺ said: "Whoever recites at night *Sūrah al-Sajdah*, *Surah Yā-Sīn*, *Sūrah al-Qamar* and *Sūrah al-Mulk*, these *Sūrah*s will be for him a light, a protection from Satan and a means of being raised in ranks on the Day of Judgement."

(*Al-Durr al-Manthūr of al-Suyūṭī*, 5: 170)

122

عَنْ عَائِشَةَ رَضِيَ اللهُ عَنْهَا، قَالَتْ: «كَانَ النَّبِيُّ صَلَّى اللهُ عَلَيْهِ وَسَلَّمَ يُقَبِّلُ وَيُبَاشِرُ وَهُو صَائِمٌ، وَكَانَ أَمْلَكَكُمْ لِإِرْبِهِ».

(صحيح البخاري:١٩٢٧)

'Ā'ishah ﵂ said: "The Prophet ﷺ used to kiss and hug [his wives] while fasting, and he had more power for self-control than anyone else amongst you."

(*Ṣaḥīḥ al-Bukhārī*: 1927)

123

عَنْ عَائِشَةَ رَضِيَ اللهُ عَنْهَا، قَالَتْ: «نَهَى رَسُولُ اللَّهِ صَلَّى اللهُ عَلَيْهِ وَسَلَّمَ عَنِ الْوِصَالِ رَحْمَةً لَهُمْ، فَقَالُوا: إِنَّكَ تُوَاصِلُ، قَالَ: إِنِّي لَسْتُ كَهيئَتِكُمْ، إِنِّي يُطْعِمُنِي رَبِّي وَيَسْقِينِي».

(صحيح البخاري:٤٦٩١)

ʿĀʾishah ﵂ said: "The Messenger of Allah ﷺ forbade fasting consecutively without breaking the fast at sunset, out of compassion for his Companions. When some Companions pointed out that he did just that, he explained: 'I am not like you; my Lord feeds me and gives me water to drink.'"

(*Ṣaḥīḥ al-Bukhārī*: 1964)

124

عَنْ عَلْقَمَةَ، قُلْتُ لِعَائِشَةَ رَضِيَ الهُ عنْهَا: «هَلْ كَانَ رَسُولُ اللَّهِ صَلَّى اللهُ عَلَيْهِ وَسَلَّمَ يَخْتَصُّ مِنَ الْأَيَّامِ شَيْئًا؟» قَالَتْ: «لَا، كَانَ عَمَلُهُ دِيمَةً، وَأَيُّكُمْ يُطِيقُ مَا كَانَ رَسُولُ اللَّهِ صَلَّى اللهُ عَلَيْهِ وَسَلَّمَ يُطِيقُ».

(صحيح البخاري:١٩٨٧)

'Alqamah asked 'Ā'ishah ﵂: "Did the Messenger of Allah ﷺ specify any particular day with a specific deed?" She replied: "No, his practice was constant and continuous, and who could measure up to to the deeds that the Messenger of Allah ﷺ regularly did?"

(*Ṣaḥīḥ al-Bukhārī*: 1987)

125

عَنْ عَائِشَةَ رَضِيَ اللهُ عنْهَا، قَالَتْ: «دَخَلَ عَلَيَّ رَسُولُ اللهِ صَلَّى اللهُ عَلَيْهِ وَسَلَّمَ يَوْمًا، فَقَالَ: صَنَعْتُ الْيَوْمَ شَيئًا لَوْ كُنْتُ اسْتَقْبَلْتُ مِنْ أَمْرِي مَا اسْتَدْبَرْتُ مَا صَنَعْتُه». قَالَتْ: «قُلْتُ: وَمَا ذَاكَ يَا رَسُولَ اللَّهِ؟» قَالَ: «دَخَلْتُ الْبَيْتَ وَخَشِيتُ أَنْ يَأْتِيَ الْآتِي مِنْ بَعْدِي فَيَقُولُ: حَجَجْتُ وَلَمْ أَدْخُلِ الْبَيْتَ، وَأَنَّهُ لَمْ يُكْتَبْ عَلَيْنَا دُخُولُهُ، إِنَّمَا كُتِبَ عَلَيْنَا طَوَافُهُ».

(حِلْيَةُ الأَوْلِيَاءِ لِأَبِي نُعَيْمٍ:٧/١١٥)

ʿĀ'ishah ﷺ said: "One day the Messenger of Allah ﷺ came home and said: 'Today I did something I would not do if I did go back in time.' I said: 'What did you do, O Messenger of Allah?' He replied: 'I entered the Kaʿbah and I feared that someone in the future might come and say: "I performed *Ḥajj* but I did not enter the Kaʿbah", when it has not been made mandatory for us to enter it; what is mandatory is to circumambulate it.'"

(*Ḥilyat al-Awliyā'* of Abū Nuʿaym al-Aṣfahānī, 7:115)

126

عَنْ عَائِشَةَ رَضِيَ اللهُ عَنْهَا، قَالَتْ: «كَانَ النَّبِيُّ صَلَّى اللهُ عَلَيْهِ وَسَلَّمَ يُصْغِي إِلَيَّ رَأْسَهُ وَهُوَ مُجَاوِرٌ فِي الْمَسْجِدِ، فَأُرَجِّلُهُ وَأَنَا حَائِضٌ».

(صحيح البخاري:٨٢٠٢)

‘Ā’ishah ﵂ said: “The Prophet ﷺ used to lean his head towards me, while in retreat (*i‘tikāf*) in the mosque [during Ramadan], to comb his hair, even though I was menstruating.”

(*Ṣaḥīḥ al-Bukhārī*: 2028)

127

عَنْ عَائِشَةَ رَضِيَ اللهُ عَنْهَا، أَنّ النَّبِيَّ صَلَّى اللهُ عَلَيْهِ وَسَلَّمَ اشْتَرَى طَعَامًا مِنْ يَهُودِيٍّ إِلَى أَجَلٍ وَرَهَنَهُ دِرْعًا مِنْ حَدِيدٍ».

(صحيح البخاري:٨٦٠٢)

ʿĀ'ishah ؓ related that once the Prophet ﷺ bought food grains from a Jewish man on credit and he pawned it against his iron armour.

(*Ṣaḥīḥ al-Bukhārī*: 2068)

128

عنْ عَائِشَةَ رَضِيَ اللهُ عَنْهَا قَالَتْ: «{وَمَنْ كَانَ غَنِيًّا فَلْيَسْتَعْفِفْ وَمَنْ كَانَ فَقِيرًا فَلْيَأْكُلْ بِالْمَعْرُوفِ} [سور النّساء آية 6)] أُنْزِلَتْ فِي وَالِي الْيَتِيمِ الَّذِي يُقِيمُ عَلَيْهِ وَيُصْلِحُ فِي مَالِهِ إِنْ كَانَ فَقِيرًا أَكَلَ مِنْهُ بِالْمَعْرُوفِ».

(صحيح البخاري:٢٢١٢)

ʿĀ'ishah ﵂ said: "The verse {Whoever (among the guardians of an orphan) is rich, should shun usurping (from the property of the orphan), but whoever (among the guardians) is poor, let him charge in a fair manner out of the orphan's belongings,} [*al-Nisā'* 4: 6] was revealed about the guardians of orphans who look after them and manage their wealth; if the guardian is poor, he may use the orphan's wealth for himself but in moderation."

(*Ṣaḥīḥ al-Bukhārī*: 2212)

129

عَنْ عَائِشَةَ رَضِيَ اللهُ عَنْهَا، قُلْتُ: «يَا رَسُولَ اللهِ، إِنَّ لِي جَارَيْنِ فَإِلَى أَيِّهِمَا أُهْدِي؟» قَالَ: «إِلَى أَقْرَبِهِمَا مِنْكِ بَابًا.»

(صحيح البخاري:٩٥٢٢)

‘Ā’ishah related that she asked: “O Messenger of Allah, I have two neighbours, to which of the two should I gift my present?” He said: “To the one whose door is closest to you.”

(*Ṣaḥīḥ al-Bukhārī*: 2259)

130

أَنَّ عَائِشَةَ رَضِيَ اللهُ عَنْهَا، زَوْجَ النَّبِيِّ صَلَّى اللهُ عَلَيْهِ وَسَلَّمَ، قَالَتْ: «وَاسْتَأْجَرَ رَسُولُ اللَّهِ صَلَّى اللهُ عَلَيْهِ وَسَلَّمَ وَأَبُو بَكْرٍ رَجُلًا مِنْ بَنِي الدِّيلِ هَادِيًا خِرِّيتًا وَهُو عَلَى دِينِ كُفَّارِ قُرَيْشٍ، فَدَفَعَا إِلَيْهِ رَاحِلَتَيْهِمَا وَوَاعَدَاهُ غَارَ ثَوْرٍ بَعْدَ ثَلَاثِ لَيَالٍ بِرَاحِلَتَيْهِمَا صُبْحَ ثَلَاثٍ».

(صحيح البخاري:٤٦٢٢)

ʿĀ'ishah ﷺ said: "The Messenger of Allah ﷺ and Abū Bakr had hired a competent man from the Banū al-Dīl tribe as a guide, who followed the religion of the unbelievers of Quraysh; they had handed over their she-camels to him and agreed to meet at the cave of Thawr after three nights and he was to bring their she-camels with him."

(*Ṣaḥīḥ al-Bukhārī*: 2264)

131

عَنْ عَائِشَةَ رَضِيَ اللهُ عَنْهَا قَالَتْ: «كَانَ رَسُولُ اللهِ صَلَّى اللهُ عَلَيْهِ وَسَلَّمَ يُصَلِّي رَكْعَتَيْنِ قَبْلَ طُلُوعِ الفَجْرِ ثُمَّ يَقُولُ: اللّهُمَّ رَبَّ جِبْرِيلَ وَمِيكَائِيلَ وَرَبَّ إِسْرَافِيلَ وَرَبَّ مُحَمَّدٍ، أَعُوذُ بِكَ مِنَ النَّارِ، ثُمَّ يَخْرُجُ إِلَى الصَّلَاةِ».

(مُسْنَد أبي يَعْلَى: ٤٧٦٠)

ʿĀ'ishah ﷺ said: "The Messenger of Allah ﷺ used to offer two units of prayer before Fajr and then say: 'O Allah, Lord of Jibrīl and Mikā'īl, Lord of Isrāfīl and Lord of Muḥammad, I seek Your refuge in You from Hell,' after which he left home for the prayer."

(*Musnad Abī Ya'lā*: 4760)

132

عَنْ عَائِشَةَ رَضِيَ اللهُ عَنْهَا، قَالَتْ: «كَانَ رَسُولُ اللَّهِ صَلَّى اللهُ عَلَيْهِ وَسَلَّمَ يَقْبَلُ الْهَدِيَّةَ وَيُثِيبُ عَلَيْهَا».

(صحيح البخاري:٢٥٨٥)

ʿĀ'ishah ﵂ said: The Prophet ﷺ used to accept gifts and used to give something in return.

(*Ṣaḥīḥ al-Bukhārī*: 2585)

133

عَنْ عَائِشَةَ رَضِيَ اللهُ عَنْهَا قَالَتْ: «كَانَ رَسُولُ اللَّهِ صَلَّى اللهُ عَلَيْهِ وَسَلَّمَ إِذَا أَرَادَ سَفَرًا أَقْرَعَ بَيْنَ نِسَائِهِ فَأَيَّتُهُنَّ خَرَجَ سَهْمُهَا خَرَجَ بِهَا مَعَهُ، وَكَانَ يَقْسِمُ لِكُلِّ امْرَأَةٍ مِنْهُنَّ يَوْمَهَا وَلَيْلَتَهَا، غَيْرَ أَنَّ سَوْدَةَ بِنْتَ زَمْعَةَ وَهَبَتْ يَوْمَهَا وَلَيْلَتَهَا لِعَائِشَةَ زَوْجِ النَّبِيِّ صَلَّى اللهُ عَلَيْهِ وَسَلَّمَ، تَبْتَغِي بِذَلِكَ رِضَا رَسُولِ اللَّهِ صَلَّى اللهُ عَلَيْهِ وَسَلَّمَ».

(صحيح البخاري:٢٥٩٣)

ʿĀ'ishah ﵂ "When the Messenger of Allah ﷺ wanted to travel he used to draw lots for selecting the wife who would accompany him. It was also his practice to fix the turn of his wives for every night and day except that Sawdah bint Zamʿah had gifted her turn to ʿĀ'ishah, she sought by doing so the good pleasure of the Messenger of Allah ﷺ."

(*Ṣaḥīḥ al-Bukhārī*: 2593)

134

عَنْ عَائِشَةَ، قَالَتْ: «تَهَجَّدَ النَّبِيُّ صَلَّى اللهُ عَلَيْهِ وَسَلَّمَ فِي بَيْتِي فَسَمِعَ صَوْتَ عَبَّادٍ يُصَلِّي فِي الْمَسْجِدِ، فَقَالَ: يَاعَائِشَةُ، أَصَوْتُ عَبَّادٍ هَذَا؟ قُلْتُ: نَعَمْ. قَالَ: اللَّهُمَّ ارْحَمْ عَبَّادًا».

(صحيح البخاري:٥٥٦٢)

'Ā'ishah ﵂ said: "Once the Prophet ﷺ prayed at night (*tahajjud*) at my house and he overheard 'Abbād praying in the mosque and so he asked me: 'O 'Ā'ishah, is this the voice of 'Abbād?' when I confirmed that it was, he said: 'O Allah, have mercy on 'Abbād.'"

(*Ṣaḥīḥ al-Bukhārī*: 2655)

135

عَنْ عَائِشَةَ رَضِيَ اللهُ عَنْهَا قَالَتْ: «قَالَ رَسُول الله صَلَّى اللهُ عَلَيْهِ وَسَلَّمَ: من قَرَأَ من سُورَ الْكَهْفِ عَشْرَ آيَاتٍ عِنْد مَنَامِهِ عُصِمَ مِنْ فِتْنَةِ الدَّجَّالِ وَمَنْ قَرَأَ خَاتِمَتَهَا عِنْد رُقَادِهِ كَانَ لَهُ نُورًا مِنْ لَدُنِ قَرْنِهِ إِلَى قَدَمِهِ يَوْمِ الْقِيَامَةِ».

(الدُّرُّ المَنْثُورُ للسُّيُوطِي: ٤/٩٠٤)

Āʾishah ﷺ related that the Messenger of Allah ﷺ said: "Whoever recites [the first] ten verses of *Sūrah al-Kahf* upon going to sleep, he will be protected from the trial of the antichrist (*al-Dajjāl*) and whoever recites the concluding part of the same *Sūrah* upon going to sleep, it will be a light for him, from head to toe, on the Day of Judgement."

(*Al-Durr al-Manthūr of al-Suyūṭī*, 4: 409)

136

عَنْ عَائِشَةَ رَضِيَ اللهُ عَنْهَا، قَالَتْ: «سَمِعَ رَسُولُ اللَّهِ صَلَّى اللهُ عَلَيْهِ وَسَلَّمَ صَوْتَ خُصُومٍ بِالْبَابِ عَالِيَةٍ أَصْوَاتُهُمَا، وَإِذَا أَحَدُهُمَا يَسْتَوْضِعُ الْآخَرَ وَيَسْتَرْفِقُهُ فِي شَيْءٍ، وَهُوَ يَقُولُ: «وَاللَّهِ لَا أَفْعَلُ». فَخَرَجَ عَلَيْهِمَا رَسُولُ اللَّهِ صَلَّى اللهُ عَلَيْهِ وَسَلَّمَ، فَقَالَ: «أَيْنَ الْمُتَأَلِّي عَلَى اللَّهِ لَا يَفْعَلُ الْمَعْرُوفَ؟» فَقَالَ: «أَنَا يَا رَسُولَ اللَّهِ وَلَهُ أَيُّ ذَلِكَ أَحَبَّ».

(صحيح البخاري:٥٠٧٢)

ʿĀ'ishah ﷺ said: "One day, the Messenger of Allah ﷺ heard the loud voices of two people who were quarrelling. One was pleading with the other to be lenient with him regarding something but the other kept saying: 'By Allah, I will not do so!' The Messenger of Allah ﷺ went out to them and said, 'Who is the one who swore by Allah that he would not do what is known to be good?' The man replied: 'I did, O Messenger of Allah, however, he [his opponent] can have whatever he wants.'"

(*Ṣaḥīḥ al-Bukhārī*: 2705)

137

عَنْ عَائِشَةَ قَالَتْ: «تُوُفِّيَ رَسُولُ اللَّهِ صَلَّى اللهُ عَلَيْهِ وَسَلَّمَ وَمَا فِي بَيْتِي مِنْ شَيْءٍ يَأْكُلُهُ ذُو كَبِدٍ إِلَّا شَطْرُ شَعِيرٍ فِي رَفٍّ لِي، فَأَكَلْتُ مِنْهُ حَتَّى طَالَ عَلَيَّ فَكِلْتُهُ فَفَنِيَ».

(صحيح البخاري:٣٠٩٧)

ʿĀ'ishah ﵂ said: "When the Messenger of Allah ﷺ died, there was nothing in my house that a live soul could eat except a portion of barley which I kept on a shelf; I ate of it for a long time; and then I used it in small measures until it was finished."

(*Ṣaḥīḥ al-Bukhārī*: 3097)

138

عَنْ عَائِشَةَ رَضِيَ اللهُ عَنْهَا، أَنّ النَّبِيَّ صَلَّى اللهُ عَلَيْهِ وَسَلَّمَ، قَالَ لَهَا: «يَا عَائِشَةُ، هَذَا جِبْرِيلُ يَقْرَأُ عَلَيْكِ السَّلَامَ»، فَقَالَتْ: «وَعَلَيْهِ السَّلَامُ وَرَحْمَةُ اللَّهِ وَبَرَكَاتُهُ، تَرَى مَا لَا أَرَى» تُرِيدُ النَّبِيَّ صَلَّى اللهُ عَلَيْهِ وَسَلَّمَ.

(صحيح البخاري:٧١٢٣)

ʿĀ'ishah ﷺ related that once the Prophet ﷺ said to her: "O ʿĀ'ishah, this is Jibrīl and he conveys the greatings of peace to you." She replied: "And on him be Allah's peace, mercy and blessings," and then she said: "You see what I cannot see," addressing the Prophet ﷺ.

(*Ṣaḥīḥ al-Bukhārī*: 3217)

139

عَنْ عَائِشَةَ رَضِيَ اللهُ عَنْهَا [فِي قَوْلِهِ تَعَالَى] {إِذْ جَاءُوكُمْ مِنْ فَوْقِكُمْ وَمِنْ أَسْفَلَ مِنْكُمْ وَإِذْ زَاغَتِ الأَبْصَارُ وَبَلَغَتِ الْقُلُوبُ الْحَنَاجِرَ} [الأحزاب:10] قَالَتْ: «كَانَ ذَاكَ يَوْمَ الْخَنْدَقِ».

(صحيح البخاري:٣٠١٤)

Regarding [the words of Allah]: {They had come upon you from above and below you. At that time your eyes became dim with horror and your hearts leapt to your throats} [*al-Aḥzāb* 33: 10], ʿĀ'ishah ﷺ said: "That was said at the battle of al-Khandaq [the Trench]."

(*Ṣaḥīḥ al-Bukhārī*: 4103)

140

عَنْ عَائِشَةَ رَضِيَ اللهُ عَنْهَا أَنّ رَسُولَ اللَّهِ صَلَّى اللهُ عَلَيْهِ وَسَلَّمَ كَانَ إِذَا اشْتَكَى نَفَثَ عَلَى نَفْسِهِ بِالْمُعَوِّذَاتِ، وَمَسَحَ عَنْهُ بِيَدِهِ، فَلَمَّا اشْتَكَى وَجَعَهُ الَّذِي تُوُفِّي فِيهِ، طَفِقْتُ أَنْفِثُ عَلَى نَفْسِهِ بِالْمُعَوِّذَاتِ الَّتِي كَانَ يَنْفِثُ وَأَمْسَحُ بِيَدِ النَّبِيِّ صَلَّى اللهُ عَلَيْهِ وَسَلَّمَ عَنْهُ»

(صحيح البخاري:٩٣٤٤)

‘Ā’ishah ﵂ related that whenever the Messenger of Allah ﷺ fell ill, he used to recite *Sūrah al-Falaq* and *Sūrah al-Nās* (the *M‘awwidhatān*) blow in his hands and then wiped over himself. And in the illness that eventually led to his death, I started reciting these two *Sūrahs*, blowing in his hands and using the hand of the Prophet ﷺ to wipe over his body.

(*Ṣaḥīḥ al-Bukhārī*: 4439)

141

عَنْ عَائِشَةَ رَضِيَ اللهُ عَنْهَا: «كَانَتْ قُرَيْشٌ وَمَنْ دَانَ دِينَهَا يَقِفُونَ بِالْمُزْدَلِفَةِ، وَكَانُوا يُسَمَّوْنَ الْحُمْسَ وَكَانَ سَائِرُ الْعَرَبِ يَقِفُونَ بِعَرَفَاتٍ، فَلَمَّا جَاءَ الْإِسْلَامُ أَمَرَ اللهُ نَبِيَّهُ صَلَّى اللهُ عَلَيْهِ وَسَلَّمَ أَنْ يَأْتِيَ عَرَفَاتٍ ثُمَّ يَقِفَ بِهَا ثُمَّ يُفِيضَ مِنْهَا، فَذَلِكَ قَوْلُهُ تَعَالَى {ثُمَّ أَفِيضُوا مِنْ حَيْثُ أَفَاضَ النَّاسُ}[البقرآية 199]»

(صحيح البخاري:٤٥٢٠)

ʿĀ'ishah ﵂ said: "The Quraysh and the tribes who followed their pagan religion used to stand at Muzdalifah as part of their pilgrimage, they used to be called al-Ḥums while the rest of the Arabs used to stand at ʿArafāh. Upon the advent of Islam, Allah commanded His Prophet ﷺ to go to ʿArafāh and stand there and proceed from there [to Muzdalifah]. That is what is meant by the words of Allah the Most High: {Then depart from the place when all the people depart...} [*al-Baqarah* 2: 199]."

(*Ṣaḥīḥ al-Bukhārī*: 4520)

142

عَنْ عَائِشَةَ رَضِيَ اللهُ عَنْهَا، قَالَتْ: «لَمَّا نَزَلَتِ الْآيَاتُ مِنْ آخِرِ سُورَ الْبَقَرَ فِي الرِّبَا قَرَأَهَا رَسُولُ اللَّهِ صَلَّى اللهُ عَلَيْهِ وَسَلَّمَ عَلَى النَّاسِ ثُمَّ حَرَّمَ التِّجَارَ فِي الْخَمْرِ».

(صحيح البخاري:٤٥٤٠)

ʿĀ’ishah ﵂ said: “When the last verses of *Sūrah al-Baqarah* about usury were revealed, the Messenger of Allah ﷺ recited these verses to people and then forbade trading in wine.”

(*Ṣaḥīḥ al-Bukhārī*: 4540)

143

عَنْ عَائِشَةَ رَضِيَ اللهُ عَنْهَا، قَالَتْ: «تَلَا رَسُولُ اللَّهِ صَلَّى اللهُ عَلَيْهِ وَسَلَّمَ هذِهِ الْآيَةَ {هُو الَّذِي أَنْزَلَ عَلَيْكَ الْكِتَابَ مِنْهُ آيَاتٌ مُحْكَمَاتٌ هُنَّ أُمُّ الْكِتَابِ وَأُخَرُ مُتَشَابِهَاتٌ فَأَمَّا الَّذِينَ فِي قُلُوبِهِمْ زَيْغٌ فَيَتَّبِعُونَ مَا تَشَابَهَ مِنْهُ ابْتِغَاءَ الْفِتْنَةِ وَابْتِغَاءَ تَأْوِيلِهِ وَمَا يَعْلَمُ تَأْوِيلَهُ إِلَّا اللهُ وَالرَّاسِخُونَ فِي الْعِلْمِ يَقُولُونَ آمَنَّا بِهِ كُلٌّ مِنْ عِنْدِ رَبِّنَا وَمَا يَذَّكَّرُ إِلَّا أُولُو الأَلْبَابِ} [سور آل عمران: آية 7] قَالَ رَسُولُ اللَّهِ صَلَّى اللهُ عَلَيْهِ وَسَلَّمَ: «فَإِذَا رَأَيْتِ الَّذِينَ يَتَّبِعُونَ مَا تَشَابَهَ مِنْهُ فَأُولَئِكِ الَّذِينَ سَمَّى اللهُ فَاحْذَرُوهُمْ».

(صحيح البخاري:٧٤٥٤)

‘Ā’ishah رضي الله عنها said: “The Messenger of Allah ﷺ read out the following Qur’ānic verse: {(O Prophet), He has sent down the Book to you. In it are absolutely clear verses (*muḥkamāt*) which are the core of the Book, and others not entirely clear (*mutashābihāt*). Those in whose hearts there is ill, they follow only its unclear verses, seeking mischief and their wrong meaning. Allah alone knows their true meaning. Those firmly grounded in knowledge say: ‘We believe in the Book; all of it is from our Lord.’ Only the men of understanding take a lesson} [*Āl ‘Imrān* 3: 7 and then he ﷺ said: ‘When you see those who are after only the unclear verses, remember that they are the ones mentioned in the above verse; so beware of them.'"

(*Ṣaḥīḥ al-Bukhārī*: 4547)

144

عَنْ عَائِشَةَ رَضِيَ اللهُ عَنْهَا أَنَّ النَّبِيَّ صَلَّى اللهُ عَلَيْهِ وَسَلَّمَ قَالَ: «ثَلَاثٌ هُنَّ عَلَيَّ فَرَائِضُ وَهُنَّ لَكُمْ سُنَّةٌ: الْوِتْرُ والسِّوَاكُ وَقِيَامُ اللَّيْلِ».

(الدُّرُّالمَنْثُورُ للسُّيُوطي: 4/196)

ʿĀ'ishah ﷺ related that the Prophet ﷺ said: "Three things are made mandatory for me but are sunnah acts for you: praying the *witr*, using the *siwāk*, and standing up at night to pray (*qiyām al-layl*)."

(*Al-Durr al-Manthūr* of al-Suyūṭī, 4: 196)

145

عَنْ عَائِشَةَ رَضِي اللهُ عَنْهَا قَالَتْ: «قَالَ رَسُولُ اللهِ صَلَّى اللهُ عَلَيْهِ وَسَلَّمَ: لَا يُنْجِي حَذَرٌ مِنْ قَدَرٍ وَإِنَّ الدُّعَاءَ يَدْفَعُ مِنَ الْبَلَاءِ».

(الدُّرُّ الْمَنْثُورُ لِلسُّيُوطِي: ٣/٨١٣)

ʿĀ'ishah related that the Messenger of Allah said: "No precautionary measure can save one from what has been destined but supplication can drive away affliction."

(*Al-Durr al-Manthūr* of al-Suyūṭī, 3: 318)

146

عَنْ عَائِشَةَ رَضِيَ اللهُ عَنْهَا [فِي قَوْلِهِ تَعَالَى:] {وَالَّذِي تَوَلَّى كِبْرَهُ} [سور النّور: آية 11]، قَالَتْ: «عَبْدُ اللَّهِ بْنُ أُبَيّ بْنُ سَلُولَ».

(صحيح البخاري:٩٤٧٤)

Regarding the Qur'ānic verse: {And he who has the greater part [in the slander campaign against 'Ā'ishah ﵂ *al-Nūr* 24: 11], 'Ā'ishah ﵂ said: "[It alluded to] 'Abdullāh ibn Ubayy ibn Salūl [the leader of the hypocrites in Madinah]."

(*Ṣaḥīḥ al-Bukhārī*: 4749)

147

عَنْ أَبِي عُبَيْدَ عَنْ عَائِشَةَ رَضِيَ اللهُ عَنْهَا، قَالَ: «سَأَلْتُهَا عَنْ قَوْلِهِ تَعَالَى {إِنَّا أَعْطَيْنَاكَ الْكَوْثَرَ} [سور الكوثر: آية 1]، قَالَتْ: «نَهْرٌ أُعْطِيَهُ نَبِيُّكُمْ صَلَّى اللهُ عَلَيْهِ وَسَلَّمَ شَاطِئَاهُ عَلَيْهِ دُرٌّ مُجَوَّفٌ آنِيَتُهُ كَعَدَدِ النُّجُومِ».

(صحيح البخاري:٥٦٩٤)

Abū ʿUbaydah related that he asked ʿĀ'ishah ﵂ about the words of Allah the Most High, {Surely We have given you abundance (*al-Kawthar*)...} [*Sūrah al-Kawthar*: 108:1], so she explicated: "*Al-Kawthar* is a river that your Prophet ﷺ has been given: on its banks are pearly tents and cups as numerous as the stars."

(*Ṣaḥīḥ al-Bukhārī*: 4965)

148

عَنْ عَائِشَةَ أَنَّ النَّبِيَّ صَلَّى اللهُ عَلَيْهِ وَسَلَّمَ كَانَ إِذَا أَوَى إِلَى فِرَاشِهِ كُلَّ لَيْلَةٍ جَمَعَ كَفَّيْهِ ثُمَّ نَفَثَ فِيهِمَا، فَقَرَأَ فِيهِمَا: {قُلْ هُو اللهُ أَحَدٌ} و{قُلْ أَعُوذُ بِرَبِّ الْفَلَقِ} و{قُلْ أَعُوذُ بِرَبِّ النَّاسِ} ثُمَّ يَمْسَحُ بِهِمَا مَا اسْتَطَاعَ مِنْ جَسَدِهِ، يَبْدَأُ بِهِمَا عَلَى رَأْسِهِ وَوَجْهِهِ وَمَا أَقْبَلَ مِنْ جَسَدِهِ، يَفْعَلُ ذَلِكَ ثَلَاثَ مَرَّاتٍ».

(صحيح البخاري:٧١٠٥)

ʿĀ'ishah ﷺ related that every night when the Prophet ﷺ retired to bed, he joined his palms and blew into them, and then recited *Sūrah al-Ikhlāṣ*, *Sūrah al-Falaq*, and *Sūrah al-Nās*, and then wiped over whatever he could reach of his body, starting with his head, then his face and then the front parts of his body - He did so thrice.

(*Ṣaḥīḥ al-Bukhārī*: 5017)

149

عَنْ عَائِشَةَ أَنَّهَا زَفَّتِ امْرَأَةً إِلَى رَجُلٍ مِنْ الْأَنْصَارِ، فَقَالَ نَبِيُّ اللَّهِ صَلَّى اللَّهُ عَلَيْهِ وَسَلَّمَ: «يَا عَائِشَةُ مَا كَانَ مَعَكُمْ لَهْوٌ فَإِنَّ الْأَنْصَارَ يُعْجِبُهُمُ اللَّهْوُ».

(صحيح البخاري:٥١٦٢)

ʿĀ'ishah ﵂ related that she accompanied a bride in the ceremony of presenting her before the bridegroom, and so the Prophet ﷺ said: "O ʿĀ'ishah, do you not have a tambourine to play? The Anṣār love it."

(*Ṣaḥīḥ al-Bukhārī*: 5162)

150

عَنْ عَائِشَةَ رَضِيَ اللهُ عَنْهَا أَنّ رَسُولَ اللَّهِ صَلَّى اللهُ عَلَيْهِ وَسَلَّمَ، قَالَ: «يَا أُمَّةَ مُحَمَّدٍ، مَا أَحَدٌ أَغْيَرَ مِنَ اللَّهِ أَنْ يَرَى عَبْدَهُ أَوْ أَمَتَهُ تَزْنِي. يَا أُمَّةَ مُحَمَّدٍ، لَوْ تَعْلَمُونَ مَا أَعْلَمُ لَضَحِكْتُمْ قَلِيلًا وَلَبَكَيْتُمْ كَثِيرًا».

(صحيح البخاري:١٢٢٥)

ʿĀ'ishah ﵂ related that the Messenger of Allah ﷺ said: "O Community of Muḥammad! None is more jealous than Allah when He sees His male servant or female servant committing adultery. O Community of Muḥammad, if you knew what I know, you would laugh very little and cry a lot."

(*Ṣaḥīḥ al-Bukhārī*: 5221)

151

عَنْ عَبْدِ الرَّحْمَنِ بْنِ عَابِسٍ، عَنْ أَبِيهِ، قَالَ: «قُلْتُ لِعَائِشَةَ: أَنَهَى النَّبِيُّ صَلَّى اللهُ عَلَيْهِ وَسَلَّمَ أَنْ تُؤْكَلَ لُحُومُ الأَضَاحِي فَوْقَ ثَلاَثٍ؟» قَالَتْ: «مَا فَعَلَهُ إِلَّا فِي عَامٍ جَاعَ النَّاسُ فِيهِ، فَأَرَادَ أَنْ يُطْعِمَ الْغَنِيُّ الْفَقِيرَ، وَإِنْ كُنَّا لَنَرْفَعُ الْكُرَاعَ فَنَأْكُلُهُ بَعْدَ خَمْسَ عَشْرَةَ». قِيلَ: «ما اضطَرَّكُمْ إِلَيْهِ؟» فَضَحِكَتْ، قَالَتْ: «مَا شَبِعَ آلُ مُحَمَّدٍ صَلَّى اللهُ عَلَيْهِ وَسَلَّمَ مِنْ خُبْزِ بُرٍّ مَأْدُومٍ ثَلَاثَةَ أَيَّامٍ حَتَّى لَحِقَ بِاللَّهِ».

(صحيح البخاري:٣٢٤٥)

ʿAbd al-Raḥmān ibn ʿĀbis related that he asked ʿĀ'ishah ﵂: "Did the Prophet ﷺ prohibit eating from the sacrificial meat for more than three days?" She said: "The Prophet ﷺ did that only in the year of famine, and so he wanted the rich to feed the poor. Otherwise, we used to store some portions of meat and eat it after fifteen days." He asked her: "What has forced you to do so?" She laughed and said: "The Household of Muḥammad (blessings and peace be upon him) never had wheat bread with seasoned sauce for three consecutive days until he joined Allah."

(*Ṣaḥīḥ al-Bukhārī*: 5221)

152

أَنَّ عَائِشَةَ رَضِيَ اللهُ عَنْهَا، قَالَتْ: «سُئِلَ رَسُولُ اللَّهِ صَلَّى اللهُ عَلَيْهِ وَسَلَّمَ عَنِ الْبِتْعِ - وَهُو نَبِيذُ الْعَسَلِ - وَكَانَ أَهْلُ الْيَمَنِ يَشْرَبُونَهُ، فَقَالَ رَسُولُ اللَّهِ صَلَّى اللهُ عَلَيْهِ وَسَلَّمَ: كُلُّ شَرَابٍ أَسْكَرَ فَهُو حَرَامٌ».

(صحيح البخاري:٦٨٥٥)

ʿĀ'ishah ﵂ related that the Messenger of Allah ﷺ was asked about *al-bitʿ* – an alcoholic drink made from honey – which the people of Yemen used to drink and so he said: "Every intoxicating drink is forbidden."

(*Ṣaḥīḥ al-Bukhārī*: 5586)

153

عَنْ عَائِشَةَ قَالَت كَانَ رَسُولُ اللهِ صَلَّى اللهُ عَلَيْهِ وَسَلَّمَ إِذَا أَتَاهُ الْأَمْرُ يَسُرُّهُ قَالَ: «الْحَمْدُ للهِ الَّذِي بِنِعْمَتِهِ تَتِمُّ الصَّالِحَاتُ» وَإِذَا أَتَاهُ الْأَمْرُ يَكْرَهُهُ قَالَ: «الْحَمْدُ للهِ عَلَى كُلِّ حَالٍ».

(الدُّرُّ المَنْثُورُ للسُّيوطي: ٣/١٨٢)

ʿĀ'ishah ﵂ related that whenever the Messenger of Allah ﷺ received some good news, he would say: "All praise be to Allah through whose grace all good deeds are completed," and whenever he received something he disliked, he would say: "Praise be to Allah in all circumstances."

(*Al-Durr al-Manthūr of al-Suyūṭī*, 3: 281)

154

عَنْ عَائِشَةَ رَضِيَ اللهُ عَنْهَا، قَالَتْ: «سَأَلَ رَسُولَ اللَّهِ صَلَّى اللهُ عَلَيْهِ وَسَلَّمَ نَاسٌ عَنِ الْكُهَّانِ، فَقَالَ: «لَيْسَ بِشَيْءٍ»، فَقَالُوا: «يَا رَسُولَ اللَّهِ إِنَّهُمْ يُحَدِّثُونَا أَحْيَانًا بِشَيْءٍ فَيَكُونُ حَقًّا»، فَقَالَ رَسُولُ اللَّهِ صَلَّى اللهُ عَلَيْهِ وَسَلَّمَ: «تِلْكَ الْكَلِمَةُ مِنَ الْحَقِّ، يَخْطَفُهَا مِنَ الْجِنِّيِّ فَيَقُرُّهَا فِي أُذُنِ وَلِيِّهِ فَيَخْلِطُونَ مَعَهَا مِائَةَ كَذْبَةٍ».

(صحيح البخاري:٥٧٦٢)

ʿĀ'ishah ﷺ related some people asked the Messenger of Allah ﷺ about soothsayers. He replied: "It [i.e., what they say] is of no consequence." They said: "O Messenger of Allah, but sometimes they tell us things which prove to be true." The Messenger of Allah ﷺ said: "What they inform of and transpires to be true is a true word that the jinns intercept and cast in the ear of the soothsayer, however, they mix it with one hundred other lies."

(*Ṣaḥīḥ al-Bukhārī*: 5762)

155

عَنْ عِمْرَانَ بْنِ حِطَّانَ، قَالَ: «سَأَلْتُ عَائِشَةَ عَنِ الْحَرِيرِ، فَقَالَتْ: ائْتِ ابْنَ عَبَّاسٍ فَسَلْهُ، قَال: فَسَأَلْتُهُ، فَقَالَ: سَلِ ابْنَ عُمَرَ، قَالَ: فَسَأَلْتُ ابْنَ عُمَرَ، فَقَالَ أَخْبَرَنِي أَبُو حَفْصٍ، يَعْنِي عُمَرَ بْنَ الْخَطَّابِ، أَنَّ رَسُولَ اللَّهِ صَلَّى اللهُ عَلَيْهِ وَسَلَّمَ قَالَ: إِنَّمَا يَلْبَسُ الْحَرِيرَ فِي الدُّنْيَا مَنْ لَا خَلَاقَ لَهُ فِي الْآخِرَةِ». فَقُلْتُ: «صَدَقَ، وَمَا كَذَبَ أَبُو حَفْصٍ عَلَى رَسُولِ اللَّهِ صَلَّى اللهُ عَلَيْهِ وَسَلَّمَ»

(صحيح البخاري:٥٣٨٥)

ʿImrān ibn Ḥiṭṭān related that he asked ʿĀ'ishah ﵂ about [men] wearing silk, and so she directed him to consult ʿAbdullāh ibn ʿUmar. When he asked ʿAbdullāh ibn ʿUmar about the same, he reported on the authority of ʿUmar ibn al-Khaṭṭāb that the Messenger of Allah ﷺ said: "Only those who have no share in the Hereafter wear silk in this world." ʿImrān ibn Ḥiṭṭān said: "He is right; Abū Ḥafṣ [i.e., ʿUmar ibn al-Khaṭṭāb] has never lyingly related a statement from the Messenger of Allah ﷺ."

(*Ṣaḥīḥ al-Bukhārī*: 5835)

156

عَنْ عَائِشَةَ رَضِيَ اللهُ عَنْهَا زَوْجِ النَّبِيِّ صَلَّى اللهُ عَلَيْهِ وَسَلَّمَ، عَنِ النَّبِيِّ صَلَّى اللهُ عَلَيْهِ وَسَلَّمَ قَالَ: «الرَّحِمُ شِجْنَةٌ فَمَنْ وَصَلَهَا وَصَلْتُهُ وَمَنْ قَطَعَهَا قَطَعْتُهُ»

(صحيح البخاري:٩٨٩٥)

Ā'ishah ﷺ related that the Prophet ﷺ said: "Ties of kinship are like the intertwined roots of a tree: whoever keeps them connected, they keep him connected, and whoever dissevers them, they dissever him."

(*Ṣaḥīḥ al-Bukhārī*: 5989)

157

عَنْ عَائِشَةَ رَضِيَ اللهُ عَنْهَا، قَالَتْ: «جَاءَ أَعْرَابِيٌّ إِلَى النَّبِيِّ صَلَّى اللهُ عَلَيْهِ وَسَلَّمَ فَقَالَ: تُقَبِّلُونَ الصِّبْيَانَ، فَمَا نُقَبِّلُهُمْ». فَقَالَ النَّبِيُّ صَلَّى اللهُ عَلَيْهِ وَسَلَّمَ: «أَوَأَمْلِكُ لَكَ أَنْ نَزَعَ اللهُ مِنْ قَلْبِكَ الرَّحْمَةَ».

(صحيح البخاري.٨٩٩٥)

ʿĀ'ishah ﵂ relates that a bedouin came to the Prophet ﷺ and said: "You kiss your children whereas we do not do so." He replied: "What can I do if Allah has your hearts bereft of mercy?'"

(*Ṣaḥīḥ al-Bukhārī*: 5998)

158

قَالَتْ عَائِشَةُ، زَوْجَ النَّبِيِّ صَلَّى اللهُ عَلَيْهِ وَسَلَّمَ، رَضِيَ اللهُ عَنْهَا: «دَخَلَ رَهْطٌ مِنَ الْيَهُودِ عَلَى رَسُولِ اللَّهِ صَلَّى اللهُ عَلَيْهِ وَسَلَّمَ فَقَالُوا: السَّامُ عَلَيْكُمْ». قَالَتْ عَائِشَةُ: «فَفَهِمْتُهَا فَقُلْتُ: وَعَلَيْكُمُ السَّامُ وَاللَّعْنَةُ». قَالَتْ: «فَقَالَ رَسُولُ اللَّهِ صَلَّى اللهُ عَلَيْهِ وَسَلَّمَ: مَهْلًا يَا عَائِشَةُ، إِنَّ اللَّهَ يُحِبُّ الرِّفْقَ فِي الْأَمْرِ كُلِّه». فَقُلْتُ: «يَا رَسُولَ اللَّهِ، أَوَلَمْ تَسْمَعْ مَا قَالُوا!». قَالَ رَسُولُ اللَّهِ صَلَّى اللهُ عَلَيْهِ وَسَلَّمَ: «قَدْ قُلْتُ: وَعَلَيْكُمْ».

(صحيح البخاري:٦٠٢٤)

ʿĀʾishah ﵂ related that a group of Jewish men called on the Messenger of Allah ﷺ and said: "*Al-sāmu ʿalaykum* (death be upon you)." I caught what they had said and so I responded, saying: "*Wa ʿalaykum al-sām wa'l-laʿnah* (death and curse be upon you)." Upon hearing this, the Messenger of Allah ﷺ told me: "O ʿĀ'ishah, hold on! Allah loves leniency in all matters." I told him: "O Messenger of Allah, did you not hear what they said?" He replied: "I have already responded, saying: '*Wa ʿalaykum* (and the same be upon you).'"

(*Ṣaḥīḥ al-Bukhārī*: 6024)

159

قَالَتْ عَائِشَةُ: «صَنَعَ النَّبِيُّ صَلَّى اللهُ عَلَيْهِ وَسَلَّمَ شَيْئًا فَرَخَّصَ فِيهِ، فَتَنَزَّهَ عَنْهُ قَوْمٌ، فَبَلَغَ ذَلِكَ النَّبِيَّ صَلَّى اللهُ عَلَيْهِ وَسَلَّمَ فَخَطَبَ فَحَمِدَ اللَّهَ، ثُمَّ قَالَ: مَا بَالُ أَقْوَامٍ يَتَنَزَّهُونَ عَنِ الشَّيْءِ أَصْنَعُهُ، فَوَاللَّهِ إِنِّي لَأَعْلَمُهُمْ بِاللَّهِ وَأَشَدُّهُمْ لَهُ خَشْيَةً».

(صحيح البخاري:٦١٠١)

ʿĀ'ishah ﵂ related: "The Prophet ﷺ did something and then gave a dispensation to everyone to do the same. However, some people held back from doing it. When this reached the Prophet ﷺ he delivered a sermon and, after praising Allah, he said: 'What is wrong with some poeple that they hold back from something I do? By Allah, I know Allah better than they do and I fear Him more than they do.'"

(*Ṣaḥīḥ al-Bukhārī*: 6101)

160

عَنْ عَائِشَةَ رَضِى الله عَنْهَا قَالَت: «قَالَ النَّبِيُّ صَلَّى اللهُ عَلَيْهِ وَسَلَّمَ: «يَا عَائِشَةُ، إِنْ أَرَدْتِ اللُّحُوقَ بِي فَلْيَكْفِكِ مِنَ الدُّنْيَا كَزَادِ الرَّاكِبِ وَلَا تَسْتَخْلِفِي ثَوْبًا حَتَّى تُرَقِّعِيهِ وَإِيَّاكِ وَمُجَالَسَةِ الْأَغْنِيَاءِ».

(الدُّرُّالمَنْثُورُ للسُّيُوطِي: ٣/٢٣٨)

ʿĀ'ishah ﷺ related that the Prophet ﷺ said to me: "O ʿĀ'ishah, if you want to join me [in Paradise] then be content in this world with only as much [provision] as a rider takes along [for his journey], and do not replace a garment [just because it is worn out] until you patch it first and beware of keeping the company of the rich."

(*Al-Durr al-Manthūr of al-Suyūṭī*, 3: 238)

161

عَنْ عَائِشَةَ أَنّ رَسُولَ اللَّهِ صَلَّى اللهُ عَلَيْهِ وَسَلَّمَ قَالَ: «سَدِّدُوا وَقَارِبُوا وَاعْلَمُوا أَنْ لَنْ يُدْخِلَ أَحَدَكُمْ عَمَلُهُ الْجَنَّةَ، وَأَنَّ أَحَبَّ الْأَعْمَالِ إِلَى اللَّهِ أَدْوَمُهَا وَإِنْ قَلَّ».

(صحيح البخاري: ٦٤٦٤)

ʿĀ'ishah ﵂ related that the Messenger of Allah ﷺ said: "Follow a middle course and strive to be close to that, and realise that none of you will enter Paradise because of his works, and that the most beloved of works to Allah are those which are constant and continuous, even if they are little."

(*Ṣaḥīḥ al-Bukhārī*: 6464)

162

عَنْ عَائِشَةَ أَنّ النَّبِيَّ صَلَّى اللهُ عَلَيْهِ وَسَلَّمَ قَالَ: «لَا نُورَثُ مَا تَرَكْنَا صَدَقَةٌ».

(صحيح البخاري:٦٧٢٧)

ʿĀ'ishah ﵂ related that the Prophet ﷺ said: "We [Messengers] are not inherited; whatever we leave behind is to be given in charity."

(*Ṣaḥīḥ al-Bukhārī*: 6727)

163

عَنْ عَائِشَةَ رَضِيَ اللهُ عَنْهَا قَالَتْ: «كَانَ النَّبِيُّ صَلَّى اللهُ عَلَيْهِ وَسَلَّمَ يُبَايِعُ النِّسَاءَ بِالْكَلَامِ بِهذِهِ الْآيَةِ: {لا يُشْرِكْنَ بِاللَّهِ شَيْئًا} [سور الممتحنة: آية 12]».
قَالَتْ: «وَمَا مَسَّتْ يَدُ رَسُولِ اللَّهِ صَلَّى اللهُ عَلَيْهِ وَسَلَّمَ يَدَ امْرَأَةٍ إِلَّا امْرَأَةً يَمْلِكُهَا».

(صحيح البخاري:٤١٢٧)

ʿĀ'ishah ﵂ said: "The Prophet ﷺ took the pledge of allegiance from women through the recitation of the Qur'ānic verse: {O Prophet, when the believing women come to you, ask them to pledge to you that they will not take any partner with Allah. Nor will they steal or have sex outside marriage. They will not kill their children. They will not slander. Nor will they invent any falsehood. They will not disobey you in anything good} [*al-Mumtaḥanah* 60: 12]." She added: "the hands of the Messenger of Allah ﷺ never touched the hand of any woman unless it be the hand of a woman who was lawful to him."

(*Ṣaḥīḥ al-Bukhārī*: 7214)

164

عَنْ عَائِشَةَ أَنَّ النَّبِيَّ صَلَّى اللهُ عَلَيْهِ وَسَلَّمَ بَعَثَ رَجُلًا عَلَى سَرِيَّةٍ وَكَانَ يَقْرَأُ لِأَصْحَابِهِ فِي صَلَاتِهِمْ فَيَخْتِمُ بِـ {قُلْ هُو اللهُ أَحَدٌ} فَلَمَّا رَجَعُوا ذَكَرُوا ذَلِكَ لِلنَّبِيِّ صَلَّى اللهُ عَلَيْهِ وَسَلَّمَ، فَقَالَ: «سَلُوهُ لِأَيِّ شَيْءٍ يَصْنَعُ ذَلِكَ؟» فَسَأَلُوهُ فَقَالَ: «لِأَنَّهَا صِفَةُ الرَّحْمَنِ وَأَنَا أُحِبُّ أَنْ أَقْرَأَ بِهَا». فَقَالَ النَّبِيُّ صَلَّى اللهُ عَلَيْهِ وَسَلَّمَ: «أَخْبِرُوهُ أَنَّ اللهَ يُحِبُّهُ».

(صحيح البخاري:٧٣٧٥)

ʿĀ'ishah ﵂ related that the Prophet ﷺ had put a man in charge of a miltary expedition and this man concluded every prayer he led with the recitation of Sūrah al-Ikhlāṣ. Upon returning from the expedition, those with him mentioned this to the Prophet ﷺ and so he said: "Go ask him why he did so." When they asked him, he said: "I do so because it is the quality of the All-Merciful and I like to recite it." The Prophet ﷺ said when he heard his answer: "Inform him that Allah loves him."

(*Ṣaḥīḥ al-Bukhārī*: 7375)

165

عَنْ عَائِشَةَ رَضِيَ اللَّهُ تَعَالَى عَنْهَا أَنَّهَا قَالَتْ: «أَمَرَنَا رَسُولُ اللَّهِ صَلَّى اللَّهُ عَلَيْهِ وَسَلَّمَ أَنْ نُنَزِّلَ النَّاسَ مَنَازِلَهُمْ، مَعَ مَا نَطَقَ بِهِ الْقُرْآنُ مِنْ قَوْلِهِ اللَّهِ تَعَالَى: {وَفَوْقَ كُلِّ ذِى عِلْمٍ عَلِيمٌ}».

(سنن أبي داود ٢٤٨٤)

‘Ā’ishah ﵂ said: “The Messenger of Allah ﷺ commanded us to treat people according to their different status along with the purport of the words of Allah the Most High in the Qur’ān: {*Over every man of knowledge is One who knows*} [*Yūsuf* 12: 76].”

(*Sunan Abū Dāwūd*: 4842)

166

عَنْ عَائِشَةَ قَالَت: «لَمَّا نَزَلَتْ {وَأَنْذِرْ عَشِيرَتَكَ الأَقْرَبِينَ} (سور الشعراء: آية 214)، قَامَ رَسُولُ اللَّهِ صَلَّى اللهُ عَلَيْهِ وَسَلَّمَ عَلَى الصَّفَا فَقَالَ: يَا فَاطِمَةُ بِنْتَ مُحَمَّدٍ، يَا صَفِيةُ بِنْتَ عَبْدِ الْمُطَّلِبِ، يَا بَنِي عَبْدِ الْمُطَّلِبِ، لَا أَمْلِكُ لكُمْ مِنَ اللَّهِ شَيْئًا، سَلُونِي مِنْ مَالِي مَا شِئْتُمْ».

(صحيح مسلم:٥٠٣)

ʿĀ'ishah ﵂ said: "When the verse: {(O Prophet), warn your close relatives} [*al-Shuʿarā'* 26: 214] was revealed, the Messenger of Allah ﷺ assembled his close relatives at al-Ṣafā and addressed them: 'O Fāṭimah, daughter of Muḥammad, O Ṣafiyyah, daughter of ʿAbd al-Muṭṭalib, and O Banū ʿAbd al-Muṭṭalib, I avail you naught vis-à-vis Allah, [even though] you can ask me to give you whatever you like of my property.'"

(*Ṣaḥīḥ Muslim*: 503)

167

عَنْ الْمِقْدَامِ بْنِ شُرَيْحٍ عَنْ أبيهِ قَالَ: «سَأَلْتُ عَائِشَةَ، قُلْتُ: بِأَيِّ شَيْءٍ كَانَ يَبْدَأُ النَّبِيُّ صَلَّى اللهُ عَلَيْهِ وَسَلَّمَ إِذَا دَخَلَ بَيْتَهُ؟» قَالَتْ: «بِالسِّوَاكِ».

(صحيح مسلم:٥٩٠)

Al-Miqdām ibn Shurayḥ related that his father asked ʿĀ'ishah ﵂: "What did the Prophet ﷺ start with when he entered his house?" She replied: "With using the *siwāk*."

(*Ṣaḥīḥ Muslim*: 590)

168

عَنْ عَائِشَةَ قَالَت: «قَالَ رَسُولُ اللَّهِ صَلَّى اللهُ عَلَيْهِ وَسَلَّمَ: عَشْرٌ مِنَ الْفِطْرَ: قَصُّ الشَّارِبِ وَإِعْفَاءُ اللِّحْيَةِ وَالسِّوَاكُ وَاسْتِنْشَاقُ الْمَاءِ وَقَصُّ الأَظْفَارِ وَغَسْلُ الْبَرَاجِمِ وَنَتْفُ الإِبِطِ وَحَلْقُ الْعَانَةِ وَانْتِقَاصُ الْمَاءِ». قَالَ زَكَرِيَّاءُ: «قَالَ مُصْعَبٌ: وَنَسِيتُ الْعَاشِرَ»، إِلَّا أَنْ تَكُونَ: الْمَضْمَضَةَ، زَادَ قُتَيْبَةُ، قَالَ وَكِيعٌ: «انْتِقَاصُ الْمَاءِ يَعْنِي الِاسْتِنْجَاءَ».

(صحيح مسلم:٤٠٦)

Āʾishah ﷺ related that the Messenger of Allah ﷺ said: "Ten things people are naturally predisposed to do: Trimming the moustache; growing the beard; using the *siwāk*; snuffing water inside of the nose and expelling it; clipping the nails; washing the finger joints; plucking the hair of the armpits; shaving pubic hair; washing the private parts with water upon going to lavatory." The narrator forgot the tenth thing, but it is established that it is rinsing the mouth.

(*Ṣaḥīḥ Muslim*: 604)

169

عَنْ عَائِشَةَ زَوْجِ النَّبِيِّ صَلَّى اللهُ عَلَيْهِ وَسَلَّمَ أَنَّ رَسُولَ اللَّهِ صَلَّى اللهُ عَلَيْهِ وَسَلَّمَ كَانَ يُؤْتَى بِالصِّبْيَانِ فَيُبَرِّكُ عَلَيْهِمْ وَيُحَنِّكُهُمْ، فَأُتِيَ بِصَبِيٍّ فَبَالَ عَلَيْهِ، فَدَعَا بِمَاءٍ فَأَتْبَعَهُ بَوْلَهُ وَلَمْ يَغْسِلْهُ».

(صحيح مسلم:٦٦٢)

ʿĀ'ishah ﵂ related that babies used to be brought to the Messenger of Allah ﷺ and he would pat them on the head and do *taḥnīk* (chewing a bit of date and passing it on to the baby's mouth). Once a baby urinated on him and he called for some water and splashed it on the spots of clothes touched by urine but he did not wash it.

(Ṣaḥīḥ Muslim: 662)

170

عَنْ عَائِشَةَ رَضِيَ اللهُ عَنْهَا قَالَتْ: «نَهَى رَسُولُ اللَّهِ صَلَّى اللهُ عَلَيْهِ وَسَلَّمَ عَنْ صَوْمَيْنِ: يَوْمِ الْفِطْرِ وَيَوْمِ الأَضْحَى».

(صحيح مسلم:٦٧٦٢)

ʿĀ’ishah said: “The Messenger of Allah ﷺ forbade fasting on two days: the day of *ʿĪd al-Fiṭr* and the day of *ʿĪd al-Aḍḥā*.”

(*Ṣaḥīḥ Muslim*: 2676)

171

عَنْ عَائِشَةَ أَنَّ امْرَأَةً قَالَتْ: «يَا رَسُولَ اللَّهِ، أَقُولُ إِنَّ زَوْجِي أَعْطَانِي مَا لَمْ يُعْطِنِي»، فَقَالَ رَسُولُ اللَّهِ صَلَّى اللهُ عَلَيْهِ وَسَلَّمَ: الْمُتَشَبِّعُ بِمَا لَمْ يُعْطَ كَلَابِسِ ثَوْبَيْ زُورٍ».

(صحيح مسلم: ٥٥٨٣)

Ā’ishah ﵂ related that a woman asked the Prophet ﷺ: “O Messenger of Allah, I often say [to co-wife] that my husband has given me something when he has not?” He said: “One who claims to have something when he does not is like a deceiving person.”

(*Ṣaḥīḥ Muslim*: 5583)

172

عَنْ إِسْمَاعِيلَ أَنَّ عَائِشَةَ كَانَتْ تَنْهَى المَرْأَةَ ذَاتِ الزَّوْجِ أَنْ تَدَعَ سَاقَيْهَا لَا تَجْعَلْ فِيهَا شَيْئًا، وَإِنَّهَا كَانَتْ تَقُولُ: لَا تَدَعِ المَرْأَةُ الخِضَابَ فَإِنَّ رَسُولَ اللهِ صَلَّى اللهُ عَلَيْهِ وَسَلَّمَ كَانَ يَكْرَهُ الرَّجِلَةَ».

كَنْزُ العُمَّالِ:١٧٤٥٧))

ʿĀ'ishah ﵂ used to advise married women against leaving their legs without wearing anything on them. She also used to say: "Let a woman not leave dying her hair, for the Messenger of Allah ﷺ disliked women who resembled men."

(*Kanz al-ʿUmmāl*: 17457)

173

عَنْ عَائِشَةَ قَالَتْ: «قَالَ رَسُولُ اللَّهِ صَلَّى اللهُ عَلَيْهِ وَسَلَّمَ: الرَّحِمُ مُعَلَّقَةٌ بِالْعَرْشِ، تَقُولُ: مَنْ وَصَلَنِي وَصَلَهُ اللهُ وَمَنْ قَطَعَنِي قَطَعَهُ اللهُ».

(صحيح مسلم:٦١٥٦)

ʿĀ'ishah ﵂ related that the Messenger of Allah ﷺ said: "The tie of kinship is attached to the Throne (of Allah) and it keeps saying: 'Whoever keeps connection with me, Allah will keep him connected to Him, and whoever dissevers me, Allah will dissever him.'"

(*Ṣaḥīḥ Muslim*: 6519)

174

عَنْ الْأَسْوَدِ قَالَ: «دَخَلَ شَبَابٌ مِنْ قُرَيْشٍ عَلَى عَائِشَةَ وَهِيَ بِمِنًى وَهُمْ يَضْحَكُونَ فَقَالَتْ: «مَا يُضْحِكُكُمْ؟» قَالُوا: «فُلَانٌ خَرَّ عَلَى طُنُبِ فُسْطَاطٍ فَكَادَتْ عُنُقُهُ، أَوْ عَيْنُهُ، أَنْ تَذْهَبَ»، فَقَالَتْ: «لَا تَضْحَكُوا، فَإِنِّي سَمِعْتُ رَسُولَ اللَّهِ صَلَّى اللهُ عَلَيْهِ وَسَلَّمَ، قَالَ: مَا مِنْ مُسْلِمٍ يُشَاكُ شَوْكَةً فَمَا فَوْقَهَا إِلَّا كُتِبَتْ لَهُ بِهَا دَرَجَةٌ وَمُحِيَتْ عَنْهُ بِهَا خَطِيئَةٌ».

(صحيح مسلم:٦٥٦١)

Al-Aswad said: "A group of young men from Quraysh went to see 'Ā'ishah ﵂ at Minā and it happened that they were laughing when they entered in on her. She asked them: "Why are you laughing?" They replied: "So-and-so was hit by a tent peg and he almost broke his neck – or lost his eye." She said: 'Do not laugh at this, for I heard the Messenger of Allah ﷺ say: 'No Muslim is pricked by a thorn or suffers more than this except that he is raised one degree, and one of his sins are effaced.'"

(*Ṣaḥīḥ Muslim*: 6561)

175

عَنْ عَائِشَةَ أَنَّ النَّبِيَّ صَلَّى اللهُ عَلَيْهِ وَسَلَّمَ كَانَ إِذَا اشْتَدَّ غَمُّهُ مَسَحَ بِيَدِهِ عَلَى رَأْسِهِ وَلِحْيَتِهِ ثُمَّ تَنَفَّسَ الصُّعَدَاءَ وَقَالَ: حَسْبِيَ اللهُ وَنِعْمَ الْوَكِيلُ».

(الدُّرُّالمَنْثُورُ لِلسُّيُوطِي: ٢/٢٩٠)

ʿĀ'ishah ﵂ related that whenever the Prophet ﷺ felt extremely distressed, he passed his hand over his head and beard, sighed deeply and said: "Allah is sufficient for me and He is the best of guardians."

(*Al-Durr al-Manthūr of al-Suyūṭī*, 2: 290)

176

عَنْ عَائِشَةَ، زَوْجِ النَّبِيِّ صَلَّى اللهُ عَلَيْهِ وَسَلَّمَ، عَنِ النَّبِيِّ صَلَّى اللهُ عَلَيْهِ وَسَلَّمَ، قَالَ: «إِنَّ الرِّفْقَ لَا يَكُونُ فِي شَيْءٍ إِلَّا زَانَه، وَلَا يُنْزَعُ مِنْ شَيْءٍ إِلَّا شَانَهُ».

(صحيح مسلم:٢٠٦٦)

ʿĀ'ishah ﵂ related that the Prophet ﷺ said: "Indeed, gentleness is not found in anything except that it makes it beautiful, and it is not taken away from anything except that it disfigures it."

(*Ṣaḥīḥ Muslim*: 6602)

177

عَنْ عَائِشَةَ قَالَتْ: «قَالَ رَسُولُ اللَّهِ صَلَّى اللهُ عَلَيْهِ وَسَلَّمَ: مَنْ أَحَبَّ لِقَاءَ اللَّهِ أَحَبَّ اللهُ لِقَاءَهُ، وَمَنْ كَرِهَ لِقَاءَ اللَّهِ كَرِهَ اللهُ لِقَاءَهُ»، فَقُلْتُ: «يَا نَبِيَّ اللَّهِ، أَكَرَاهِيَةُ الْمَوْتِ فَكُلُّنَا نَكْرَهُ الْمَوْتَ». فَقَالَ: «لَيْسَ كَذَلِكِ، وَلَكِنَّ الْمُؤْمِنَ إِذَا بُشِّرَ بِرَحْمَةِ اللَّهِ وَرِضْوَانِهِ وَجَنَّتِهِ أَحَبَّ لِقَاءَ اللَّهِ، فَأَحَبَّ اللهُ لِقَاءَهُ، وَإِنَّ الْكَافِرَ إِذَا بُشِّرَ بِعَذَابِ اللَّهِ وَسَخَطِهِ كَرِهَ لِقَاءَ اللَّهِ وَكَرِهَ اللهُ لِقَاءَهُ».

(صحيح مسلم:٢٢٨٦)

ʿĀ'ishah ﷺ related that the Messenger of Allah ﷺ said: "Whoever loves to meet Allah, Allah loves to meet him too and whoever does not love to meet Allah, Allah does not love to meet him either." I said: "O Messenger of Allah, if it is a question of disliking death, then we all dislike death." He said: "It is not like that; rather when the believer is given the glad tiding of Allah's mercy, of His good pleasure and of Paradise, he loves to meet Allah and Allah loves to meet him. On the other hand, when the disbeliever is given the news of Allah's chastisement and detestation, he dislikes meeting Allah and Allah, too, dislikes meeting him."

(*Ṣaḥīḥ Muslim*: 6822)

178

عَنْ عَائِشَةَ أَنّ النَّبِيَّ صَلَّى اللهُ عَلَيْهِ وَسَلَّمَ كَانَ يَقُولُ فِي دُعَائِهِ: اللَّهُمَّ إِنِّي أَعُوذُ بِكَ مِنْ شَرِّ مَا عَمِلْتُ وَشَرِّ مَا لَمْ أَعْمَلْ».

(صحيح مسلم:٦٨٩٨)

ʿĀ'ishah ﷺ related that the Prophet ﷺ used to say in his supplication: "O Allah, I seek refuge in You from the evil I have committed and also from the evil I did not commit."

(*Ṣaḥīḥ Muslim*: 6898)

179

عَنْ عَائِشَةَ قَالَتْ: «سَأَلْتُ رَسُولَ اللَّهِ صَلَّى اللهُ عَلَيْهِ وَسَلَّمَ عَنْ قَوْلِهِ عَزَّ وَجَلَّ {يَوْمَ تُبَدَّلُ الأَرْضُ غَيْرُ الأَرْضِ وَالسَّمَوَاتُ} [سور إبراهيم: آية 48] فَأَيْنَ يَكُونُ النَّاسُ يَوْمَئِذٍ يَا رَسُولَ اللَّهِ؟»، فَقَالَ: «عَلَى الصِّرَاطِ».

(صحيح مسلم:٦٥٠٧)

ʿĀ'ishah ﷺ said: "I asked the Messenger of Allah ﷺ about the words of Allah, glorified and exalted is He: {On the Day of Judgement, the Earth and the heavens will be altogether changed} [*Ibrāhīm* 14: 48] and enquired: 'Where will all the people be on that Day, O Messenger of Allah?' He replied: 'On the Bridge over Hell (*al-Ṣirāṭ*).'"

(*Ṣaḥīḥ Muslim*: 7056)

180

عَنْ عَائِشَةَ قَالَتْ: «كَانَ رَسُولُ اللَّهِ صَلَّى اللهُ عَلَيْهِ وَسَلَّمَ يَأْكُلُ طَعَامًا فِي سِتَّةِ نَفَرٍ مِنْ أَصْحَابِهِ، فَجَاءَ أَعْرَابِيٌّ فَأَكَلَهُ بِلُقْمَتَيْنِ، فَقَالَ رَسُولُ اللَّهِ صَلَّى اللهُ عَلَيْهِ وَسَلَّمَ: أَمَا أَنَّهُ لَوْ كَانَ قَالَ: بِسْمِ اللَّهِ لَكَفَاكُمْ، فَإِذَا أَكَلَ أَحَدُكُمْ طَعَامًا فَلْيَقُلْ: بِسْمِ اللَّهِ، فَإِنْ نَسِيَ أَنْ يَقُول بِسْمِ اللَّهِ فِي أَوَّلِهِ، فَلْيَقُلْ: بِسْمِ اللَّهِ فِي أَوَّلِهِ وَآخِرِهِ».

(سنن ابن ماجه:٣٢٦٤)

ʿĀ'ishah ﵂ related that one day the Messenger of Allah ﷺ was having a meal along with six Companions when a Bedouin joined them and he ate all the food there was there in only two morsels. Upon seeing this, the Messenger of Allah ﷺ said: "Had he said: 'in the name of Allah' [before he started], the food would have sufficed for all of you. So, when one of you takes food, one should start with 'in the name of Allah [*bismillāh*]' and, if he forgets, let him say: 'in the name of Allah, at its beginning and at its end [*bismillāh fī awwalihi wa ākhirihi*'."

(*Sunan Ibn Mājah*: 3264)

181

عَنْ عَائِشَةَ عَنْ رَسُولِ اللَّهِ صَلَّى اللهُ عَلَيْهِ وَسَلَّمَ قَالَ: «مَنْ شَرِبَ فِي إِنَاءِ فِضَّةٍ فَكَأَنَّمَا يُجَرْجِرُ فِي بَطْنِهِ نَارَ جَهَنَّمَ».

(سنن ابن ماجه:٣٤١٥)

'Āishah ﵂ related that the Messenger of Allah ﷺ said: "Whoever drinks from a silver pot, it is as if he fills his belly with Hellfire."

(*Sunan Ibn Mājah*: 3415)

182

عَنْ عَائِشَةَ قَالَتْ: «قَالَ رَسُولُ اللَّهِ صَلَّى اللهُ عَلَيْهِ وَسَلَّمَ: إِنَّ أَعْظَمَ النَّاسِ فِرْيَةً لَرَجُلٌ هَاجَى رَجُلًا فَهَجَا الْقَبِيلَةَ بِأَسْرِهَا، وَرَجُلٌ انْتَفَى مِنْ أَبِيهِ وَزَنَّى أُمَّهُ».

(سنن ابن ماجه:١٦٧٣)

ʿĀ'ishah ﵂ related that the Messenger of ﷺ said: "The worst slanderer is a man who exchanges disparaging words with another man and this leads him to disparage his whole tribe, and a man who calls someone else as his father and thus accuses his mother of adultery."

(*Sunan Ibn Mājah*: 3761)

183

عَنْ عَائِشَةَ قَالَتْ: «سَمِعْتُ رَسُولَ اللَّهِ صَلَّى اللهُ عَلَيْهِ وَسَلَّمَ يَقُولُ: مُرُوا بِالْمَعْرُوفِ وَانْهَوْا عَنِ الْمُنْكَرِ قَبْلَ أَنْ تَدْعُوا فَلَا يُسْتَجَابَ لَكُمْ».

(سنن ابن ماجه:٤٠٠٤)

ʿĀ'ishah ﷺ related that the Messenger of Allah ﷺ said: "Enjoin good and forbid evil before you make supplication and it is answered."

(*Sunan Ibn Mājah*: 4004)

184

عَنْ عَائِشَةَ قَالَتْ: «قُلْتُ: يَا رَسُولَ اللَّهِ {وَالَّذِينَ يُؤْتُونَ مَا آتَوْا وَقُلُوبُهُمْ وَجِلَةٌ} [سور المؤمنون: آية 60]، أَهُوَ يُضَافُ الرَّجُلُ الَّذِي يَزْنِي وَيَسْرِقُ وَيَشْرَبُ الْخَمْرَ؟» قَالَ: «لَا، يَا بِنْتَ أَبِي بَكْرٍ- أَوْ يَا بِنْتَ الصِّدِّيقِ - وَلَكِنَّهُ الرَّجُلُ يَصُومُ وَيَتَصَدَّقُ وَيُصَلِّي وَهُو يَخَافُ أَنْ لَا يُتَقَبَّلَ مِنْهُ».

(سنن ابن ماجه:٤١٩٨)

ʿĀ'ishah ﷺ related that she said: "O Messenger of Allah does, {And those who give that which they give, with their hearts fearing that they have to return to their Lord} [*al-Mu'minūn* 23: 60] refer to the person who fornicates, steals and drink wine?" He said: 'No, O daughter of Abū Bakr - or he said: O daughter of al-Siddiq - it is about the person who fasts, gives in charity, and prays and yet he fears that it will not be accepted from him by Allah."

(*Sunan Ibn Mājah*: 4198)

185

عَنْ عَائِشَةَ رَضِيَ اللهُ عَنْهَا أَنّ رَسُولَ اللَّهِ صَلَّى اللهُ عَلَيْهِ وَسَلَّمَ قَالَ: «رُفِعَ الْقَلَمُ عَنْ ثَلَاثَةٍ: عَنِ النَّائِمِ حَتَّى يَسْتَيْقِظَ وَعَنِ الْمُبْتَلَى حَتَّى يَبْرَأَ وَعَنِ الصَّبِيِّ حَتَّى يَكْبَرَ».

(سنن أبي داود:٤٣٩٨)

ʿĀ'ishah ﵂ related that the Messenger of Allah ﷺ said: "The pen is lifted from three people [i.e., they are not taken to task]: The sleeping person until he wakes up; the afflicted until he is healed; and the young child until he comes of age."

(*Sunan Abī Dāwūd*: 4398)

186

عَنْ عَائِشَةَ قَالَت: «كَانَ النَّبِيُّ صَلَّى اللهُ عَلَيْهِ وَسَلَّمَ إِذَا بَلَغَهُ عَنِ الرَّجُلِ الشَّيْءُ لَمْ يَقُلْ: مَا بَالُ فُلَانٍ يَقُولُ، وَلَكِنْ يَقُولُ: مَا بَالُ أَقْوَامٍ يَقُولُونَ كَذَا وَكَذَا».

(سنن أبي داود:٨٨٧٤)

ʿĀ’ishah related that whenever the Prophet ﷺ was informed that someone did something that he should not have done, he did not name that person [upon addressing his community]. Rather, he used to say: “What is it with some people that they say such-and-such and such-and-such?”

(*Sunan Abī Dāwūd*: 4788)

187

عَنْ عَائِشَةَ قَالَت: «قَالَ رَسُولُ اللهِ صَلَّى اللهُ عَلَيْهِ وَسَلَّمَ: إِنَّ اللهَ أَمَرَنِي بِمُدَارَاةِ النَّاسِ كَمَا أَمَرَنِي بِإِقَامَةِ الْفَرَائِضِ».

(الدُّرُّالمَنْثُورُ للسُّيُوطي:٢/٠٩)

Āʾishah ﵂ related that the Messenger of Allah ﷺ said: "Allah has commanded me to be affable with people in the same way He commanded me to establish the obligatory acts."

(*Al-Durr al-Manthūr of al-Suyūṭī*, 2: 90)

188

عَنْ عَائِشَةَ أَنَّ رَسُولَ اللهِ صَلَّى اللهُ عَلَيْهِ وَسَلَّمَ قَالَ: «مَنْ أَنْظَرَ مُعْسِرًا أَظَلَّهُ اللهُ فِي ظِلِّهِ يَوْمَ الْقِيَامَةِ».

(الدُّرُّالمَنْثُورُ للسُّيُوطي:١/٢٦٦)

'Āishah ﵂ related that the Messenger of Allah ﷺ said: "Whoever gives respite to a borrower who is facing hard times, Allah will shade him under His shade on the Day of Judgement."

(*Al-Durr al-Manthūr of al-Suyūṭī*, 1: 266)

189

عَنْ عَائِشَةَ رَضِيَ اللهُ عَنْهَا أَنّ رَسُولَ اللَّهِ صَلَّى اللهُ عَلَيْهِ وَسَلَّمَ قَالَ: «لَا يَكُونُ لِمُسْلِمٍ أَنْ يَهْجُرَ مُسْلِمًا فَوْقَ ثَلَاثَةٍ فَإِذَا لَقِيَهُ سَلَّمَ عَلَيْهِ ثَلَاثَ مِرَارٍ كُلُّ ذَلِكَ لَا يَرُدُّ عَلَيْهِ فَقَدْ بَاءَ بِإِثْمِهِ».

(سنن أبي داود:٣١٩٤)

ʿĀʾishah ﵂ related that the Messenger of Allah ﷺ said: "It is not permitted for a Muslim to be estranged from another fellow Muslim for more than three days. On meeting him, he should offer him the greeting of peace (*salām*) thrice and if he does not return the greeting, the latter would be sinning."

(*Sunan Abī Dāwūd*: 4913)

190

عَنْ عَائِشَةَ قَالَتْ: «قَالَ رَسُولُ اللَّهِ صَلَّى اللهُ عَلَيْهِ وَسَلَّمَ: خَيْرُكُمْ خَيْرُكُمْ لِأَهْلِهِ وَأَنَا خَيْرُكُمْ لِأَهْلِي وَإِذَا مَاتَ صَاحِبُكُمْ فَدَعُوهُ».

(سنن الترمذي:٥٩٨٣)

ʿĀ’ishah ﵂ related that the Messenger of Allah ﷺ said: “The best among you is the one who is best with his family, and I am the best to my family; and when one of you dies, leave him be.”

(*Sunan al-Tirmidhī*: 3895)

191

عَنْ عَائِشَةَ عَنْ النَّبِيِّ صَلَّى اللهُ عَلَيْهِ وَسَلَّمَ قَالَ: «مَنْ نَذَرَ أَنْ يُطِيعَ اللَّهَ جَلَّ وَعَزَّ فَلْيُطِعْهُ وَمَنْ نَذَرَ أَنْ يَعْصِيَ اللَّهَ جَلَّ وَعَزَّ فَلَا يَعْصِهِ».

(مسند أحمد: ٤٠٦٠)

'Āʾishah ﷺ related that the Prophet ﷺ said: "Whoever vows to obey Allah, glorified and exalted is He, let him obey Him, but whoever vows to disobey Allah, glorified and exalted is He, let him not disobey Him."

(*Musnad Aḥmad*: 4060)

192

عَنْ عَائِشَةَ سَمِعَ النَّبِيُّ صَلَّى اللهُ عَلَيْهِ وَسَلَّمَ قِرَاءَ أَبِي مُوسَى فَقَالَ: «لَقَدْ أُوتِيَ هَذَا مِنْ مَزَامِيرِ آلِ دَاوُدَ».

(مسند أحمد: ٢٨٠٤)

ʿĀ'ishah ﷺ related that, when the Prophet ﷺ heard Abū Mūsā [al-Ashʿarī] recite the Qur'ān, he said: "This one has been gifted with one of the pipes of the Household of [Prophet] Dāwūd."

(*Musnad Aḥmad*: 4082)

193

عَنْ عَائِشَةَ تَبْلُغُ بِهِ النَّبِيَّ صَلَّى اللهُ عَلَيْهِ وَسَلَّمَ: «إِذَا ظَهَرَ السُّوءُ فِي الْأَرْضِ أَنْزَلَ اللهُ بِأَهْلِ الْأَرْضِ بَأْسَهُ»، قَالَتْ: «وَفِيهِمْ أَهْلُ طَاعَةِ اللَّهِ عَزَّ وَجَلَّ؟» قَالَ: «نَعَمْ، ثُمَّ يَصِيرُونَ إِلَى رَحْمَةِ اللَّهِ تَعَالَى».

(مسند أحمد: ٧١١٤)

'Ā'ishah ﵂ related that the Prophet ﷺ said: "When evil spreads in the Earth, Allah sends down His punishment on the people of Earth." 'Ā'ishah ﵂ asked: "Would this happen notwithstanding the presence of the people of obedience to Allah?" He replied: "Yes; and then they would proceed to the mercy of Allah Most High."

(*Musnad Aḥmad*: 4117)

194

عَنْ عَائِشَةَ قَالَتْ: «كَانَ النَّبِيُّ صَلَّى اللهُ عَلَيْهِ وَسَلَّمَ يُحْرَسُ حَتَّى نَزَلَتْ هذِهِ الْآيَةَ: {وَاللهُ يَعْصِمُكَ مِنَ النَّاسِ} [سور المائد: آية 67] فَأَخْرَجَ رَسُولُ اللَّهِ صَلَّى اللهُ عَلَيْهِ وَسَلَّمَ رَأْسِهِ مِنَ الْقُبَّةِ، فَقَالَ لَهُمْ: يَا أَيُّهَا النَّاسُ، انْصَرِفُوا فَقَدْ عَصَمَنِي اللهُ».

(سنن الترمذي :٣٠٤٦)

Ā'ishah ﵂ related that the Prophet ﷺ used to have guards to protect him until the following verse was revealed: {Allah will protect you from people} [*al-Mā'idah* 5: 67], upon which the Messenger of Allah popped his head out of his tent and said to his guards: "Disperse, for Allah shall be protecting me."

(*Sunan al-Tirmidhī*: 3046)

195

قَالَتْ عَائِشَةُ: «سَمِعْتُ رَسُولَ اللَّهِ صَلَّى اللهُ عَلَيْهِ وَسَلَّمَ يَقُولُ: لَا يُصَلِّي بِحَضْرَةِ الطَّعَامِ وَلَا وَهُوَ يُدَافِعُهُ الْأَخْبَثَانِ».

(مسند أحمد:١٥١٤)

ʿĀ'ishah ﷺ reports: 'I heard the Prophet ﷺ say: "One should not offer prayer when food is served or when he has to answer the call of nature."'

(Musnad Aḥmad, Hadith: 4151)

196

قَالَتْ عَائِشَةُ: «قَالَ رَسُولُ اللَّهِ صَلَّى اللهُ عَلَيْهِ وَسَلَّمَ فِي مَرَضِهِ الَّذِي مَاتَ فِيهِ: يَا عَائِشَةُ، مَا فَعَلَتْ الذَّهَبُ؟» فَجَاءَتْ مَا بَيْنَ الْخَمْسَةِ إِلَى السَّبْعَةِ أَوْ الثَّمَانِيَةِ أَوْ التِّسْعَةِ، فَجَعَلَ يُقَلِّبُهَا بِيَدِهِ وَيَقُولُ: «مَا ظَنُّ مُحَمَّدٍ بِاللَّهِ عَزَّ وَجَلَّ لَوْ لَقِيَهُ وَهذِهِ عِنْدَهُ؟ أَنْفِقِيهَا».

(مسند أحمد:٣٠٢٤)

‘Ā’ishah ﵂ related that, in the illness that culminated in his death, the Messenger of Allah ﷺ called out: “O ‘Ā’ishah, what has become of the gold?” It was five to nine gold coins, and he kept turning these coins in his hand and then said: “How does Muḥammad think of his Lord if he meets Him while these gold coins are still in his possession? Give them in charity!”

(*Musnad Aḥmad*: 4203)

197

عَنْ عَائِشَةَ عَنْ النَّبِيِّ صَلَّى اللهُ عَلَيْهِ وَسَلَّمَ قَالَ: «لَا يَقُولَنَّ أَحَدُكُمْ خَبُثَتْ نَفْسِي وَلَكِنْ لِيَقُلْ لَقِسَتْ».

(مسند أحمد:٤٢٢٤)

ʿĀ'ishah ﷺ related that the Prophet ﷺ said: "Let no one say: 'My soul has become wicked,' rather one should say: 'My soul has become exasperated.'"

(*Musnad Aḥmad*: 4224)

198

عَنْ عَائِشَةَ قَالَتْ: «تَزَوَّجَنِي رَسُولُ اللَّهِ صَلَّى اللهُ عَلَيْهِ وَسَلَّمَ فِي شَوَّالٍ وَأُدْخِلْتُ عَلَيْهِ فِي شَوَّالٍ فَأَيُّ نِسَائِهِ كَانَ أَحْظَى عِنْدَهُ مِنِّي، فَكَانَتْ تَسْتَحِبُّ أَنْ تُدْخِلَ نِسَائَهَا فِي شَوَّالٍ».

(مسند أحمد:١٥٢٤)

ʿĀ'ishah said: "The Messenger of Allah ﷺ married me in the month of Shawwāl and I moved to his house in Shawwāl. And who among the wives of Allah's Messenger ﷺ was dearer to him than I?" She encouraged that the bride should move to her husband's house in Shawwāl.

(*Musnad Aḥmad*: 4251)

199

عَنْ عَبْدِ الْوَهَّابِ بْنِ الْوَرْدِ، عَنْ رَجُلٍ مِنْ أَهْلِ الْمَدِينَةِ، قَالَ: «كَتَبَ مُعَاوِيَةُ إِلَى عَائِشَةَ أُمِّ الْمُؤْمِنِينَ رَضِيَ اللهُ عَنْهَا أَنِ اكْتُبِي إِلَيَّ كِتَابًا تُوصِينِي فِيهِ وَلَا تُكْثِرِي عَلَيَّ»، فَكَتَبَتْ عَائِشَةُ رَضِيَ اللهُ عَنْهَا إِلَى مُعَاوِيَةَ: «سَلَامٌ عَلَيْكَ، أَمَّا بَعْدُ فَإِنِّي سَمِعْتُ رَسُولَ اللَّهِ صَلَّى اللهُ عَلَيْهِ وَسَلَّمَ يقُولُ: «مَنِ التَمَسَ رِضَاءَ اللَّهِ بِسَخَطِ النَّاسِ كَفَاهُ اللهُ مُؤْنَةَ النَّاسِ، وَمَنِ الْتَمَسَ رِضَاءِ النَّاسِ بِسَخَطِ اللَّهِ وَكَلَهُ اللهُ إِلَى النَّاسِ، وَالسَّلَامُ عَلَيْكَ».

(سنن الترمذي:٢٤١٤)

ʿAbd al-Wahhāb ibn Ward related from a Madinan man that Muʿāwiyah ﵁ wrote a letter to ʿĀ'ishah ﵂ requesting her to write to him a concise piece of advice, so she wrote: "Peace be upon you. To proceed: I heard the Messenger of Allah ﷺ say: 'Whoever seeks Allah's good pleasure despite people's displeasure, Allah will suffice him the burden of people, and whoever seeks good pleasure of people despite Allah's displeasure, Allah will consign him people.' Peace be upon you."

(*Sunan al-Tirmidhī*: 2414)

200

قَالَ أَبُو عَبْدِ اللَّهِ الْجَدَلِيُّ: «سَأَلْتُ عَائِشَةَ عَنْ خُلُقِ رَسُولِ اللَّهِ صَلَّى اللهُ عَلَيْهِ وَسَلَّمَ، فَقَالَتْ: لَمْ يَكُنْ فَاحِشًا وَلَا مُتَفَحِّشًا وَلَا صَخَّابًا فِي الْأَسْوَاقِ، وَلَا يَجْزِي بِالسَّيِّئَةِ السَّيِّئَةَ، وَلَكِنْ يَعْفُو وَيَصْفَحُ».

(سنن الترمذي:٢٠١٦)

Abū ʿAbdullāh al-Jadalī related that he asked ʿĀ'ishah ﷺ about the character of the Messenger of Allah ﷺ, so she said: "He was not foul in speech nor indecent nor foul-mouthed in the marketplaces. Moreover, he did not meet something bad with another bad thing, instead he pardoned and forgave."

(*Sunan al-Tirmidhī*: 2016)

201

عَنْ عَائِشَةَ، قَالَتْ: «لَمَّا قُبِضَ رَسُولُ اللَّهِ صَلَّى اللهُ عَلَيْهِ وَسَلَّمَ اخْتَلَفُوا فِي دَفْنِهِ، فَقَالَ أَبُو بَكْرٍ: سَمِعْتُ مِنْ رَسُولِ اللَّهِ صَلَّى اللهُ عَلَيْهِ وَسَلَّمَ شَيْئًا مَا نَسِيتُهُ، قَالَ: مَا قَبَضَ اللهُ نَبِيًّا إِلَّا فِي الْمَوْضِعِ الَّذِي يُحِبُّ أَنْ يُدْفَنَ فِيهِ. ادْفِنُوهُ فِي مَوْضِعِ فِرَاشِهِ».

(سنن الترمذي:٨١٠١)

ʿĀ'ishah ﷺ related that when the Messenger of Allah ﷺ passed away, there was disagreement about where he should be buried. But Abū Bakr ﷺ said: "I heard something from the Messenger of Allah ﷺ which I have not forgotten; he said: 'Allah does not take away the soul of any Prophet except in the spot where He wants him to be buried.' Bury him at the spot where his bed is."

(*Sunan al-Tirmidhī*: 1018)

202

عَنْ عَائِشَةَ أَنّ رَسُولَ اللَّهِ صَلَّى اللهُ عَلَيْهِ وَسَلَّمَ أَتَى سَعْدًا يَعُودُهُ، فَقَالَ لَهُ سَعْدٌ: «يَا رَسُولَ اللَّهِ، أُوصِي بِثُلُثَيْ مَالِي؟» قَالَ: «لَا». قَالَ: «فَأُوصِي بِالنِّصْفِ؟» قَالَ: «لَا». قَالَ: «فَأُوصِي بِالثُّلُثِ؟» قَالَ: نَعَمْ، الثُّلُثُ، وَالثُّلُثُ كَثِيرٌ أَوْ كَبِيرٌ، إِنَّكَ أَنْ تَدَعَ وَرَثَتَكَ أَغْنِيَاءَ خَيْرٌ مِنْ أَنْ تَدَعَهُمْ فُقَرَاءَ يَتَكَفَّفُونَ».

(سنن النَّسائي:٣٦٦٣)

ʿĀ'ishah ﵂ related that the Messenger of Allah ﷺ visited Saʿd [ibn Abī Waqqāṣ ﵁] when he was sick. Saʿd ﵁ said: "O Messenger of Allah, can I bequeath two-thirds of my wealth?" He replied by saying: "No!". Saʿd ﵁: "Can I bequeath half of it?" The reply was: "No!". Saʿd ﵁ said: "How about one-third of it?" He said: "Yes, you can bequeath one third of it, and one third is quite a lot; it is better to leave behind your heirs rich than to leave them impoverished and begging from others."

(*Sunan al-Nasā'ī*: 3663)

203

عَنْ عَائِشَةَ قَالَتْ: «قَالَ رَسُولُ اللَّهِ صَلَّى اللهُ عَلَيْهِ وَسَلَّمَ: السِّوَاكُ مَطْهَرَةٌ لِلْفَمِ مَرْضَاةٌ لِلرَّبِّ».

(سنن الدارمي:٧٠٧)

ʿĀ'ishah ﵂ related that the Messenger of Allah ﷺ said: "The *siwāk* cleanses the mouth and pleases the Lord."

(*Sunan al-Dārimī*: 707)

204

عَنْ عَائِشَةَ قَالَتْ: «أُصِيبَ سَعْدٌ يَوْمَ الْخَنْدَقِ رَمَاهُ رَجُلٌ مِنْ قُرَيْشٍ يُقَالُ لَهُ حِبَّانُ بْنُ الْعَرِقَةِ فِي الْأَكْحَلِ فَضَرَبَ عَلَيْهِ رَسُولُ اللَّهِ صَلَّى اللهُ عَلَيْهِ وَسَلَّمَ خَيْمَةً فِي الْمَسْجِدِ لِيَعُودَهُ مِنْ قَرِيبٍ».

(مسند أحمد:٣٧٢٤)

ʿĀ'ishah ﵂ related that Saʿd [ibn Muʿādh ﵁] was hit by an arrow thrown by a man called Hibban ibn al-ʿAriqqah at the Battle of the Trench. The arrow pierced through a vein in his arm. And so the Messenger of Allah ﷺ erected a tent for him at his mosque so that he may closely see to his recovery.

(*Musnad Aḥmad*: 4273)

205

قَالَتْ عَائِشَةُ: «قَالَ رَسُولُ اللَّهِ صَلَّى اللهُ عَلَيْهِ وَسَلَّمَ إِنَّ كَسْرَ عَظْمِ الْمُؤْمِنِ مَيْتًا مِثْلُ كَسْرِهِ حَيًّا».

(مسند أحمد :٢٤٦٨٦)

'Ā'ishah ﵂ related that the Messenger of Allah ﷺ said: "Breaking the bone of a dead believer is no different than breaking the bone of a believer who is alive."

(*Musnad Aḥmad*: 4286)

206

عَنْ عَائِشَةَ قَالَتْ: «قَالَ رَسُولُ اللَّهِ صَلَّى اللهُ عَلَيْهِ وَسَلَّمَ صَلَاةُ الْجَالِسِ عَلَى النِّصْفِ مِنْ صَلَاةِ الْقَائِمِ».

(مسند أحمد:٥٠٣٤)

ʿĀ'ishah ﷺ related that the Messenger of Allah ﷺ said: "The reward for the prayer of a person who is seated is half that of the prayer of a person who performs it standing."

(*Musnad Aḥmad*: 4305)

207

عَنْ عَائِشَةَ قَالَتْ: «قَالَ رَسُولُ اللَّهِ صَلَّى اللهُ عَلَيْهِ وَسَلَّمَ: مَا مِنْ رَجُلٍ تَكُونُ لَهُ سَاعَةٌ مِنَ اللَّيْلِ يَقُومُهَا فَيَنَامُ عَنْهَا إِلَّا كُتِبَ لَهُ أَجْرُ صَلَاتِهِ وَكَانَ نَوْمُهُ عَلَيْهِ صَدَقَةً تُصُدِّقَ بِهِ عَلَيْهِ».

(مسند أحمد:٩١٣٤)

ʿĀ’ishah ﵂ related that the Messenger of Allah ﷺ said: “No man who usually sets up a regular time at night in which he wakes up to pray and then happens to fail to wake up for it except that he gets the reward of the prayer that he usually performs at that time, and his sleep is considered a charity that has been given to him.”

(*Musnad Aḥmad*: 4319)

208

عَنْ عَائِشَةَ أَن النَّبِيَّ صَلَّى اللهُ عَلَيْهِ وَسَلَّمَ قَالَ: «قِرَاءَ الْقُرْآنِ فِي الصَّلَا أَفْضَلُ مِنْ قِرَاءَ الْقُرْآنِ فِي غَيْرِ الصَّلَا وَقِرَاءَ الْقُرْآنِ فِي غَيْرِ الصَّلَا أَفْضَلُ مِنَ التَّسْبِيحِ وَالتَّكْبِير وَالتَّسْبِيحِ أَفْضَلُ مِنَ الصَّدَقَةِ وَالصَّدَقَةُ أَفْضَلُ مِنَ الصَّوْمِ وَالصَّوْمُ جُنَّةٌ مِنَ النَّارِ».

(الدُّرُّالمَنْثُورُ للسُّيُوطي:١/٣٥٤)

ʿĀʾishah ﵂ related that the Prophet ﷺ said: "Reciting the Qur'ān in one's prayer is superior to one's recitation of it outside of the prayer. And the recitation of the Qur'ān outside of the prayer is better than glorifying Allah and saying: *Allāhu akbar*. And glorifying Allah is superior to giving alms while the latter is superior to [superregatory] fasting, and fasting is a protection from Hellfire."

(*Al-Durr al-Manthūr of al-Suyūṭī*, 1: 354)

209

قَالَتْ عَائِشَةُ زَوْجُ النَّبِيِّ صَلَّى اللهُ عَلَيْهِ وَسَلَّمَ: «قَالَ رَسُولُ اللهِ صَلَّى اللهُ عَلَيْهِ وَسَلَّمَ: الْإِمَامُ ضَامِنٌ وَالْمُؤَذِّنُ مُؤْتَمَنٌ فَأَرْشَدَ اللهُ الْإِمَامَ وَعَفَا عَنِ الْمُؤَذِّنِ».

(مسند أحمد :١٤٣٤)

ʿĀ'ishah ﵂ related that the Messenger of Allah ﷺ said: "The imam (the prayer leader) is a guarantor and the muezzin (the person who calls to prayer) is a confidant, and so Allah guides the imam and pardons the muezzin."

(*Musnad Aḥmad*: 4341)

210

عَنْ عَائِشَةَ أَنَّ رَسُولَ اللَّهِ صَلَّى اللهُ عَلَيْهِ وَسَلَّمَ كَانَ يَقُولُ: «اجْعَلُوا مِنْ صَلَاتِكُمْ فِي بُيُوتِكُمْ وَلَا تَجْعَلُوهَا عَلَيْكُمْ قُبُورًا».

(مسند أحمد:٤٤٣٤)

ʿĀ'ishah ﵂ related that the Messenger of Allah ﷺ said: "Offer some of your prayers at homes, and do not turn them into graveyards."

(*Musnad Aḥmad*: 4344)

211

عَنْ عَائِشَةَ زَوْجِ النَّبِيِّ صَلَّى اللهُ عَلَيْهِ وَسَلَّمَ أَنَّ رَجُلًا تَلَا هذِهِ الْآيَةَ {مَنْ يَعْمَلْ سُوءًا يُجْزَ بِهِ} قَالَ: إِنَّا لَنُجْزَى بِكُلِّ عَمَلِنَا هَلَكْنَا إِذًا». فَبَلَغَ ذَاكَ رَسُولَ اللَّهِ صَلَّى اللهُ عَلَيْهِ وَسَلَّمَ فَقَالَ: «نَعَمْ، يُجْزَى بِهِ الْمُؤْمِنُونَ فِي الدُّنْيَا فِي مُصِيبَةٍ فِي جَسَدِهِ فِيمَا يُؤْذِيهِ».

(مسند أحمد :٦٤٣٤)

ʿĀ'ishah ﷺ related that a man recited {One who does evil will be punished for it}[*al-Nisā'* 4: 123] and exclaimed: "If we are requitted for every single action we would be destroyed." When the Messenger of Allah ﷺ was told about this, he said: "True, but the believer is punished in this world in the form of physical harm."

(*Musnad Aḥmad*: 4346)

212

عَنْ سَعِيدِ بْنِ الْمُسَيَّبِ وَسُلَيْمَانَ بْنِ يَسَارٍ أَنَّ خَالِدَ بْنَ سَعِيدِ بْنِ الْعَاصِ الْمَخْزُومِي هَجَرَ امْرَأَتَهُ سَنَةً وَلَمْ يَكُنْ حلَفَ، فَقَالَتْ لَهُ عَائِشَةُ: «أَمَا تَقْرَأُ آيَةَ الإِيلَاءِ؟ إِنَّهُ لَا يَنْبَغِي أَنْ تَهْجُرَ أَكْثَرَ مِنْ أَرْبَعَةِ أَشْهُرٍ».

(الدُّرُّالمَنْثُورُ للسُّيُوطي:١/٢٧٠)

Sa'īd ibn al-Musayyib and Sulaymān ibn Yasār related that Khālid ibn Sa'īd ibn al-'Āṣ al-Makhzūmī kept away from his wife for a year even though he did not take any oath regarding separating himself from her. When 'Ā'ishah ﵁ learnt about it, she said: "Do you not read the verse concerning those who say to their wives 'be as my mother's back' (*al-Ilā'*) [*al-Mujādalah*, 58: 1-5]? You ought not keep away from your wife for more than four months."

(*Al-Durr al-Manthūr of al-Suyūṭī*, 1: 270)

213

عَنْ عَائِشَةَ قَالَتْ: «كَانَ الرُّكْبَانُ يَمُرُّونَ بِنَا وَنَحْنُ مَعَ رَسُولِ اللَّهِ صَلَّى اللهُ عَلَيْهِ وَسَلَّمَ مُحْرِمَاتٌ فَإِذَا حَاذَوْا بِنَا أَسْدَلَتْ إِحْدَانَا جِلْبَابِهَا مِنْ رَأْسِهَا عَلَى وَجْهِهَا فَإِذَا جَاوَزَنَا كَشَفْنَاهُ».

(مسند أحمد: ٢٤٠٠٨)

ʿĀ'ishah ﵂ said: "Riders used to pass by us when we were with the Messenger of Allah ﷺ while in a state of ritual consecration, and as they came closer, we covered our faces by lowering our head scarf, and uncovered our faces when they went past us."

(*Musnad Aḥmad*: 8004)

214

عَنْ عَائِشَةَ قَالَتْ: «قَالَ رَسُولُ اللَّهِ صَلَّى اللهُ عَلَيْهِ وَسَلَّمَ: هذِهِ الدُّنْيَا خَضِرَةٌ حُلْوَةٌ فَمَنْ آتَيْنَاهُ مِنْهَا شَيْئاً بِطِيبِ نَفْسٍ مِنَّا وَطِيبِ طُعْمَةٍ وَلَا إِشْرَاهٍ بُورِكَ لَهُ فِيهِ، وَمَنْ آتَيْنَاهُ مِنْهَا شَيْئاً بِغَيْرِ طِيبِ نَفْسٍ مِنَّا وَغَيْرِ طِيبِ طُعْمَةٍ وَإِشْرَاهٍ مِنْهُ لَمْ يُبَارَكْ لَهُ فِيهِ».

(مسند أحمد:٢٧٣٤)

ʿĀ'ishah ﵂ related that the Messenger of Allah ﷺ said: "This world is verdant and sweet and, so, if we willingly and gladly give of it to anyone, without him coveting it, it will be blessed for him. But if we unwillingly and unhapilly give of it to anyone, while he covets it, it will not be blessed for him."

(*Musnad Aḥmad*: 4372)

215

عَنْ عَائِشَةَ عَنِ النَّبِيِّ صَلَّى اللهُ عَلَيْهِ وَسَلَّمَ قَالَ: «مَنْ كَانَ يُؤْمِنُ بِاللهِ وَالْيَوْمِ الْآخِرِ فَلَا يُؤْذِ جَارَهُ، وَمَنْ كَانَ يُؤْمِنُ بِاللَّهِ وَالْيَوْمِ الْآخِرِ فَلْيَقُلْ خَيْرًا أَوْ لِيَصْمُتْ، وَمَنْ كَانَ يُؤْمِنُ بِاللَّهِ وَالْيَوْمِ الْآخِرِ فَلْيُكْرِمْ ضَيْفَهُ».

(مسند أحمد: ٤٣٨٢)

ʿĀ'ishah ﵂ related that the Prophet ﷺ said: "Whoever believes in Allah and the Last Day let him not harm his neighbour; and whoever believes in Allah and the Last Day let him say something good or be silent; and whoever believes in Allah and the Last Day let him honour his guest."

(*Musnad Aḥmad*: 4382)

216

عَنْ عَائِشَةَ قَالَتْ: «قَالَ رَسُولُ اللَّهِ صَلَّى اللهُ عَلَيْهِ وَسَلَّمَ: مَنْ وَلَّاهُ اللهُ عَزَّ وَجَلَّ مِنْ أَمْرِ الْمُسْلِمِينَ شَيئًا فَأَرَادَ بِهِ خَيْرًا جَعَلَ لَهُ وَزِيرَ صِدْقٍ فَإِنْ نَسِيَ ذَكَّرَهُ وَإِنْ ذَكَرَ أَعَانَهُ».

(مسند أحمد:٢٩٣٤)

ʿĀ'ishah ﵂ related that the Messenger of Allah ﷺ said: "When Allah, glorified and exalted is He, entrusts someone with overseeing some of the affairs of Muslims and He wants good for him, He helps him with a sincere deputy who reminds him when he forgets and assists him when he remembers."

(*Musnad Aḥmad*: 4392)

217

عَنْ عَائِشَةَ أَنَّ سَائِلًا سَأَلَ، قَالَتْ: «فَأَمَرْتُ الْخَادِمَ فَأَخْرَجَ لَهُ شَيْئًا». قَالَتْ: «فَقَالَ النَّبِيُّ صَلَّى اللهُ عَلَيْهِ وَسَلَّمَ لَهَا: يَاعَائِشَةُ، لَا تُحْصِي فَيُحْصِيَ اللهُ عَلَيْكِ».

(مسند أحمد:٦٩٣٤)

ʿĀ’ishah ﵂ related that once a begger asked her to give him something and so she said: “I ordered the servant and he got something out to give him.” She said: “The Prophet ﷺ then said to her: ‘Do not be stringent in what you give [in charity] lest Allah be stringent in what He gives you.’”

(*Musnad Aḥmad*: 4396)

218

عَنْ عَائِشَةَ أَنَّهَا قَالَتْ: «قَالَ رَسُولُ اللَّهِ صَلَّى اللهُ عَلَيْهِ وَسَلَّمَ: إِذَا أَرَادَ اللهُ عَزَّ وَجَلَّ بِأَهْلِ بَيْتٍ خَيْرًا أَدْخَلَ عَلَيْهِمُ الرِّفْقَ».

(مسند أحمد:٤٠٤٤)

Ā’ishah ﵂ related that the Messenger of Allah ﷺ said: “When Allah wants good for any members of a household, He makes them lenient.”

(*Musnad Aḥmad*: 4404)

219

قَالَتْ عَائِشَةُ: «قَالَ رَسُولُ اللَّهِ صَلَّى اللهُ عَلَيْهِ وَسَلَّمَ: لَا تَشْرَبُوا إِلَّا فِيمَا أُوكِئَ عَلَيْهِ».

(مسند أحمد:٠١٤٤)

ʿĀ’ishah ﵂ related that the Messenger of Allah ﷺ said: “Do not drink water except from properly covered containers.”

(*Musnad Aḥmad*: 4410)

220

عَنْ عَائِشَةَ قَالَتْ: «قَالَ رَسُولُ اللَّهِ صَلَّى اللهُ عَلَيْهِ وَسَلَّمَ: مَنْ حُمِّلَ مِنْ أُمَّتِي دَيْنًا ثُمَّ جَهِدَ فِي قَضَائِهِ فَمَاتَ وَلَمْ يَقْضِهِ فَأَنَا وَلِيُّهُ».

(مسند أحمد:٠٣٤٤)

ʿĀ’ishah (raḍiya Allāhu ʿanhā) related that the Messenger of Allah ﷺ said: “If a member of my community becomes indebted and he exerts all efforts to repay it but then dies before he does so, I will be his guardian [and repay it for him].”

(*Musnad Aḥmad*: 4430)

221

قَالَ عِمْرَانُ بْنُ حِطَّانَ: «دَخَلْتُ عَلَى عَائِشَةَ فَذَاكَرْتُهَا حَتَّى ذَكَرْنَا الْقَاضِيَ، فَقَالَتْ عَائِشَةُ: سَمِعْتُ رَسُولَ اللَّهِ صَلَّى اللهُ عَلَيْهِ وَسَلَّمَ يَقُولُ: لَيَأْتِيَنَّ عَلَى الْقَاضِي الْعَدْلِ يَوْمَ الْقِيَامَةِ سَاعَةٌ يَتَمَنَّى أَنَّهُ لَمْ يَقْضِ بَيْنَ اثْنَيْنِ فِي تَمْرٍ قَطُّ»

(مسند أحمد.٨١٤٤)

ʿImrān ibn Ḥiṭṭān said: "One day I visited ʿĀ'ishah ﵂ and asked her some questions of knowledge until reference to the *qāḍī* (judge) came up. ʿĀ'ishah ﵂ then said: I heard the Messenger of Allah ﷺ say: 'On the Day of Judgement there will be a moment, for even the just *qāḍī*, when he would wish he had never judged a case between two people, even if it involved a single date.'"

(*Musnad Aḥmad*: 4438)

222

عَنْ عَائِشَةَ أَنَّ رَسُولَ اللَّهِ صَلَّى اللهُ عَلَيْهِ وَسَلَّمَ قَالَ: «إِنَّ مِنْ يُمْنِ الْمَرْأَةِ تَيْسِيرَ خِطْبَتِهَا وَتَيْسِيرَ صَدَاقِهَا وَتَيْسِيرَ رَحِمِهَا».

(مسند أحمد:٢٤٤٥٢)

Āʾishah ﷺ related that the Messenger of Allah ﷺ said: "Indeed, of the good fortune of a woman is that she is married easily and her dower is facilitated [i.e., not exaggerated] and she bears children easily and has quite a few of them."

(*Musnad Aḥmad*: 4452)

223

عَنِ الْمُطَّلِبِ بْنِ حَنْطَبٍ أَنَّ عَبْدَ اللَّهِ بْنَ عَامِرٍ بَعَثَ إِلَى عَائِشَةَ بِنَفَقَةٍ وَكِسْوَةٍ فَقَالَتْ لِلرَّسُولِ: «إِنِّي يَا بُنَيَّ لَا أَقْبَلُ مِنْ أَحَدٍ شَيْئًا». فَلَمَّا خَرَجَ قَالَتْ: «رُدُّوهُ عَلَيَّ»، فَرَدُّوهُ فَقَالَتْ: «إِنِّي ذَكَرْتُ شَيْئًا قَالَهُ لِي رَسُولُ اللَّهِ صَلَّى اللهُ عَلَيْهِ وَسَلَّمَ. قَالَ: يَا عَائِشَةُ، مَنْ أَعْطَاكِ عَطَاءً بِغَيْرِ مَسْأَلَةٍ فَاقْبَلِيهِ فَإِنَّمَا هُوَ رِزْقٌ عَرَضَهُ اللهُ لَكِ».

(مسند أحمد:٤٥٤٤)

Al-Muṭṭalib ibn Ḥanṭab related that ʿAbdullāh ibn ʿĀmir sent some money and clothes to ʿĀ'ishah ﵂ but she said to the courier: "O my son, I do not accept anything from anybody." However, when the courier left, she asked that he be brought back, and then she said to him: "I remembered something that the Messenger of Allah ﷺ said to me. He said: 'O ʿĀ'ishah, if someone gives you something without you asking for it, then accept it for it is a provision that Allah has sent you.'"

(*Musnad Aḥmad*: 4454)

224

عَنْ عَائِشَةَ قَالَتْ: «لَمَّا نَزَلَتْ آيَةُ الْخِيَارِ دَعَانِي رَسُولُ اللَّهِ صَلَّى اللهُ عَلَيْهِ وَسَلَّمَ فَقَالَ: يَا عَائِشَةُ، إِنِّي أُرِيدُ أَنْ أَذْكُرَ لَكِ أَمْرًا فَلَا تَقْضِينَ فِيهِ شَيْئًا دُونَ أَبَوَيْكِ. فَقَالَتْ: وَمَا هُوَ؟ قَالَتْ: فَدَعَانِي رَسُولُ اللَّهِ صَلَّى اللهُ عَلَيْهِ وَسَلَّمَ فَقَرَأَ عَلَيَّ هذِهِ الْآيَةَ {يَا أَيُّهَا النَّبِيُّ قُلْ لِأَزْوَاجِكَ إِنْ كُنْتُنَّ تُرِدْنَ اللَّهَ وَرَسُولَهُ وَالدَّارَ الْآخِرَ} الْآيَةَ كُلَّهَا: قَالَتْ: فَقُلْتُ قَدْ اخْتَرْتُ اللَّهَ عَزَّ وَجَلَّ وَرَسُولَهُ. قَالَتْ: فَفَرِحَ بِذَلِكَ رَسُولُ اللَّهِ صَلَّى اللهُ عَلَيْهِ وَسَلَّمَ».

(مسند أحمد:٤٤٣٤)

ʿĀ'ishah ﵂ said: "When the verse relating 'to making a choice' (*āyat al-khiyār*) was revealed, the Messenger of Allah ﷺ called me and said: 'O 'Ā'ishah, I want to mention something to you, so do not make a decision until you consult your parents.' I asked him: 'What is it?' So the Messenger of Allah ﷺ recited to me the following verse: {O Prophet, tell your wives: 'If you desire this world and its glitter, then come, and I will give you some provision and release you in an honourable way} [*al-Aḥzāb* 33: 2}. I said: 'I have chosen Allah, glorified and exalted is He, and His Messenger.' The Messenger of Allah ﷺ was delighted with my response."

(*Musnad Aḥmad*: 4344)

225

عَنْ عَائِشَةَ أَنَّ رَسُولَ اللَّهِ صَلَّى اللهُ عَلَيْهِ وَسَلَّمَ قَالَ لَهَا: «يَا عَائِشَةُ اسْتَتِرِى مِنْ النَّارِ وَلَوْ بِشِقِّ تَمْرٍ فَإِنَّهَا تَسُدُّ مِنْ الْجَائِعِ مَسَدَّهَا مِنْ الشَّبْعَانِ».

(مسند أحمد:٥٧٤٤)

ʿĀ'ishah ﷺ related that the Messenger of Allah ﷺ said to her: "O ʿĀ'ishah, shield yourself from the Hellfire even if it be a with a date [given in charity], for it does to one what it does to a hungry person who becomes full."

(*Musnad Aḥmad*: 4475)

226

عَائِشَةَ تَقُولُ: «قَالَ رَسُولُ اللَّهِ صَلَّى اللهُ عَلَيْهِ وَسَلَّمَ: الْفَارُّ مِنْ الطَّاعُونِ كَالْفَارِّ مِنْ الزَّحْفِ».

(مسند أحمد:٤٥٠٠)

ʿĀ'ishah ﵂ related that the Messenger of Allah ﷺ said: "Someone who flees from a place afflicted with the plague is like a deserter from the battleground."

(*Musnad Aḥmad*: 4500)

227

عَنْ عَائِشَةَ أَنَّ رَسُولَ اللَّهِ صَلَّى اللهُ عَلَيْهِ وَسَلَّمَ قَالَ: «إِنَّ أَعْظَمَ النِّكَاحِ بَرَكَةً أَيْسَرُهُ مُؤْنَةً».

(مسند أحمد:٢٠٥٤)

ʿĀ'ishah ﵂ related that the Messenger of Allah ﷺ said: "The marriage that is blessed most is that which involves the least of expenses."

(*Musnad Aḥmad*: 4502)

228

عَنْ عَائِشَةَ أَنَّ رَسُولَ اللَّهِ صَلَّى اللهُ عَلَيْهِ وَسَلَّمَ قَالَ: «مَنْ أَخَذَ السَّبْعَ الْأُوَلَ مِنْ الْقُرْآنِ فَهُو حَبْرٌ».

(مسند أحمد:٤٠٥٤)

Ā'ishah ﷺ related that the Messenger of Allah ﷺ said: "Whoever learns the first seven *sūrah*s of the Qur'ān is an erudite sage."

(*Musnad Aḥmad*: 4504)

229

قَالَتْ عَائِشَةُ: «قَالَ رَسُولُ اللَّهِ صَلَّى اللَّهُ عَلَيْهِ وَسَلَّمَ الشُّؤْمُ سُوءُ الْخُلُقِ».

(مسند أحمد:٢٢٥٤)

ʿĀ'ishah ﵂ related that the Messenger of Allah ﷺ said: "Ill-fortune is bad character."

(*Musnad Aḥmad*: 4522)

230

عَنْ عَائِشَةَ قَالَتْ: «شَرِبَ رَسُولُ اللَّهِ صَلَّى اللهُ عَلَيْهِ وَسَلَّمَ قَائِمًا وَقَاعِدًا وَمَشَى حَافِيًا وَنَاعِلًا وَانْصَرَفَ عَنْ يَمِينِهِ وَعَنْ شِمَالِهِ».

(مسند أحمد:٢٤٥٤)

ʿĀ'ishah ﵂ said: "The Messenger of Allah ﷺ drank water both while standing and also while sitting, and he walked both bare-footed and with shoes on, and walked out both from his right and left sides."

(*Musnad Aḥmad*: 4542)

231

عَنْ عَائِشَةَ قَالَتْ: «مَا مِنْ يَوْمٍ مِنَ السَّنَةِ أَصُومُهُ أَحَبُّ إِلَيَّ مِنْ يَوْمِ عَرَفَةَ».

(المُصَنَّفُ لِابْنِ أَبِي شَيْبَةَ: ٣/٩٦)

Ā'ishah ﵂ said: "The Day of 'Arafah [9th Dhū'l-Ḥijjah] for me is the best day of the year to fast."

(*Al-Muṣannaf* of Ibn Abī Shaybah, 3: 96)

232

عَنْ عَائِشَةَ أَنَّ رَسُولَ اللَّهِ صَلَّى اللهُ عَلَيْهِ وَسَلَّمَ قَالَ: «مَنْ أَتَى إِلَيْهِ مَعْرُوفٌ فَلْيُكَافِئْ بِهِ وَمَنْ لَمْ يَسْتَطِعْ فَلْيَذْكُرْهُ فَمَنْ ذَكَرَهُ فَقَدْ شَكَرَهُ وَمَنْ تَشَبَّعَ بِمَا لَمْ يَنَلْ فَهُو كَلَابِسِ ثَوْبَيْ زُورٍ».

(مسند أحمد:٦٦٥٤)

Ā'ishah ﵂ related that the Messenger of Allah ﷺ said: "Whoever receives something good should reward it with something in exchange. But if he is unable to do so, he should, at least, remember this act, for whoever remembers an act of kindness has given his thanks. Moreover, whoever pretends to possess something which he does not have is like someone who gives a false testimony."

(*Musnad Aḥmad*: 4566)

233

عَنْ عَائِشَةَ رَضِيَ اللهُ عَنْهَا عَنْ رَسُولِ اللَّهِ صَلَّى اللهُ عَلَيْهِ وَسَلَّمَ قَالَ: «إِذَا قَضَى أَحَدُكُمْ حَجَّهُ فَلْيَجْعَلِ الرِّحْلَةَ إِلَى أَهْلِهِ، فَإِنَّهُ أَعْظَمُ لِأَجْرِهِ».

(المُستدرك للحاكم:١٨٠٥)

Ā'ishah ﷺ related that the Messenger of Allah ﷺ said: "When one of you completes his *ḥajj*, he should rush back to his family for this would make his reward greater."

(*Al-Mustadrak* of al-Ḥākim: 1805)

234

عَنْ عَائِشَةَ قَالَتْ: «أُهْدِيَتْ لِحَفْصَةَ شَاةٌ وَنَحْنُ صَائِمَتَانِ فَأَفْطَرَتْنِي وَكَانَتْ ابْنَةُ أبيهَا فَدَخَلَ عَلَيْنَا رَسُولُ اللَّهِ صَلَّى اللهُ عَلَيْهِ وَسَلَّمَ فَذَكَرْنَا ذَلِكَ لَهُ فَقَالَ: «أَبْدِلَا يَوْمًا مَكَانَهُ».

(مسند أحمد:٥٩٢٨)

ʿĀ'ishah ﷺ said: "Once Ḥafṣah ﷺ was given a sheep as a present while we were both fasting [a voluntary fast], and so she, forceful as her father was, made me break my fast. When the Messenger of Allah ﷺ came in and we mentioned to him what happened, he said: 'Fast another instead of today.'"

(*Musnad Aḥmad*: 8295)

235

عَنْ عَائِشَةَ رَضِيَ اللهُ عَنْهَا قَالَتْ: «مَا شَرِبَ أَبُو بَكْرٍ خَمْرًا فِي جَاهِلِيَّةٍ وَلَا إِسْلَامٍ».

(كَنْزُ العُمَّالِ:٩٩٥٥٣)

‘Ā’ishah رضي الله عنها said: “Abū Bakr never drank wine: neither in the pre-Islamic pagan period nor after the advent of Islam.”

(*Kanz al-‘Ummāl*: 35599)

236

عَنْ عَائِشَةَ رَضِيَ اللهُ عَنْهَا قَالَتْ: «قَالَ رَسُولِ اللَّهِ صَلَّى اللهُ عَلَيْهِ وَسَلَّمَ: «إِنَّ اللهَ تَصَدَّقَ بِفِطْرِ رَمَضَانَ عَلَى مَرِيضِ أُمَّتِي وَمُسَافِرِهَا».

(الدُرُّ المَنْثُورُ لِلسُّيُوطِي: ١/١٩١)

'Ā'ishah ﷺ related that the Messenger of Allah ﷺ said: "Allah has given a dispensation to those members of my community who are ill or travelling not to fast in Ramadan."

(*Al-Durr al-Manthūr of al-Suyūṭī*, 1: 191)

237

عَنْ عَائِشَةَ قَالَتْ: «قِيلَ: يَا رَسُولَ اللَّهِ، مَاتَتْ فُلَانَةُ وَاسْتَرَاحَتْ»، فَغَضِبَ رَسُولُ اللَّهِ صَلَّى اللهُ عَلَيْهِ وَسَلَّمَ وَقَالَ: «إِنَّمَا يَسْتَرِيحُ مَنْ غُفِرَ لَهُ».

(مسند أحمد:٥٨٦٤)

ʿĀ'ishah ﵂ said: "It was once said: 'O Messenger of Allah, so-and-so has died and is now resting in peace,' so the Messenger of Allah ﷺ got angry and said: 'Only the one who has been forgiven rests in peace.'"

(*Musnad Aḥmad*: 4685)

238

عَنْ عَائِشَةَ أَنَّ رَسُولَ اللَّهِ صَلَّى اللهُ عَلَيْهِ وَسَلَّمَ قَالَ: «لَا يُحَاسَبُ يَوْمَ الْقِيَامَةِ أَحَدٌ فَيُغْفَرَ لَهُ، يَرَى الْمُسْلِمُ عَمَلَهُ فِي قَبْرِهِ وَيَقُولُ اللهُ عَزَّ وَجَلَّ: {فَيَوْمَئِذٍ لَا يُسْأَلُ عَنْ ذَنْبِهِ إِنْسٌ وَلَا جَانٌّ}، {يُعْرَفُ الْمُجْرِمُونَ بِسِيمَاهُمْ}».

(مسند أحمد :٨٨٦٤)

Ā'ishah ﵂ related that the Messenger of Allah ﷺ said: "On the Day of Judgement no one will be taken to task and be forgiven; The Muslim will see his deeds in his grave and Allah shall say: {On that Day there will be no need to ask any human being or jinn about their sins} and {The sinners will be known by their marks} [*al-Raḥmān* 55: 39, 41]."

(*Musnad Aḥmad*: 4688)

239

عَنْ عَائِشَةَ أَنَّ النَّبِيَّ صَلَّى اللهُ عَلَيْهِ وَسَلَّمَ نَهَى عَنْ نَقِيعِ الْبُسْرِ - وَهُو الزَّهْوُ.

(مسند أحمد:٢١٧٤)

ʿĀ'ishah related that the Prophet ﷺ forbade drinking the juice resulting from soaking dates in water.

(*Musnad Aḥmad*: 4712)

240

عَنْ عَائِشَةَ رَضِيَ اللهُ عَنْهَا قَالَتْ: «شَكَوْا إِلَى رَسُولِ اللَّهِ صَلَّى اللهُ عَلَيْهِ وَسَلَّمَ مَا يَجِدُونَ مِنَ الْوَسْوَسَةِ وَقَالُوا: «يَا رَسُولَ اللَّهِ إِنَّا لَنَجِدُ شَيْئًا لَوْ أَنَّ أَحَدَنَا خَرَّ مِنَ السَّمَاءِ كَانَ أَحَبَّ إِلَيْهِ مِنْ أَنْ يَتَكَلَّمَ بِهِ». فَقَالَ النَّبِيُّ صَلَّى اللهُ عَلَيْهِ وَسَلَّمَ: «ذَاكَ مَحْضُ الْإِيمَانِ».

(مسند أحمد :٣٢٧٤)

ʿĀ'ishah ﵂ said: "Some Companions complained to the Messenger of Allah ﷺ about some of the misgivings that occur to their minds, saying: 'Sometimes we prefer to be thrown to our death from a very high place than to utter one word about some of the thoughts that cross our minds.' The Prophet ﷺ said: 'That is a sign of pure faith.'"

(*Musnad Aḥmad*: 4723)

241

عَنْ هِشَامِ بْنِ عُرْوَ عَنْ أَبِيهِ عَنْ عَائِشَةَ أَنَّ رَسُولَ اللَّهِ صَلَّى اللهُ عَلَيْهِ وَسَلَّمَ قَالَ: «إِنَّ الرَّجُلَ لَيَعْمَلُ بِعَمَلِ أَهْلِ الْجَنَّةِ وَإِنَّهُ لَمَكْتُوبٌ فِي الْكِتَابِ مِنْ أَهْلِ النَّارِ فَإِذَا كَانَ قَبْلَ مَوْتِهِ تَحَوَّلَ فَعَمِلَ بِعَمَلِ أَهْلِ النَّارِ فَمَاتَ فَدَخَلَ النَّارَ، وَإِنَّ الرَّجُلَ لَيَعْمَلُ بِعملِ أَهلِ النَّارِ وَإِنَّهُ لَمَكْتُوبٌ فِي الْكِتَابِ مِنْ أَهْلِ الْجَنَّةِ فَإِذَا كَانَ قَبْلَ مَوْتِهِ تَحَوَّلَ فَعَمِلَ بِعَمَلِ أَهْلِ الْجَنَّةِ فَمَاتَ فَدَخَلَهَا».

(مسند أحمد :٢٣٧٤)

ʿĀʾishah ﵂ related that the Messenger of Allah ﷺ said: "Indeed, it may well happen that a man acts as befits all the dwellers of Paradise, but he is inscribed in the register of the dwellers of Hell, and so just before he dies, he changes and acts as befits the dwellers of Hell and he enters Hell. And it may well happen that a man acts as befits the dwellers of Hell, but he is inscribed in the register of the dwellers of Paradise, and so just before he dies, he chages and acts as befits the dwellers of Paradise, and he enters Paradise."

(*Musnad Aḥmad*: 4732)

242

عن عَائِشَةَ أَنَّ النَّبِيَّ صَلَّى اللهُ عَلَيْهِ وَسَلَّمَ بَعَثَ إِلَى عُثْمَانَ بْنِ مَظْعُونٍ، فَجَاءَهُ، فَقَالَ: "يَا عُثمانُ، أَرَغِبْتَ عَنْ سُنَّتِي؟" قال: "لَا وَاللهِ يَا رَسولَ اللهِ، وَلَكِنْ سُنَّتَكَ أطلُبُ". قالَ: "فَإِنِّي أَنَامُ وأُصَلِّي وأَصُومُ وَأُفطِرُ وَأَنْكِحُ النِّسَاءَ، فَاتَّقِ اللهَ يَا عُثْمَانُ فَإِنَّ لِأَهْلِكَ عليْكَ حقًّا، وَإِنَّ لِضَيْفِكَ عَلَيْكَ حقًّا، وإِنَّ لنَفْسِك عَلَيْكَ حقًّا. فصُمْ وَأَفْطِرْ وَصَلِّ وَنَمْ".

(سنن أبي داود:٩٦٣١)

ʿĀʾishah ﵂ related that the Prophet ﷺ summoned ʿUthmān ibn Maẓʿūn ﵁ and when he came he asked him: "O ʿUthmān, have you shunned my practice?" ʿUthmān ibn Maẓʿūn said: "No, by Allah, O Messenger of Allah; it is your practice that I seek to emulate." So the Prophet ﷺ said to him: "In that case, I sleep as well as pray at night; I fast sometimes and sometimes I don't, and I marry women. Fear Allah, O ʿUthmān, for your wife has a right over you, your guest has a right over you, and your own soul has a right over you. So fast sometimes and not others, pray at night but also sleep."

(*Sunan Abī Dāwūd*: 1369)

243

عَنْ عَائِشَةَ قَالَتْ: «قَالَ رَسُولُ اللَّهِ صَلَّى اللَّهُ عَلَيْهِ وَسَلَّمَ: مَنْ غَسَّلَ مَيِّتًا فَأَدَّى فِيهِ الْأَمَانَةَ وَلَمْ يُفْشِ عَلَيْهِ مَا يَكُونُ مِنْهُ عِنْدَ ذَلِكَ خَرَجَ مِنْ ذُنُوبِهِ كَيَوْمِ وَلَدَتْهُ أُمُّهُ». قَالَ: «لِيَلِهِ أَقْرَبُكُمْ مِنْهُ إِنْ كَانَ يَعْلَمُ فَإِنْ كَانَ لَا يَعْلَمُ فَمَنْ تَرَوْنَ أَنَّ عِنْدَهُ حَظًّا مِنْ وَرَعٍ وَأَمَانَةٍ».

(مسند أحمد:٩٤٨٤)

Ā'ishah related that the Messenger of Allah said: "Whoever washes a dead person and does so in a trustworthy manner, such that he does not divulge what he sees upon washing the dead, all his sins shall be forgiven and he will be like the day his mother gave birth to him." He further directed: "The closest relative of the deceased amongst you should wash him if he has the knowledge of how to do it. And if he does not have the knowledge, then you should appoint anyone with a share of scrupulousness and trustworthiness."

(*Musnad Aḥmad*: 4849)

244

عَنْ عَائِشَةَ قَالَتْ: «سَمِعْتُ رَسُولَ اللَّهِ صَلَّى اللهُ عَلَيْهِ وَسَلَّمَ يَقُولُ: إِنِّي عَلَى الْحَوْضِ أَنْتَظِرُ مَنْ يَرِدُهُ عَلَيَّ مِنْكُمْ، فَلَيُقَطَّعَنَّ رِجَالٌ دُونِي، فَلَأَقُولَنَّ: يَا رَبِّ أُمَّتِي أُمَّتِي! فَلَيُقَالَنَّ لِي: إِنَّكَ لَا تَدْرِي مَا عَمِلُوا بَعْدَكَ، مَا زَالُوا يَرْجِعُونَ عَلَى أَعْقَابِهِمْ».

(مسند أحمد:٤٨٦٨)

ʿĀ'ishah ﷺ said: "I heard the Messenger of Allah ﷺ say: 'Indeed, I shall be at the Pool [Kawthar] waiting for those of you who will proceed to it. Some will be stopped from reaching me and I shall say: "O my Lord, [they are of] my community, [they are of] my community." But it would be said to me: 'You do not know what they have done after you; they kept sliding back [in their commitment to Islam].'"

(*Musnad Aḥmad*: 4868)

245

قَالَ أَخْبَرَنَا عَطَاءٌ الْخُرَاسَانِيُّ أَنَّ عَبْدَ الرَّحْمَنِ بْنَ أَبِي بَكْرٍ دَخَلَ عَلَى عَائِشَةَ يَوْمَ عَرَفَةَ وَهِيَ صَائِمَةٌ وَالْمَاءُ يُرَشُّ عَلَيْهَا فَقَالَ لَهَا عَبْدُ الرَّحْمَنِ: «أَفْطِرِي!» فَقَالَتْ: «أُفْطِرُ وَقَدْ سَمِعْتُ رَسُولَ اللَّهِ صَلَّى اللهُ عَلَيْهِ وَسَلَّمَ يَقُولُ: إِنَّ صَوْمَ يَوْمِ عَرَفَةَ يُكَفِّرُ الْعَامَ الَّذِي قَبْلَهُ».

(مسند أحمد:٦٣٩٤)

ʿAṭā' al-Khurāsānī related that once ʿAbd al-Raḥmān ibn Abī Bakr ﷺ went to see his sister ʿĀ'ishah on the Day of ʿArafāh while she was fasting and he saw people sprinkling water on her [due to the scorching heat]. He asked her to break her fast but she responded: "How can I break my fast when I have heard the Messenger of Allah ﷺ say: 'Fasting on the Day of ʿArafāh expiates all the sins that one has committed the previous year?'"

(*Musnad Aḥmad*: 4936)

246

عَنْ عَائِشَةَ أَنَّ النَّبِيَّ صَلَّى اللهُ عَلَيْهِ وَسَلَّمَ قَالَ: «لَا يَبْقَى بَعْدِي مِنَ النُّبُوَّةِ شَيْءٌ إِلَّا الْمُبَشِّرَاتُ». قَالُوا: «يَا رَسُولَ اللَّهِ، وَمَا الْمُبَشِّرَاتُ؟» قَالَ: «الرُّؤْيَا الصَّالِحَةُ يَرَاهَا الرَّجُلُ أَوْ تُرَى لَهُ».

(مسند أحمد:٣٤٩٤)

ʿĀ'ishah ﵂ related that the Prophet ﷺ said: "Nothing of prophethood shall remain after me except auspicious glad tidings." The Companions asked: "What are these auspicious glad tidings?" He said: "True dreams that a man sees or other people see about him."

(*Musnad Aḥmad*: 4943)

247

عَنْ عَائِشَةَ أَنَّ رَسُولَ اللَّهِ صَلَّى اللهُ عَلَيْهِ وَسَلَّمَ كَانَ يَقُولُ: «اللَّهُمَّ اجْعَلْنِي مِنَ الَّذِينَ إِذَا أَحْسَنُوا اسْتَبْشَرُوا وَإِذَا أَسَاءُوا اسْتَغْفَرُوا».

(مسند أحمد: ٢٤٩٤٦)

ʿĀ'ishah ﷺ said: The Messenger of Allah ﷺ used to say: "O Allah, make me among those who are hopeful when they do something good and of those who seek forgiveness when they lapse."

(*Musnad Aḥmad*: 4946)

248

عَنْ عَائِشَةَ أَنَّ رَسُولَ اللَّهِ صَلَّى اللهُ عَلَيْهِ وَسَلَّمَ عَلَّمَهَا هَذَا الدُّعَاءَ: "اللَّهُمَّ إِنِّي أَسْأَلُكَ مِنَ الْخَيْرِ كُلِّهِ عَاجِلِهِ وَآجِلِهِ مَا عَلِمْتُ مِنْهُ وَمَا لَمْ أَعْلَمْ، اللَّهُمَّ إِنِّي أَسْأَلُكَ مِنْ خَيْرِ مَا سَأَلَكَ عَبْدُكَ وَنَبِيُّكَ مُحَمَّدٌ صَلَّى اللهُ عَلَيْهِ وَسَلَّمَ وَأَعُوذُ بِكَ مِنْ شَرِّ مَا عَاذَ مِنْهُ عَبْدُكَ وَنَبِيُّكَ؛ اللَّهُمَّ إِنِّي أَسْأَلُكَ الْجَنَّةَ وَمَا قَرَّبَ إِلَيْهَا مِنْ قَوْلٍ أَوْ عَمَلٍ وَأَسْأَلُكَ أَنْ تَجْعَلَ كُلَّ قَضَاءٍ تَقْضِيهِ لِي خَيْرًا».

(مسند أحمد:٤٨٩٤)

ʿĀ'ishah ﷺ related that the Messenger of Allah ﷺ taught her this supplication: "O Allah, I ask of You goodness, all of it; that which is immediate and that which comes later, that which I know and that which I do not know. O Allah, I ask of You the good that Your servant and Prophet Muḥammad ﷺ asked of You and I seek refuge in You from the evil that Your servant and Prophet sought refuge in You. O Allah, I ask of You Paradise and that which makes one draw close to it of deed or word, and I ask You to make everthing that You decree for me to be good."

(*Musnad Aḥmad*: 4984)

249

عَنْ أُمِّ بَكْرٍ أَنَّ عَبْدَ الرَّحْمَنِ بْنَ عَوْفٍ بَاعَ أَرْضًا لَهُ مِنْ عُثْمَانَ بْنِ عَفَّانَ بِأَرْبَعِينَ أَلْفَ دِينَارٍ فَقَسَمَهُ فِي فُقَرَاءِ بَنِي زُهْرَةَ وَفِي ذِي الْحَاجَةِ مِنَ النَّاسِ وَفِي أُمَّهَاتِ الْمُؤْمِنِينَ. قَالَ الْمِسْوَرُ: «فَدَخَلْتُ عَلَى عَائِشَةَ بِنَصِيبِهَا مِنْ ذَلِكَ فَقَالَتْ: مَنْ أَرْسَلَ بِهَذَا؟ قُلْتُ: عَبْدُ الرَّحْمَنِ بْنُ عَوْفٍ. فَقَالَتْ إِنَّ رَسُولَ اللَّهِ صَلَّى اللهُ عَلَيْهِ وَسَلَّمَ قَالَ: لَا يَحِنُّ عَلَيْكُمْ بَعْدِي إِلَّا الصَّابِرُونَ سَقَى اللهُ ابْنَ عَوْفٍ مِنْ سَلْسَبِيلِ الْجَنَّةِ».

(مسند أحمد :٧٩٩٤)

Umm Bakr ibn al-Miswar ﵂ related that ʿAbd al-Raḥmān ibn ʿAwf ﵁ sold his land to ʿUthmān ibn ʿAffān ﵁ for 40,000 gold pieces and then divided this amount amongst the poor of Banū Zuhrah, other needy people, and the Prophet's wives. Al-Miswar said: "When I took ʿĀ'ishah's share to her, she asked: 'Who sent it?' I said: ''Abd al-Raḥmān ibn ʿAwf.' She said: 'I heard the Messenger of Allah ﷺ say: 'No one will show kindness to you after me except those who are patient.' May Allah make ʿAbd al-Raḥmān ibn ʿAwf drink from the Salsabīl of Paradise.'"

(*Musnad Aḥmad*: 4997)

250

عَنْ عَائِشَةَ قَالَت: «أُنْزِلَتِ الصُّحُفُ الأُولَى فِي أَوَّلِ يَوْمٍ مِنْ رَمَضَانَ وَأُنْزِلَتِ التَّوْرَاةُ فِي سِتٍّ مِنْ رَمَضَانَ وَأُنْزِلَ الإِنْجِيلُ فِي اثْنَتَيْ عَشْرَ مِنْ رَمَضَانَ وَأُنْزِلَ الزَّبُورُ فِي ثَمَانِي عَشْرَ مِنْ رَمَضَانَ وَأُنْزِلَ الْقُرْآن فِي أَرْبَعٍ وَعِشْرِينَ مِنْ رَمَضَان».

(الدُرُّ المَنْثورُ لِلسُّيوطي:١/١٨٩)

Āʾishah ﷺ said: "The earlier scriptures were revealed on the first days of Ramadan, the Torah on the 6th day of Ramadan, the Gospels on the 12th day of Ramadan, the Psalms on the 18th of Ramadan and the Qur'ān on the 24th of Ramadan."

(*Al-Durr al-Manthūr* of al-Suyūṭī, 1:189)

251

أَنَّ عَائِشَةَ حَكَتْ امْرَأً عِنْدَ النَّبِيِّ صَلَّى اللهُ عَلَيْهِ وَسَلَّمَ ذَكَرَتْ قِصَرَهَا فَقَالَ النَّبِيُّ صَلَّى اللهُ عَلَيْهِ وَسَلَّمَ: «قَدْ اغْتَبْتِيهَا».

(مسند أحمد :٢١٠٥)

‘Ā’ishah رضي الله عنها imitated a woman, in the presence of the Prophet ﷺ, and mentioned her short height, and so the Prophet ﷺ said: “You have backbited her.”

(*Musnad Aḥmad*: 5012)

252

عَنْ عَائِشَةَ أَنَّهُ سُرِقَ ثَوْبٌ لَهَا فَدَعَتْ عَلَى صَاحِبِهَا فَقَالَ رَسُولُ اللَّهِ صَلَّى اللهُ عَلَيْهِ وَسَلَّمَ: «لَا تُسَبِّخِي عَنْهُ».

(مسند أحمد:٥١٠٥)

ʿĀ'ishah ﷺ related that once her garment was stolen and so she prayed against the thief, but the Messenger of Allah ﷺ told her: "Do not lighten his sin for him."

(*Musnad Aḥmad*: 5015)

253

عَنْ عَائِشَةَ قَالَتْ سَمِعْتُ رَسُولَ اللَّهِ صَلَّى اللهُ عَلَيْهِ وَسَلَّمَ نَهَى أَنْ يُمْنَعَ نَقْعُ الْبِئْرِ. قَالَ يَزِيدُ: يَعْنِي فَضْلَ الْمَاءِ».

(مسند أحمد:٥٠٥٠)

ʿĀ’ishah رضي الله عنها related that she heard the Messenger of Allah ﷺ warn against denying others the excess water of a well.

(*Musnad Aḥmad*: 5050)

254

عَنْ عَائِشَةَ أَنَّ رَسُولَ اللَّهِ صَلَّى اللهُ عَلَيْهِ وَسَلَّمَ قَالَ: «ثَلَاثٌ أَحْلِفُ عَلَيْهِنَّ لَا يَجْعَلُ اللهُ عَزَّ وَجَلَّ مَنْ لَهُ سَهْمٌ فِي الْإِسْلَامِ كَمَنْ لَا سَهْمَ لَهُ. فَأَسْهُمُ الْإِسْلَامِ ثَلَاثَةٌ الصَّلَاةُ وَالصَّوْمُ وَالزَّكَاةُ، وَلَا يَتَوَلَّى اللهُ عَزَّ وَجَلَّ عَبْدًا فِي الدُّنْيَا فَيُوَلِّيهِ غَيْرَهُ يَوْمَ الْقِيَامَةِ، وَلَا يُحِبُّ رَجُلٌ قَوْمًا إِلَّا جَعَلَهُ اللهُ عَزَّ وَجَلَّ مَعَهُمْ وَالرَّابِعَةُ، لَوْ حَلَفْتُ عَلَيْهَا رَجَوْتُ أَنْ لَا آثَمَ: لَا يَسْتُرُ اللهُ عَزَّ وَجَلَّ عَبْدًا فِي الدُّنْيَا إِلَّا سَتَرَهُ يَوْمَ الْقِيَامَةِ».

(مسند أحمد:٢٨٠٥)

Ā'ishah ﵂ related that the Messenger of Allah ﷺ said: "I can swear that three things are true and will come to pass: (1) Allah, glorified and exalted is He, will not make the person who has a share in Islam like the person who does not. And so, the shares of Islam are three: the prayer, fasting Ramadan and *zakāt*. (2) Allah, glorified and exalted is He, will not protect and befriend a servant in this world and then entrust him to anyone other than Him on the Day of Judgement. (3) No one loves a group of people except that Allah, glorified and exalted is He, puts him with them. There is a fourth thing which, were I to swear on it, I hope I would not be commiting a sin, namely that Allah will not conceal [the faults of] His servant in this world except that He will conceal them on the Day of Judgement."

(*Musnad Aḥmad*: 5082)

255

عَنْ عَائِشَةَ أَنَّهَا قَالَتْ: «مَا رَأَيْتُ صَانِعَةَ طَعَامٍ مِثْلَ صَفِيَّةَ، أَهْدَتْ إِلَى النَّبِيِّ صَلَّى اللهُ عَلَيْهِ وَسَلَّمَ إِنَاءً فِيهِ طَعَامٌ فَمَا مَلَكْتُ نَفْسِي أَنْ كَسَرْتُهُ فَقُلْتُ: يَا رَسُولَ اللَّهِ مَا كَفَّارَتُهُ؟ فَقَالَ: إِنَاءٌ كَإِنَاءٍ وَطَعَامٌ كَطَعَامٍ».

(مسند أحمد:٥١١٤)

'Ā'ishah ﵂ said: "I did not see a better cook than Ṣafiyyah. One day she sent a dish of food to the Prophet ﷺ and I could not control myself, so I broke that dish. Then I asked the Prophet ﷺ: 'What is the expiation for such an act?'. He said: 'A dish like (that) dish, and food like (that) food.'"

(*Musnad Aḥmad*: 5114)

256

عَنْ عَائِشَةَ قَالَتْ: «قَالَ رَسُولُ اللَّهِ صَلَّى اللهُ عَلَيْهِ وَسَلَّمَ: نِمْتُ فَرَأَيْتُنِي فِي الْجَنَّةِ فَسَمِعْتُ صَوْتَ قَارِئٍ يَقْرَأُ فَقُلْتُ: مَنْ هَذَا؟ قَالُوا: هَذَا حَارِثَةُ بْنُ النُّعْمَانِ. فَقَالَ لَهَا رَسُولُ اللَّهِ صَلَّى اللهُ عَلَيْهِ وَسَلَّمَ: كَذَاكَ الْبِرُّ! كَذَاكَ الْبِرُّ!» وَكَانَ أَبَرَّ النَّاسِ بِأُمِّهِ».

(مسند أحمد:٥١٤٠)

ʿĀ'ishah ﵂ related that the Messenger of Allah ﷺ said: "I slept and saw in a dream that I was in Paradise and I heard someone reciting the Qur'ān. I said: 'Who is this?' They said: 'It is Ḥārithah ibn al-Nuʿmān.'" The Messenger of Allah ﷺ then said to ʿĀ'ishah ﵂: "This is what dutifulness does! This is what dutifulness does!" Indeed, Ḥārithah ibn al-Nuʿmān was very dutiful to his mother.

(*Musnad Aḥmad*: 5140)

257

أعَنْ عَائِشَةَ قَالَتْ: «مَا كَانَ خُلُقٌ أَبْغَضَ إِلَى أَصْحَابِ رَسُولِ اللَّهِ صَلَّى اللهُ عَلَيْهِ وَسَلَّمَ مِنْ الْكَذِبِ، وَلَقَدْ كَانَ الرَّجُلُ يَكْذِبُ عِنْدَ رَسُولِ اللَّهِ صَلَّى اللهُ عَلَيْهِ وَسَلَّمَ الْكَذِبَةَ فَمَا يَزَالُ فِي نَفْسِهِ عَلَيْهِ حَتَّى يَعْلَمَ أَنْ قَدْ أَحْدَثَ مِنْهَا تَوْبَةً».

(مسند أحمد:١٤١٥)

ʿĀ'ishah ﷺ said: "No trait was more loathsome to the Companions of the Messenger of Allah ﷺ than lying. If anyone ever told a lie in the presence of the Messenger of Allah ﷺ, he would keep it in his heart until he learns that he has sincerely repented from it."

(*Musnad Aḥmad*: 5141)

258

عَنْ عَائِشَةَ أَنَّ رَسُولَ اللَّهِ صَلَّى اللهُ عَلَيْهِ وَسَلَّمَ قَالَ: «تُزَوَّجُ الْمَرْأَةُ لِثَلَاثٍ لِمَالِهَا وَجَمَالِهَا وَدِينِهَا، فَعَلَيْكَ بِذَاتِ الدِّينِ تَرِبَتْ يَدَاكَ».

(مسند أحمد :٩٤١٥)

'Āishah ﵂ related that the Messenger of Allah ﷺ said: "A woman is married because of three things: her wealth, her beauty, and her religiousness, so choose the one who is religious and you shall succeed."

(*Musnad Aḥmad*: 5149)

259

عَنْ عَائِشَةَ أَنَّهَا قَالَتْ: «أُتِيَ النَّبِيُّ صَلَّى اللهُ عَلَيْهِ وَسَلَّمَ بِظَبْيَةٍ خَرَزٍ فَقَسَمَهَا لِلْحُرَّ وَلِلْأَمَةِ». وَقَالَتْ: «كَانَ أَبِي يَقْسِمُ لِلْحُرِّ وَالْعَبْدِ».

(مسند أحمد:٤٨١٥)

ʿĀ'ishah ﵂ said: "A sack full of diamonds was brought to the Prophet ﷺ and he distributed them among free and enslaved women. My father also used to distribute things amongst freemen and enslaved ones."

(*Musnad Aḥmad*: 5184)

260

عَنْ عَائِشَةَ قَالَتْ دَخَلَ رَسُولُ اللَّهِ صَلَّى اللهُ عَلَيْهِ وَسَلَّمَ فَعَرَفْتُ فِي وَجْهِهِ أَنْ قَدْ حَفَزَهُ شَيْءٌ فَتَوَضَّأَ ثُمَّ خَرَجَ فَلَمْ يُكَلِّمْ أَحَدًا فَدَنَوْتُ مِنَ الْحُجُرَاتِ فَسَمِعْتُهُ يَقُولُ: «يَا أَيُّهَا النَّاسُ إِنَّ اللَّهَ عَزَّ وَجَلَّ يَقُولُ: مُرُوا بِالْمَعْرُوفِ وَانْهَوْا عَنِ الْمُنْكَرِ مِنْ قَبْلِ أَنْ تَدْعُونِي فَلَا أُجِيبُكُمْ وَتَسْأَلُونِي فَلَا أُعْطِيكُمْ وَتَسْتَنْصِرُونِي فَلَا أَنْصُرُكُمْ».

(مسند أحمد:٨٠٢٥)

Āʾishah ﷺ said: “Once the Messenger of Allah ﷺ came home and I noticed from his facial expression that something was bothering him. He performed *wuḍūʾ* and went out, without talking to anyone and then I heard him say: ‘O people! Allah, glorified and exalted is He, says: enjoin good and forbid evil lest you invoke Me and I do not answer you, and ask Me and I do not give you, and seek My help and I do not help you.’”

(*Musnad Aḥmad*: 5208)

261

عَنْ عَائِشَةَ أَنَّ النَّبِيَّ صَلَّى اللهُ عَلَيْهِ وَسَلَّمَ قَالَ لَهَا إِنَّهُ مَنْ أُعْطِيَ حَظَّهُ مِنْ الرِّفْقِ فَقَدْ أُعْطِيَ حَظَّهُ مِنْ خَيْرِ الدُّنْيَا وَالْآخِرَ وَصِلَةُ الرَّحِمِ وَحُسْنُ الْخُلُقِ وَحُسْنُ الْجِوَارِ يَعْمُرَانِ الدِّيَارَ وَيَزِيدَانِ فِي الْأَعْمَارِ».

(مسند أحمد:٢١٢٥)

ʿĀ’ishah ﵂ related that the Prophet ﷺ said to her that whoever is given leniency has been given his fair share of both this world and the next; moreover keeping ties of kinship, good character, and good treatment of one’s neighbours make polities thrive and prolongs lifespans.

(*Musnad Aḥmad*: 5212)

262

عَنْ عَائِشَةَ فِي قَوْلِهِ عَزَّ وَجَلَّ {إِنَّ الصَّفَا وَالْمَرْوَ مِنْ شَعَائِرِ اللَّهِ}، قَالَتْ: «كَانَ رِجَالٌ مِنْ الْأَنْصَارِ مِمَّنْ يُهِلُّ لِمَنَا فِي الْجَاهِلِيَّةِ وَمَنَا صَنَمٌ بَيْنَ مَكَّةَ وَالْمَدِينَةِ، قَالُوا: يَا نَبِيَّ اللَّهِ، إِنَّا كُنَّا نَطُوفُ بَيْنَ الصَّفَا وَالْمَرْوَ تَعْظِيمًا لِمَنَا فَهَلْ عَلَيْنَا مِنْ حَرَجٍ أَنْ نَطُوفَ بِهِمَا؟ فَأَنْزَلَ اللهُ عَزَّ وَجَلَّ: {إِنَّ الصَّفَا وَالْمَرْوَ مِنْ شَعَائِرِ اللَّهِ فَمَنْ حَجَّ الْبَيْتَ أَوْ اعْتَمَرَ فَلَا جُنَاحَ عَلَيْهِ أَنْ يَطَّوَّفَ بِهِمَا}».

(مسند أحمد:٩٤٢٥)

Regarding Allah's words: {*Verily, Safa and Marwah are sites of Allah's worship. So whoever makes pilgrimage to the Sacred House or the lesser visitation, there is no wrong or harm in making many a round between them*} [*al-Baqarah* 2:158], 'Ā'ishah ﵂ said: "Men from the Anṣār used to make pilgrimage to the idol Manāt between Makkah and Madinah in the pre-Islamic period. [After embracing Islam] they said to the Prophet ﷺ: 'O Prophet of Allah, we used to go between al-Ṣafā and al-Marwah in veneration of Manāt, so is it sinful for us to go between them?' Allah, glorified and exalted is He, then revealed the verse: {*Verily, Safa and Marwah are sites of Allah's worship. So whoever makes pilgrimage to the Sacred House or the lesser visitation, there is no wrong or harm in making many a round between them}.*"

(*Musnad Aḥmad*: 5249)

263

عَنْ عَائِشَةَ قَالَتْ: «أَبْطَأْتُ عَلَى النَّبِيِّ صَلَّى اللهُ عَلَيْهِ وَسَلَّمَ فَقَالَ: مَا حَبَسَكِ يَا عَائِشَةُ؟» قَالَتْ: «يَا رَسُولَ اللَّهِ، إِنَّ فِي الْمَسْجِدِ رَجُلًا مَا رَأَيْتُ أَحَدًا أَحْسَنَ قِرَائَةً مِنْهُ». فَذَهَبَ رَسُولُ اللَّهِ صَلَّى اللهُ عَلَيْهِ وَسَلَّمَ فَإِذَا هُوَ سَالِمٌ مَوْلَى أَبِي حُذَيْفَةَ، فَقَالَ رَسُولُ اللَّهِ صَلَّى اللهُ عَلَيْهِ وَسَلَّمَ: «الْحَمْدُ لِلَّهِ الَّذِي جَعَلَ فِي أُمَّتِي مِثْلَكَ».

(مسند أحمد:٠٧٢٥)

‘Ā’ishah ؓ said: “Once I came late to the Prophet ﷺ and he asked me: ‘What is it that has delayed you, O ‘Ā’ishah?’. I replied: ‘O Messenger of Allah, there was a man in the mosque and I have not seen anyone recite [the Qur’ān] better than him.’ So the Messenger of Allah ﷺ went out and found out that it was Sālim, the client of Abū Ḥudhayfah. The Messenger of Allah ﷺ then said to him: ‘Praise be to Allah who has made someone like you in my community.’”

(*Musnad Aḥmad*: 5270)

264

قَالَتْ عَائِشَةُ: «يَا نَبِيَّ اللَّهِ أَرَأَيْتَ إِنْ وَافَقْتُ لَيْلَةَ الْقَدْرِ مَا أَقُولُ؟» قَالَ: «تَقُولِينَ: اللَّهُمَّ إِنَّكَ عَفُوٌّ تُحِبُّ الْعَفْوَ فَاعْفُ عَنِّي».

(مسند أحمد:٩٢٣٥)

'Ā'ishah ﵂ related that she asked: "O Prophet of Allah, What shall I say if I were to witness the Night of Power (*Laylat al-Qadr*)?" He replied: "You should recite this supplication: O Allah, indeed You are most pardoning, and You like the act of pardoning, so pardon me (*Allāhumma innaka 'afuwwun tuḥibbu al-'afwa fa'fū 'annī*)."

(*Musnad Aḥmad*: 5329)

265

عَنْ عَائِشَةَ قَالَت: «كَانَ رَسُولُ رَسُولُ اللَّهِ صَلَّى اللهُ عَلَيْهِ وَسَلَّمَ إِذَا دَخَلَ شَهْرُ رَمَضَانَ تَغَيَّرَ لَوْنُهُ وَكَثُرَتْ صَلَاتُهُ وَابْتَهَلَ فِي الدُّعَاءِ وَأَشْفَقَ مِنْهُ».

(الدُّرُّ المَنْثُورُ لِلسُّيُوطي: ١/١٨٥)

ʿĀ'ishah ﷺ said: "Upon the start of the month of Ramadan, the Messenger of Allah ﷺ used to change in complexion, his prayers increased, his supplication became more fervent and he showed more insistence in it."

(*Al-Durr al-Manthūr of al-Suyūṭī*, 1: 185)

266

عَنْ جُبَيْرِ بْنِ نُفَيْرٍ قَالَ: «دَخَلْتُ عَلَى عَائِشَةَ، فَقَالَتْ: هَلْ تَقْرَأُ سُورَ الْمَائِدَةِ؟ قَالَ: قُلْتُ نَعَمْ. قَالَتْ: فَإِنَّهَا آخِرُ سُورَةٍ نَزَلَتْ، فَمَا وَجَدْتُمْ فِيهَا مِنْ حَلَالٍ فَاسْتَحِلُّوهُ وَمَا وَجَدْتُمْ فِيهَا مِنْ حَرَامٍ فَحَرِّمُوهُ. وَسَأَلْتُهَا عَنْ خُلُقِ رَسُولِ اللَّهِ صَلَّى اللهُ عَلَيْهِ وَسَلَّمَ فَقَالَتْ: الْقُرْآنُ».

(مسند أحمد:٥٨٤٥)

Jubayr ibn Nufayr said: "When I visited 'Ā'ishah ﵂, she asked me: 'Do you memorise *Sūrah al-Mā'idah*?' When I replied in the affirmative, she said: 'This was the last *Sūrah* to be revealed. So whatever is stated there as lawful, accept it as lawful; and whatever is stated there as unlawful, accept it as unlawful.'" He continued: "And I asked her about the character of the Messenger of Allah ﷺ, and she replied: '[His character was] the Qur'ān.'"

(*Musnad Aḥmad*: 5485)

267

عَنْ عَائِشَةَ أَنَّ رَجُلًا قَالَ لَهَا: «إِنِّي أُرِيد أَن أوصِي». قَالَت: «كَمْ مَالُكَ؟» قَالَ: «ثَلَاثَةُ آلَافٍ». قَالَت: «كَمْ عِيَالُكَ؟» قَالَ: «أَرْبَعَةٌ». قَالَت: «قَالَ الله {إِنْ تَرَكَ خَيْرًا...}، وَهَذَا شَيْءٌ يَسِيرٌ فَاتْرُكْهُ لِعِيَالِكَ فَهُوَ أَفْضَلُ»

(الدُّرُّ الْمَنْثُورُ لِلسُّيُوطي:١/٤٧١)

Ā'ishah ﵂ related that a man said to her: "I want to bequeath some of my wealth." She asked him: "How much wealth do you have?" He replied: "3000 gold pieces." Again she asked him: "How many dependents do you have?" He said: "I have four." she said to him: "Allah says: {... is to make a testament in favour of his parents and kinsmen honourably...} [al-Baqarah: 180] and what you have is only a small amount, so it is better to leave it for your dependents."

(*Al-Durr al-Manthūr of al-Suyūṭī*, 1: 174)

268

عَنْ أُمَيَّةَ أَنَّهُ قَالَ: «سَأَلَتُ عَائِشَةَ عَنْ هذِهِ الْآيَةِ {إِنْ تُبْدُوا مَا فِي أَنْفُسِكُمْ أَوْ تُخْفُوهُ يُحَاسِبْكُمْ بِهِ اللَّهُ} وَعَنْ هذِهِ الْآيَةِ {مَنْ يَعْمَلْ سُوءًا يُجْزَ بِهِ}، فَقَالَتْ: مَا سَأَلَنِي عَنْهُمَا أَحَدٌ مُنْذُ سَأَلْتُ رَسُولَ اللَّهِ صَلَّى اللهُ عَلَيْهِ وَسَلَّمَ عَنْهُمَا فَقَالَ: يَا عَائِشَةُ، هذِهِ مُتَابَعَةُ اللَّهِ عَزَّ وَجَلَّ الْعَبْدَ بِمَا يُصِيبُهُ مِنَ الْحُمَّةِ وَالنَّكْبَةِ وَالشَّوْكَةِ حَتَّى الْبِضَاعَةُ يَضَعُهَا فِي كُمِّهِ فَيَفْقِدُهَا فَيَفْزَعُ لَهَا فَيَجِدُهَا فِي ضِبْنِهِ حَتَّى إِنَّ الْمُؤْمِنَ لَيَخْرُجُ مِنْ ذُنُوبِهِ كَمَا يَخْرُجُ التِّبْرُ الْأَحْمَرُ مِنَ الْكِيرِ».

(مسند أحمد:٥٦٧٥)

Umayyah related that he asked ʿĀ'ishah ﷺ about these two Qur'ānic verses: {Allah will call you to account for it whether you declare or hide what is in your hearts} [*al-Baqarah* 2: 284] and {One who does evil will be punished for it} [*al-Nisā'* 4: 123]. She said: "No one has asked me about these two verses since the time I had asked the Messenger of Allah ﷺ about them. He said: 'O ʿĀ'ishah, this refers to the calamities that Allah repeatedly sends to His servant, such as fevers, setbacks, being pricked by thorns, even the loss of a merchandise that he places in his long sleeve, and becomes alarmed because of its loss, consequently finding it under his arm – all these calamities purify him from his sins just as gold is extracted from dust.'"

(*Musnad Aḥmad*: 5765)

269

عَائِشَةَ قَالَتْ: «كَانَ رَسُولُ اللَّهِ صَلَّى اللهُ عَلَيْهِ وَسَلَّمَ إِذَا ضَحَّى اشْتَرَى كَبْشَيْنِ عَظِيمَيْنِ سَمِينَيْنِ أَقْرَنَيْنِ أَمْلَحَيْنِ مَوْجُوأَيْنِ فَيَذْبَحُ أَحَدَهُمَا عَنْ أُمَّتِهِ مِمَّنْ أَقَرَّ بِالتَّوْحِيدِ وَشَهِدَ لَهُ بِالْبَلَاغِ وَيَذْبَحُ الْآخَرَ عَنْ مُحَمَّدٍ وَآلِ مُحَمَّدٍ».

(مسند أحمد:٤٧٧٥)

‘Ā’ishah رضي الله عنها said: “When the Messenger of Allah ﷺ intended to make a sacrifice on ‘Id day, he bought two plump and healthy horned rams and sacrificed one of them on behalf of the members of his community – who confess monotheism and testify that he ﷺ had conveyed Allah’s message, and the second one on his own behalf and that of his Household.”

(*Musnad Aḥmad*: 5774)

270

عَنْ عَائِشَةَ قَالَتْ: «نَهَانَا رَسُولُ اللَّهِ صَلَّى اللهُ عَلَيْهِ وَسَلَّمَ عَنْ خَمْسٍ: لُبْسِ الْحَرِيرِ وَالذَّهَبِ وَالشُّرْبِ فِي آنِيَةِ الذَّهَبِ وَالْفِضَّةِ وَالْمِيثَرِ الْحَمْرَاءِ وَلُبْسِ الْقَسِّيِّ». فَقَالَتْ عَائِشَةُ: «يَا رَسُولَ اللَّهِ، شَيْءٌ رَقِيقٌ مِنَ الذَّهَبِ يُرْبَطُ بِهِ الْمِسْكُ أَوْ يُرْبَطُ بِهِ؟». قَالَ: «لَا اجْعَلِيهِ فِضَّةً وَصَفِّرِيهِ بِشَيْءٍ مِنْ زَعْفَرَانٍ».

(مسند أحمد:٧٣٨٥)

ʿĀ'ishah ﷺ said: "The Messenger of Allah ﷺ forbade five (things) for us: Wearing silk and gold [i.e., for men]; drinking from gold and silver utensils; [using] pack-saddles lined with silk and linen clothes embroidered with silk." She asked him: "O Messenger of Allah, what about a fine thread of gold to tie [bottles of] Musk or other things?' He replied: 'No, make the thread from silver and dye it with saffron."

(*Musnad Aḥmad*: 5837)

271

رُوِيَ عَنْ أَنَّ عَائِشَةَ نَزَلَتْ عَلَى أُمِّ طَلْحَةَ الطَّلْحَاتِ فَرَأَتْ بَنَاتِهَا يُصَلِّينَ بِغَيْرِ خُمُرٍ فَقَالَتْ: «إِنِّي لَأَرَى بَنَاتِكِ قَدْ حِضْنَ أَوْ حَاضَ بَعْضُهُنَّ». قَالَتْ: «أَجَلْ». قَالَتْ: «فَلَا تُصَلِّيَنَّ جَارِيَةٌ مِنْهُنَّ وَقَدْ حَاضَتْ إِلَّا وَعَلَيْهَا خِمَارٌ، فَإِنَّ رَسُولَ اللَّهِ صَلَّى اللهُ عَلَيْهِ وَسَلَّمَ دَخَلَ عَلَيَّ وَعِنْدِي فَتَاةٌ فَأَلْقَى إِلَيَّ حَقْوَهُ فَقَالَ شُقِّيهِ بَيْنَ هذِهِ وَبَيْنَ الْفَتَاةِ الَّتِي عِنْدَ أُمِّ سَلَمَةَ فَإِنِّي لَا أُرَاهُمَا إِلَّا قَدْ حَاضَتَا أَوْ لَا أُرَاهَا إِلَّا قَدْ حَاضَتْ».

(مسند أحمد:٧٣٩٥)

It is related that one day ʿĀʾishah ﵂ was a guest at the house of Umm Ṭalḥah al-Ṭalḥāt and she noticed her daughters were praying without wearing scarves, and so she remarked: "I have noticed that your daughters are praying without covering their heads!" When their mother confirmed this, ʿĀʾishah ﵂ added: "No girl who has reached the age of puberty should pray without wearing a scarf, for the Messenger of Allah ﷺ once came to my room when I had a girl with me, so he threw to me his loin-cloth and said: 'Cut it into two pieces and divide them between this girl and the girl who is with

Umm Salamah; for I think they have reached the age of puberty.'"

(*Musnad Aḥmad*: 5937)

272

عَنْ عَائِشَةَ قَالَتْ: «قَالَ رَسُولُ اللَّهِ صَلَّى اللهُ عَلَيْهِ وَسَلَّمَ: الدَّوَاوِينُ عِنْدَ اللَّهِ عَزَّ وَجَلَّ ثَلَاثَةٌ: دِيوَانٌ لَا يَعْبَأُ اللهُ بِهِ شَيئًا، وَدِيوَانٌ لَا يَتْرُكُ اللهُ مِنْهُ شَيْئًا وَدِيوَانٌ لَا يَغْفِرُهُ اللهُ. فَأَمَّا الدِّيوَانُ الَّذِي لَا يَغْفِرُهُ اللهُ فَالشِّرْكُ بِاللَّهِ، قَالَ اللهُ عَزَّ وَجَلَّ {إِنَّهُ مَنْ يُشْرِكْ بِاللَّهِ فَقَدْ حَرَّمَ اللهُ عَلَيْهِ الْجَنَّةَ}. وَأَمَّا الدِّيوَانُ الَّذِي لَا يَعْبَأُ اللهُ بِهِ شَيْئًا فَظُلْمُ الْعَبْدِ نَفْسَهُ فِيمَا بَيْنَهُ وَبَيْنَ رَبِّهِ مِنْ صَوْمِ يَوْمٍ تَرَكَهُ أَوْ صَلَاةٍ تَرَكَهَا، فَإِنَّ اللَّهَ عَزَّ وَجَلَّ يَغْفِرُ ذَلِكَ وَيَتَجَاوَزُ إِنْ شَاءَ. وَأَمَّا الدِّيوَانُ الَّذِي لَا يَتْرُكُ اللهُ مِنْهُ شَيْئًا فَظُلْمُ الْعِبَادِ بَعْضِهِمْ بَعْضًا: الْقِصَاصُ لَا مَحَالَةَ»

(مسند أحمد:٢٥٩٥٠)

'Āishah ﵂ related that the Messenger of Allah ﷺ said: "There are three types of registers [of deeds] with Allah: there is one register He does not pay too much attention to; a second register that He does not overlook a single thing written in it; and a third register that He does not forgive anything in it at all. As for the register that Allah does not forgive, it is that of associating partners with Allah the Most High; he says: {Verily who so associates with Allah anything, Allah shall prohibit him entrance to Paradise} [*al- Mā'idah* 5: 72]. As for the register that Allah will not pay too much attention to, it is the wrong that the slave commits against himself regarding that which is between him and his Lord, such as missing a day of fasting or a prayer, for Allah will forgive such matters and overlook them if He wills. As for the register He will not overlook, it concerns the wrong that people have committed against each other. Here, retribution must necessarily be applied."

(*Musnad Aḥmad*: 5952)

273

عَنْ عَائِشَةَ قَالَتْ: «قَالَ رَسُولُ اللَّهِ صَلَّى اللهُ عَلَيْهِ وَسَلَّمَ: وَالَّذِي نَفْسُ مُحَمَّدٍ بِيَدِهِ لَخُلُوفُ فَمِ الصَّائِمِ أَطْيَبُ عِنْدَ اللَّهِ مِنْ رِيحِ الْمِسْكِ».

(مسند أحمد:٥٩٥٦)

ʿĀ'ishah ﷺ related that the Messenger of Allah ﷺ said: "By Him in whose Hand is Muḥammad's soul, the smell of the mouth of a fasting person is more fragrant with Allah than the scent of musk."

(*Musnad Aḥmad*: 5956)

274

عَنْ عَائِشَةَ أَنَّ رَسُولَ اللَّهِ صَلَّى اللهُ عَلَيْهِ وَسَلَّمَ كَانَ يَكْرَهُ أَنْ يُوجَدَ مِنْهُ رِيحٌ يُتَأَذَّى مِنْه.

(مسند أحمد:٨٣٠٦)

Āʾishah ﷺ related that the Messenger of Allah ﷺ used to hate that people smell in him anything that may offend them.

(*Musnad Aḥmad*: 6038)

275

عَنْ عَائِشَةَ رَضِيَ اللهُ عَنْهَا قَالَتْ: «كَانَ رَسُولُ اللَّهِ صَلَّى اللهُ عَلَيْهِ وَسَلَّمَ يَقْرَأُ كُلَّ لَيْلَةٍ تَنْزِيلُ السَّجْدَ».

(المَطَالِبُ العَالِيَةِ:٣٦٨٢)

ʿĀ'ishah ﷺ said: "The Messenger of Allah ﷺ used to recite *Sūrah al-Sajdah* every night."

(*Al-Maṭālib al-ʿĀliyah*: 3682)

276

عَنْ عَائِشَةَ أَنَّ رَسُولَ اللَّهِ صَلَّى اللهُ عَلَيْهِ وَسَلَّمَ قَالَ: «إِنَّ اللَّهَ لَيُرَبِّي لِأَحَدِكُمْ التَّمْرَ وَاللُّقْمَةَ كَمَا يُرَبِّي أَحَدُكُمْ فَلُوَّهُ أَوْ فَصِيلَهُ حَتَّى يَكُونَ مِثْلَ أُحُدٍ».

(مسند أحمد:٦٠٥٤)

ʿĀ'ishah ﷺ related that the Messenger of Allah ﷺ said: "Indeed, Allah tends a single date or morsel from you until it grows, just as you tend to your foal or young camel until it grows in size."

(*Musnad Aḥmad*: 6054)

277

عَنْ عَائِشَةَ أَنَّ النَّبِيَّ صَلَّى اللهُ عَلَيْهِ وَسَلَّمَ كَانَ يَخْرُجُ إِلَى الْبَقِيعِ فَيَدْعُو لَهُمْ فَسَأَلَتْهُ عَنْ ذَلِكَ فَقَالَ: «إِنِّي أُمِرْتُ أَنْ أَدْعُوَ لَهُمْ».

(مسند أحمد:٦٠٦٦)

ʿĀ'ishah ﷺ related that the Prophet ﷺ used to go to al-Baqīʿ graveyard and make supplications for all those buried there. When she asked him about this, he replied: "I have been commanded to make supplications for them."

(*Musnad Aḥmad*: 6066)

278

عَنْ عَائِشَةَ أَنَّ النَّبِيَّ صَلَّى اللهُ عَلَيْهِ وَسَلَّمَ نَهَى عَنْ التَّبَتُّلِ.

(مسند أحمد:٦٠٦٨)

Āʾishah ﷺ related that the Prophet ﷺ forbade leading a life of retreat and seclusion from people in devotion to Allah.

(*Musnad Aḥmad*: 6068)

279

عَنْ عَائِشَةَ قَالَتْ: «قَالَ رَسُولُ اللَّهِ صَلَّى اللهُ عَلَيْهِ وَسَلَّمَ: قَالَ اللهُ عَزَّ وَجَلَّ: مَنْ أَذَلَّ لِي وَلِيًّا فَقَدْ اسْتَحَلَّ مُحَارَبَتِي وَمَا تَقَرَّبَ إِلَيَّ عَبْدِي بِمِثْلِ أَدَاءِ الْفَرَائِضِ وَمَا يَزَالُ الْعَبْدُ يَتَقَرَّبُ إِلَيَّ بِالنَّوَافِلِ حَتَّى أُحِبَّهُ إِنْ سَأَلَنِي أَعْطَيْتُهُ وَإِنْ دَعَانِي أَجَبْتُهُ ومَا تَرَدَّدْتُ عَنْ شَيْءٍ أَنَا فَاعِلُهُ تَرَدُّدِي عَنْ وَفَاتِهِ لِأَنَّهُ يَكْرَهُ الْمَوْتَ وَأَكْرَهُ مَسَاءَتَهُ».

(مسند أحمد:٦١١١)

Āʾishah ﷺ related that the Messenger of Allah ﷺ said: "Allah, glorified and exalted is He, says: 'Who humiliates a friend of Mine has declared war against Me; and My servant does not draw closer to Me with anything better than what I have made obligatory on him. And the servant keeps drawing closer to Me with supererogatory acts until I love him, [and when I do] I shall certainly give to him when he calls upon Me. And I do not hesitate in doing anything like I hesitate when I take his soul away, for he does not like to die, and I dislike hurt him.'"

(*Musnad Aḥmad*: 6111)

280

عَنْ عَائِشَةَ أَنَّ رَسُولَ اللَّهِ صَلَّى اللهُ عَلَيْهِ وَسَلَّمَ قَالَ: «إِنَّ أَحَدَكُمْ يَأْتِيهِ الشَّيْطَانُ فَيَقُولُ: مَنْ خَلَقَكَ؟ فَيَقُولُ: اللهُ، فَيَقُولُ: فَمَنْ خَلَقَ اللَّهَ؟ فَإِذَا وَجَدَ ذَلِكَ أَحَدُكُمْ فَلْيَقْرَأْ: آمَنْتُ بِاللَّهِ وَرُسُلِهِ فَإِنَّ ذَلِكَ يُذْهِبُ عَنْهُ».

(مسند أحمد:٠٢١٦)

'Ā'ishah ﵂ related that the Messenger of Allah ﷺ said: "The devil may come to one of you and whisper to him: 'Who created you?' and he says: 'Allah,' but then he whispers to him again: 'And who created Allah?' If this does happen to anyone of you, then let him say: 'I believe in Allah and His Messengers,' for that will drive away that thought from him."

(*Musnad Aḥmad*: 6120)

281

عَنْ عَائِشَةَ عَنِ النَّبِيِّ صَلَّى اللهُ عَلَيْهِ وَسَلَّمَ قَالَ: «يُرَدُّ مِنْ صَدَقَةِ الجَانِفِ فِي حَيَاتِهِ مَا يُرَدُّ مِنْ وَصِيَّةِ المُجْنِفِ عِنْدَ مَوْتِهِ».

(الدُّرُّ المَنْثُورُ لِلسُّيُوطِي: ١/١٧٥)

'Ā'ishah ﵂ related that the Prophet ﷺ said: "The charity act of a transgressor is rejected while still alive just as the unfair bequest of a person is rejected upon his death."

(*Al-Durr al-Manthūr* of al-Suyūṭī, 1: 175)

282

عَنْ عَائِشَةَ زَوْجِ النَّبِيِّ صَلَّى اللهُ عَلَيْهِ وَسَلَّمَ قَالَتْ: «كَانَتْ فِي حِجْرِي جَارِيَةٌ مِنْ الْأَنْصَارِ فَزَوَّجْتُهَا». قَالَتْ: «فَدَخَلَ عَلَيَّ رَسُولُ اللَّهِ صَلَّى اللهُ عَلَيْهِ وَسَلَّمَ يَوْمَ عُرْسِهَا فَلَمْ يَسْمَعْ لَعِبًا، فَقَالَ: يَاعَائِشَةُ، إِنَّ هَذَا الْحَيَّ مِنْ الْأَنْصَارِ يُحِبُّونَ كَذَا وَكَذَا».

(مسند أحمد:٣٢٢٦)

ʿĀ'ishah ﵂ said: "A girl from the Ansar was under my care and eventually I got her married. On the day of her wedding, the Messenger of Allah ﷺ came to me and, when he did not hear any signs of merriment, he said: 'O 'Ā'ishah, this neighbourhood of the Anṣār loves this and that.'"

(*Musnad Aḥmad*: 6223)

283

عَنْ عَائِشَةَ قَالَتْ: «أقْبَلَ رَسُولُ اللَّهِ يَمْشي وقَدْ لَدَغَتْهُ شَوْكَةٌ في إبْهامِهِ، فَجَعَلَ يَسْتَرْجِعُ مِنها ويَمْسَحُها، فَلَمّا سَمِعْتُ اسْتِرْجاعَهُ دَنَوْتُ مِنهُ، فَنَظَرْتُ فَإذا أثَرٌ حَقِيرٌ، فَضَحِكْتُ، فَقُلْتُ: يا رَسُولَ اللَّهِ، بِأبِي أنْتَ وأُمِّي، أكُلُّ هَذا الِاسْتِرْجاعِ مِن أجْلِ هَذِهِ الشَّوْكَةِ؟ فَتَبَسَّمَ، ثُمَّ ضَرَبَ عَلى مَنكِبِي، فَقالَ: يا عائِشَةُ، إنَّ اللَّهَ عَزَّ وجَلَّ إذا أرَادَ أنْ يَجْعَلَ الصَّغِيرَ كَبِيرًا جَعَلَهُ، وَإذَا أَرَادَ أنْ يَجْعَلَ الكَبِيرَ صَغِيرًا جَعَلَهُ».

(الدُّرُّ المَنْثُورُ لِلسُّيُوطِي: ١/٧٥١)

'Ā'ishah ﷺ said: "One day the Messenger of Allah ﷺ came home while he was rubbing his thumb which was pricked by a thorn, saying: 'We all are from Allah and to Him we shall return.' When I heard this, I went closer to him and saw it was only a minor thorn prick and so I laughed and said: 'O Messenger of Allah, may my parents be sacrificed for you, all this reaction over just this minor thorn prick?' Upon this, he smiled, patted me on the shoulder and said: 'O 'Ā'ishah, if Allah, glorified and exalted is He, wants to turn something small into something big, He can do so; and if He wants to turn something big into something small, He can do so too.'"

(*Al-Durr al-Manthūr* of al-Suyūṭī, 1: 157)

284

عَنْ عَائِشَةَ زَوْجِ النَّبِيِّ صَلَّى اللهُ عَلَيْهِ وَسَلَّمَ عَنْ النَّبِيِّ صَلَّى اللهُ عَلَيْهِ وَسَلَّمَ أَنَّهُ قَالَ: «فَضْلُ الصَّلَاةِ بِالسِّوَاكِ عَلَى الصَّلَاةِ بِغَيْرِ سِوَاكٍ سَبْعِينَ ضِعْفًا».

(مسند أحمد:٢٦٢٤٩)

'Āʾishah ﷺ related that the Prophet ﷺ said: "The merit of a prayer performed after one uses the *siwāk* (toothbrush) is greater than the prayer performed without first using the *siwāk* by seventy times."

(*Musnad Aḥmad*: 6249)

285

عَنْ مُحَمَّدِ بْنِ عُبَيْدِ بْنِ أَبِي صَالِحٍ الْمَكِّيِّ قَالَ: «حَجَجْتُ مَعَ عَدِيِّ بْنِ عَدِيٍّ الْكِنْدِيِّ فَبَعَثَنِي إِلَى صَفِيَّةَ بِنْتِ شَيْبَةَ ابْنَةِ عُثْمَانَ صَاحِبِ الْكَعْبَةِ أَسْأَلُهَا عَنْ أَشْيَاءَ سَمِعَتْهَا مِنْ عَائِشَةَ زَوْجِ النَّبِيِّ صَلَّى اللَّهُ عَلَيْهِ وَسَلَّمَ عَنْ رَسُولِ اللَّهِ صَلَّى اللَّهُ عَلَيْهِ وَسَلَّمَ فَكَانَ فِيمَا حَدَّثَتْنِي أَنَّهَا سَمِعَتْ عَائِشَةَ تَقُولُ: سَمِعْتُ رَسُولَ اللَّهِ صَلَّى اللَّهُ عَلَيْهِ وَسَلَّمَ يَقُولُ: لَا طَلَاقَ وَلَا عِتَاقَ فِي إِغْلَاقٍ».

(مسند أحمد:٠٧٢٦)

Muḥammad ibn ʿUbayd ibn Abī Ṣāliḥ al-Makkī said: "I went to perform Ḥajj along with ʿAdī ibn ʿAdī al-Kindī, and while there he sent me to Ṣafiyyah, the daughter of Shaybah ibn ʿUthmān who was the gatekeeper of the Kaʿbah, to ask about what she had heard ʿĀ'ishah رضي الله عنها relating from the Messenger of Allah ﷺ. Among what she told me is that she heard ʿĀ'ishah رضي الله عنها saying: 'I heard the Messenger of Allah ﷺ say: 'Any divorce or freeing of slaves that takes place under duress is legally invalid.'"

(*Musnad Aḥmad*: 6270)

286

عَنْ عَائِشَةَ زَوْجِ النَّبِيِّ صَلَّى اللهُ عَلَيْهِ وَسَلَّمَ قَالَتْ: «لَمَّا بَعَثَ أَهْلُ مَكَّةَ فِي فِدَاءِ أَسْرَاهُمْ، بَعَثَتْ زَيْنَبُ بِنْتُ رَسُولِ اللَّهِ صَلَّى اللهُ عَلَيْهِ وَسَلَّمَ فِي فِدَاءِ أَبِي الْعَاصِ بْنِ الرَّبِيعِ بِمَالٍ وَبَعَثَتْ فِيهِ بِقِلَادَةٍ لَهَا كَانَتْ لِخَدِيجَةَ أَدْخَلَتْهَا بِهَا عَلَى أَبِي الْعَاصِ حِينَ بَنَى عَلَيْهَا». قَالَتْ: «فَلَمَّا رَآهَا رَسُولُ اللَّهِ صَلَّى اللهُ عَلَيْهِ وَسَلَّمَ رَقَّ لَهَا رِقَّةً شَدِيدَةً وَقَالَ: إِنْ رَأَيْتُمْ أَنْ تُطْلِقُوا لَهَا أَسِيرَهَا وَتَرُدُّوا عَلَيْهَا الَّذِي لَهَا فَافْعَلُوا. فَقَالُوا: نَعَمْ يَا رَسُولَ اللَّهِ. فَأَطْلَقُوهُ وَرَدُّوا عَلَيْهَا الَّذِي لَهَا».

(مسند أحمد:٢٧٢٦)

ʿĀ'ishah ﵂ said: When the Makkans sent representatives to pay ransom for their captives, Zaynab, the daughter of the Messenger of Allah ﷺ, sent money, including her mother's [Khadījah] necklace which she had when she married Abū al-ʿĀṣ ibn al-Rabīʿ, to secure her husband's release. When the Messenger of Allah ﷺ saw it, he was deeply moved for her and he said to the Companions: 'If you deem it fit, release her captive and give her back the ransom she sent.' They all agreed and released her husband and returned to her what she had paid.

(*Musnad Aḥmad*: 6272)

287

عَنْ عَائِشَةَ قَالَتْ: «قَالَ رَسُولُ اللَّهِ صَلَّى اللَّهُ عَلَيْهِ وَسَلَّمَ: مَا أَنْعَمَ اللَّهُ عَلَى عَبْدٍ نِعْمَةً فَعَلِمَ أَنَّهَا مِنْ عِنْدِ اللَّهِ إِلَّا كَتَبَ اللَّهُ لَهُ بِهَا شُكْرَهُ قَبْلَ أَنْ يَحْمَدَهُ عَلَيْهَا، وَمَا أَذْنَبَ عَبْدٌ ذَنْبًا فَنَدِمَ عَلَيْهِ إِلَّا كَتَبَ اللَّهُ لَهُ مَغْفِرَتَهُ قَبْلَ أَنْ يَسْتَغْفِرَهُ، وَمَا اشْتَرَى عَبْدٌ ثَوْبًا بِدِينَارٍ أَوْ نِصْفِ دِينَارٍ فَحَمِدَ اللَّهَ حِينَ يَلْبَسُهُ إِلَّا لَمْ يَبْلُغْ رُكْبَتَيْهِ حَتَّى يَغْفِرَ اللَّهُ لَهُ".

(الدُّرُّ المَنْثُورُ لِلسُّيُوطي:١/٣٥١)

Āʾishah ﵂ related that the Messenger of Allah ﷺ said: "Whenever Allah bestows a blessing on a servant and the latter recognises that it is from Allah, Allah will inscribe this recognition as an act of praising Him even before the servant praises Him for it. And whenever a servant commits a sin and then regrets it, Allah will forgive him even before the servant asks forgiveness of Him. And whenever a servant buys a dress for a gold piece or half a gold piece and then praises Allah upon putting it on, Allah will forgive his lapses before the dress reaches his knees."

(*Al-Durr al-Manthūr* of al-Suyūṭī, 1: 153)

288

عَنْ عَائِشَةَ أَنَّ رَسُولَ اللَّهِ صَلَّى اللهُ عَلَيْهِ وَسَلَّمَ أَمَرَ بِبِنَاءِ الْمَسَاجِدِ فِي الدُّورِ وَأَمَرَ بِهَا أَنْ تُنَظَّفَ وَتُطَيَّبَ.

(مسند أحمد:٦٩٢٦)

ʿĀ’ishah رضي الله عنها related that the Messenger of Allah ﷺ comanded that places of worship be built in houses, and that they should be kept clean and perfumed.

(*Musnad Aḥmad*: 6296)

289

عَنْ عَائِشَةَ قَالَتْ: «كَانَ رَسُولُ اللَّهِ صَلَّى اللهُ عَلَيْهِ وَسَلَّمَ لَمَّا بَدَّنَ وَثَقُلَ يَقْرَأُ مَا شَاءَ اللهُ عَزَّ وَجَلَّ وَهُو جَالِسٌ فَإِذَا غَبَرَ مِنْ السُّورِ ثَلَاثُونَ أَوْ أَرْبَعُونَ آيَةً قَامَ فَقَرَأَهَا ثُمَّ سَجَدَ».

(مسند أحمد:٥٧١٤)

ʿĀ’ishah ؓ said: “When the Messenger of Allah ﷺ put on weight over time, he started reciting as much as Allah willed [of the Qur’ān] in his prayer sitting down, but after reciting 30 or 40 verses, he stood up and recited some more verses before bowing.”

(*Musnad Aḥmad*: 4175)

290

عَنْ عَائِشَةَ أَنّهَا سَمِعَتْ رَسُولَ اللهِ صَلَّى اللهُ عَلَيْهِ وَسَلَّمَ يَقُول: «مَا مِنْ سَاعَةٍ تَمُرُّ بِابْنِ آدَمَ لَمْ يَذْكُرِ اللهَ فِيهَا إِلَّا خَسِرَ عَلَيْهَا يَوْمَ القِيَامَةِ».

(الدُرُّ المَنْثُورُ لِلسُّيُوطِي: ١/١٥٠)

ʿĀ'ishah ﷺ related that she heard the Messenger of Allah ﷺ say: "Any moment that passes the son of Adam without him remembering Allah in it will be a loss for him on the Day of Judgement."

(*Al-Durr al-Manthūr* of al-Suyūṭī, 1: 150)

291

عَن عَائِشَةَ قَالَت: "قَالَ رَسُولُ اللهِ صَلَّى اللهُ عَلَيْهِ وَسَلَّمَ: سِتَّةٌ لَعَنْتُهُم ولَعَنَهُمْ اللهُ وَكُلُّ نَبِيٍّ مُجابٌ: الزَائِدُ فِي كِتَابِ اللهِ والمُكذِّبُ بقَدَرِ اللهِ وَالمُتسلِّطُ بِالجَبَرُوتِ لِيُعِزَّ مَنْ أَذَلَّ اللهُ وَيُذِلَّ مَنْ أَعَزَّ اللهُ والمُستحِلُّ لِحُرُمِ اللهِ والمُستحِلُّ مِنْ عِتْرَتِي مَا حَرَّم اللهُ والتَارِكُ لِسُنَّتِي».

(الدُرُّ المَنْثُورُ لِلسُّيُوطِي: ١/١٢٢)

ʿĀ'ishah ﵂ related that the Messenger of Allah ﷺ said: "I have cursed six types of people, just as every Prophet before me did, and the prayer of every Prophet is accepted: (1) The one who interpolates something into the Book of Allah; (2) the one who denies Allah's Decree; (3) the tyrant who elevates those whom Allah has abased and abases those whom Allah has elevated; (4) the one who violates what Allah has made inviolable; (5) the one from my household who declares to be lawful what Allah has made unlawful; and (6) the one who shuns my Practice."

(*Al-Durr al-Manthūr* of al-Suyūṭī, 1: 122)

292

عَنْ عَائِشَةَ رَضِيَ اللَّهُ عَنْهَا أَنَّ رَسُولَ اللَّهِ صَلَّى اللَّهُ عَلَيْهِ وَسَلَّمَ كَانَ إِذَا سَافَرَ سَافَرَ بِسِتٍّ: بِالْمِرْآةِ وَالْقَارُورَةِ وَالْمُشْطِ وَالْمِقْرَاضِ وَالسِّوَاكِ وَالْمُكْحُلَةِ".

(الدُّرُّ المَنْثُورُ لِلسُّيُوطِي: ١/١١٤)

ʿĀ'ishah ﵂ related that whenever the Messenger of Allah ﷺ set out for a journey he took with him six things: a mirror, a glass utensil, a comb, scissors, a *siwāk* (toothbrush), and a *kohl* container.

(*Al-Durr al-Manthūr of al-Suyūṭī*, 1: 114)

293

عَنْ عَائِشَةَ رَضِيَ اللهُ عَنْهَا قَالَتْ: «يَرْحَمُ اللهُ نِسَاءَ الْمُهَاجِرَاتِ الْأُوَلَ لَمَّا أَنْزَلَ اللهُ: {وَلْيَضْرِبْنَ بِخُمُرِهِنَّ عَلَى جُيُوبِهِنَّ} [سور النور آية ١٣] شَقَّقْنَ مُرُوطَهُنَّ فَاخْتَمَرْنَ بِهَا».

(صحيح البخاري:٨٥٧٤)

‘Ā’ishah رضي الله عنها said: “May Allah have mercy on the believing women who had migrated in the first phase. When Allah revealed, “*And let them pitch their head covers fast down over their collars...*” (*al-Nūr* 24: 31), they tore their sheets and made scarves out of them.”

(*Ṣaḥīḥ al-Bukhārī*: 4758)

294

عَنْ عَائِشَةَ رَضِيَ اللهُ عَنْهَا، قَالَتْ: «هَلَكَتْ قِلَادَةٌ لِأَسْمَاءَ، فَبَعَثَ النَّبِيُّ صَلَّى اللهُ عَلَيْهِ وَسَلَّمَ فِي طَلَبِهَا رِجَالًا، فَحَضَرَتِ الصَّلَاةُ وَلَيْسُوا عَلَى وُضُوءٍ وَلَمْ يَجِدُوا مَاءً، فَصَلَّوْا وَهُمْ عَلَى غَيْرِ وُضُوءٍ، فَأَنْزَلَ اللهُ، يَعْنِي آيَةَ التَّيَمُّمِ».

(صحيح البخاري:٣٨٥٤)

ʿĀ'ishah ﷺ said: "A necklace belonging to Asmā' was lost, and so the Prophet ﷺ sent some men to look for it. When the time for the prayer entered, they were without ritual ablution and they could not find water to perform *wuḍū'*, therefore they prayed without ritual ablution. Following this incident Allah revealed the verse of dry ablution (tayammum)."

(*Ṣaḥīḥ al-Bukhārī*: 4583)

295

عَنْ عَائِشَةَ رَضِيَ اللهُ عَنْهَا قَالَت: «مَا صَلَّى النَّبِيُّ صَلَّى اللهُ عَلَيْهِ وَسَلَّمَ صَلَاةً بَعْدَ أَنْ نَزَلَتْ عَلَيْهِ {إِذَا جَاءَ نَصْرُ اللَّهِ وَالْفَتْحُ} [سور النصر آية ١] إِلَّا يَقُولُ فِيهَا : سُبْحَانَكَ رَبَّنَا وَبِحَمْدِكَ، اللَّهُمَّ اغْفِرْ لِي».

(صحيح البخاري:٧٦٩٤)

'Āishah ﷺ said: "After "*When the victorious help of Allah is come...*" [*al-Naṣr* 110: 1] was revealed to him, the Messenger of Allah ﷺ never prayed any prayer except that he said during it: "Glory be to You, O our Lord, All praise is Yours; O Allah, forgive me."

(*Ṣaḥīḥ al-Bukhārī*)

296

عَنْ عُرْوَ أَنَّ عَائِشَةَ رَضِيَ اللهُ عَنْهَا قَالَتْ: «أَوَّلُ مَا بُدِئَ بِهِ رَسُولُ اللَّهِ صَلَّى اللهُ عَلَيْهِ وَسَلَّمَ الرُّؤْيَا الصَّالِحَةُ فَجَاءَهُ الْمَلَكُ، فَقَالَ: {اقْرَأْ بِاسْمِ رَبِّكَ الَّذِي خَلَقَ خَلَقَ الإِنْسَانَ مِنْ عَلَقٍ اقْرَأْ وَرَبُّكَ الأَكْرَمُ} [سور العلق آية ١-٣]».

(صحيح البخاري:٥٥٩٤)

ʿĀ'ishah ﵂ said: "First the Messenger of Allah ﷺ started having true dream visions, and then the angel came to him and said: {Recite: In the Name of your Lord who created, created Man of a blood-clot. Recite: And your Lord is the Most Generous} [*al-ʿAlaq* 96: 1-3]."

(*Ṣaḥīḥ al-Bukhārī* : 4955)

297

قَالَتْ عَائِشَةَ رَضِيَ اللهُ عَنْهَا: «سَمِعْتُ رَسُولَ اللَّهِ صَلَّى اللهُ عَلَيْهِ وَسَلَّمَ يَقُولُ: «مَنْ صَلَّى الْفَجْرَ، أَوْ قَالَ الْغَدَاءَ، فَقَعَدَ مَقْعَدَهُ فَلَمْ يَلْغُ بِشَيْءٍ مِنْ أَمْرِ الدُّنْيَا وَيَذْكُرُ اللَّهَ حَتَّى يُصَلِّيَ الضُّحَى أَرْبَعَ رَكَعَاتٍ، خَرَجَ مِنْ ذُنُوبِهِ كَيَوْمِ وَلَدَتْهُ أُمُّهُ لاَ ذَنْبَ لَهُ».

(المطالب العالية:٧٩٣٣)

ʿĀ'ishah ﷺ related that she heard the Messenger of Allah ﷺ say: "Whoever performs the Fajr prayer and remains seated in his place, without indulging in any worldly matter, and remembering Allah, and then performs four units of prayer after the sun rises, such a person will come out of his sins and becomes like the day his mother gave birth to him."

(*Al-Maṭālib al-ʿĀliyah*: 3397)

298

عَنْ عَائِشَةَ رَضِيَ اللهُ عَنْهَا قَالَتْ: «كَانَ رَسُولُ اللَّهِ صَلَّى اللهُ عَلَيْهِ وَسَلَّمَ يُفَضِّلُ الذِّكْرَ الخَفِيَّ الَّذِي لاَ تَسْمَعُهُ الحَفَظَةُ بِسَبْعِينَ ضِعْفًا، وَيَقُولُ: إِذَا كَانَ يَوْمُ الْقِيَامَةِ جَمَعَ اللهُ تَعَالَى الخَلاَئِقَ لِحِسَابِهِمْ، وَجَاءَتِ الحَفَظَةُ بِمَا حَفِظُوا أَوْ كَتَبُوا، قَالَ اللهُ تَعالَى لَهُمْ: انْظُرُوا، هَلْ بَقِيَ لَهُ مِنْ شَيْءٍ؟ فَيَقُولُونَ: رَبَّنَا مَا تَرَكْنَا شَيْئًا مِمَّا عَلِمْنَاهُ وَحَفِظْنَاهُ إِلاَّ وَقَدْ أَحْصَيْنَاهُ وَكَتَبْنَاهُ. فَيَقُولُ اللهُ تَبَارَكَ وَتَعَالَى: إِنَّ لَكَ عِنْدِي خَبِيئًا لاَ تَعْلَمُهُ، وَأَنَا أَجْزِيكَ بِهِ وَهُو الذِّكْرُ الخَفِيُّ».

(المطالب العالية:١١٤٣)

ʿĀ'ishah ﷺ said: The Messenger of Allah ﷺ used to prefer silent remembrance of Allah, which cannot be heard even by the guardian angels, as being seventy times superior [to loud remembrance of Allah]. He used to say: "On the Day of Judgement, Allah would gather all created beings for their reckoning, and the guardian angels would bring what they had recorded and written down. Allah Most High shall say to them: 'Check if he has anything else [i.e., any other good deed]?'. They would submit: 'O our Lord, we have not left out anything and have recorded and written down everything.' Then Allah, glorified and exalted is He, would say [to His servant]:

‘I have with Me something for you which I have kept aside for you and which you are not aware of; and today I will reward you for it: it is [your] silent remembrance [of Me].’”

(*Al-Maṭālib al-‘Āliyah*: 3411)

299

عَنْ عَائِشَةَ رَضِيَ اللهُ عَنْهَا، فِي قَوْلِهِ تَعَالَى: {وَمَنْ كَانَ غَنِيًّا فَلْيَسْتَعْفِفْ وَمَنْ كَانَ فَقِيرًا فَلْيَأْكُلْ بِالْمَعْرُوفِ} [سور النساء آية ٦] أَنَّهَا نَزَلَتْ فِي وَالِي الْيَتِيمِ إِذَا كَانَ فَقِيرًا أَنَّهُ يَأْكُلُ مِنْهُ مَكَانَ قِيَامِهِ عَلَيْهِ بِمَعْرُوفٍ.

(صحيح البخاري:٥٧٥٤)

Āʾishah ﷺ related, regarding Allah's words {If the guardian (of an orphan) is wealthy, he should not charge anything. But if he is poor, he may take what is fair,} [*al-Nisā'* 4: 6], that it was revealed about the guardianship of the orphan; if the guardian is poor, he may moderately use the orphan's wealth.

(*Ṣaḥīḥ al-Bukhārī*: 4575)

300

عَنْ عَائِشَةَ قَالَتْ: «قَالَ رَسُولُ اللَّهِ صَلَّى اللهُ عَلَيْهِ وَسَلَّمَ: إِنَّ اللَّهَ عَزَّ وَجَلَّ وَمَلَائِكَتَهُ عَلَيْهِمْ السَّلَام يُصَلُّونَ عَلَى الَّذِينَ يَصِلُونَ الصُّفُوفَ وَمَنْ سَدَّ فُرْجَةً رَفَعَهُ اللهُ بِهَا دَرَجَةً».

(مسند أحمد:٤٥٦٠)

ʿĀ'ishah ﷺ related that the Messenger of Allah ﷺ said: "Indeed, Allah, glorified and exalted is He, and His angels (peace be upon them) send mercy on those who join rows [in congregational prayer]; and whoever fills a gap in a row, Allah raises his rank."

(*Musnad Aḥmad*: 4560)

301

عَنْ عَائِشَةَ قَالَتْ: «جَاءَتْ عَجُوزٌ إِلَى النَّبِيِّ صَلَّى اللهُ عَلَيْهِ وَآلِهِ وَسَلَّمَ وَهُوَ عِندِي فَقَالَ لَهَا رَسُولُ اللهِ صَلَّى اللهُ عَلَيْهِ وَآلِهِ وَسَلَّمَ: مَنْ أَنْتِ؟ قَالَتْ: أنا جَثَّامةُ المُزَنِيَّةُ. فَقَالَ: بَلْ أَنْتِ حَسَّانَةُ المُزَنِيَّةُ. كَيْفَ أَنْتُمْ؟ كَيْفَ حَالُكُمْ؟ كَيْفَ كُنْتُمْ بَعْدَنَا؟ قَالَتْ: بِخَيْرٍ بِأَبِي أَنْتَ وَأُمِّي يَا رَسُولَ اللهِ. فَلَمَّا خَرَجَتْ قلتُ: يَا رَسُولَ اللهِ، تُقبِلُ عَلَى هَذِهِ العَجُوزِ هَذَا الإِقْبَالَ، فَقَالَ: إِنَّهَا كَانَتْ تَأْتِينَا زَمَنَ خَدِيجَةَ وَإِنَّ حُسْنَ العَهْدِ مِنَ الإِيمَانِ».

(المستدرك للحاكم:١/٦٦١)

ʿĀ'ishah ﵂ said: "An old woman came to see the Prophet ﷺ while he was with me and so the Messenger of Allah ﷺ asked her: 'Who are you?' She said: 'I am Jaththāmah al-Muzaniyyah.' He exclaimed: 'No, you are Ḥassānah al-Muzaniyyah! How are you? How are you doing? What has become of you after us?' She replied: 'We are well, may my parents be sacrificed for you, O Messenger of Allah.' When she left, I said: 'O Messenger, why all this warm welcome for this old woman?' He replied: 'She used to visit us when Khadījah was alive, and maintaining ties with old acquaintances is part of true faith.'"
(*Al-Mustadrak* of al-Ḥākim, 1: 166)

302

قَالَ عُقْبَةُ بْنُ صُهْبَانَ الْهُنَائِيُّ: «سَأَلْتُ عَائِشَةَ رَضِيَ اللهُ عَنْهَا عَنْ قَوْلِ اللهِ عَزَّ وَجَلَّ: {ثُمَّ أَوْرَثْنَا الْكِتَابَ الَّذِينَ اصْطَفَيْنَا مِنْ عِبَادِنَا فَمِنْهُمْ ظَالِمٌ لِّنَفْسِهِ وَمِنْهُم مُّقْتَصِدٌ وَمِنْهُمْ سَابِقٌ بِالْخَيْرَاتِ بِإِذْنِ اللَّهِ ذَٰلِكَ هُوَ الْفَضْلُ الْكَبِيرُ} [فاطر:٣٢]، فَقَالَتْ لِي: يَا بُنَيَّ، كُلُّ هَؤُلَاءِ فِي الْجَنَّةِ، فَأَمَّا السَّابِقُ بِالْخَيْرَاتِ فَمَنْ مَضَى عَلَى عَهْدِ رَسُولِ اللَّهِ صَلَّى اللهُ عَلَيْهِ وَآلِهِ وَسَلَّمَ، فَشَهِدَ لَهُ رَسُولُ اللَّهِ صلى الله عليه وسلم بِالْحَيَا وَالرِّزْقِ، وَأَمَّا الْمُقْتَصِدُ فَمَنِ اتَّبَعَ أَثَرَهُ مِنْ أَصْحَابِهِ حَتَّى يَلْحَقَ بِهِ، وَأَمَّا الظَّالِمُ لِنَفْسِهِ فَمِثْلِي وَمِثْلُكَ، قَالَ: فَجَعَلَتْ نَفْسَهَا رَضِيَ اللهُ عَنْهَا مَعَنَا».

(المطالب العالية:٣٨٦٣)

'Uqbah ibn Ṣuhbān al-Hunā'ī related that he asked 'Ā'ishah ﷺ about the words of Allah, glorified and exalted is He {Allah gave the Book to some of His servants whom He chose. Some people are wrongdoers; some follow the middle path; and some, by Allah's permission, excel in doing good. This is indeed a great blessing}' [*Fāṭir* 35: 32], so she said: "O my son, all of them are in Paradise. As for the one who excels in doing good, he is the one who is faithful to the covenant he made with the Messenger of Allah ﷺ and the Messenger of Allah ﷺ testifies in his favour that he shall live and be bestowed provision. As for the one who follows the middle path, it is any Companion who follows in his footsteps until he joins him. As for the one who wrongs himself, it is popele like me and you." The narrator adds: "She placed herself رضي الله عنها on the same footing as us."

(*Al-Maṭālib al-'Āliyah*: 3688)

303

عن عَائِشَةَ رَضِيَ اللهُ عَنْهَا قَالَتْ: «لَمَّا حَلَفَ أَبُو بَكْرٍ رَضِيَ اللهُ عَنْهُ أَنْ لَا يُنْفِقَ عَلَى مِسْطَحٍ رَضِيَ اللهُ عَنْهُ، فَأَنْزَلَ اللهُ عَزَّ وَجَلَّ {قَدْ فَرَضَ اللهُ لَكُمْ تَحِلَّةَ أَيْمَانِكُمْ} [التحريم: ٢] فَأَحَلَّ يَمِينَهُ وَأَنْفَقَ عَلَيْهِ».

(المطالب العالية:٣٧٦٠)

ʿĀ'ishah ﵂ said: "When Abū Bakr ﵁ swore not to financially support Misṭaḥ ﵁ [because of taking part in the slander of 'Ā'ishah ﵂], and Allah, glorified and exalted is He, revealed {Allah has prescribed for you a way for dissolving your oaths}" [*al-Taḥrīm* 66: 2], he [i.e., Abū Bakr] recanted his oath and resumed his financial assistance to him."

(*Al-Maṭālib al-ʿĀliyah*: 3760)

304

عَنْ عَائِشَةَ رَضِيَ اللهُ عَنْهَا قَالَتْ أَنّ رَسُولَ اللَّهِ صَلَّى اللهُ عَلَيْهِ وَآلِهِ وَسَلَّمَ سَمِعَ رَجُلًا يُلَبِّي عَنْ شُبْرُمَةَ، فَقَالَ: «وَمَا شُبْرُمَةُ؟» فَذَكَرَهُ قَرَابَةً لَهُ صَلَّى اللهُ عَلَيْهِ وَآلِهِ وَسَلَّمَ، قَالَ: «حَجَجْتَ عَنْ نَفْسِكَ؟» قَالَ: «لا»، قَالَ: «فَاحْجُجْ عَنْ نَفْسِكَ، ثُمَّ حُجَّ عَنْ شُبْرُمَةَ».

(المطالب العالية:١٥١١)

ʿĀʾishah ﷺ related that the Messenger of Allah ﷺ overheard someone during *Ḥajj* making invocations on behalf of Shubrumah and, when he asked who Shubrumah might be, he informed him that he was one of his relatives. The Prophet ﷺ asked the man: "Have you performed *Ḥajj* yourself?" When the man said that he had not, he said to him: "Perform Hajj as your own personal obligation first and then perform Hajj on behalf Shubrumah."

(*Al-Maṭālib al-ʿĀliyah*: 1151)

305

عَنْ أَبِي حَازِمٍ قَالَ: «جَعَلَ عُرْوَةُ بْنُ الزُّبَيْرِ رَضِيَ اللهُ عَنْهُمَا لِعَائِشَةَ رَضِيَ اللهُ عَنْهَا طَعَامًا، فَجَعَلَ يَرْفَعُ قَصْعَةً وَيَضَعُ قَصْعَةً»، قَالَ: «فَحَوَّلَتْ رَضِيَ اللهُ عَنْهَا وَجْهَهَا إِلَى الْحَائِطِ تَبْكِي، فَقَالَ لَهَا عُرْوَةُ رَضِيَ اللهُ عَنْهُ: كَدَّرْتِ عَلَيْنَا، فَقَالَتْ: وَالَّذِي بَعَثَهُ بِالْحَقِّ، مَا رَأَى الْمَنَاخِلَ مُنْذُ بَعَثَهُ اللهُ تَبَارَكَ وَتَعَالَى حَتَّى قُبِضَ».

(المطالب العالية:٩٥١٣)

Abū Ḥāzim related that once ʿUrwah ibn al-Zubayr ﵄ prepared food for ʿĀ'ishah ﵄ and placed on the table for her one dish after another. Upon seeing this, she turned her face towards a wall and started crying. ʿUrwah ﵄ said to her: "You have spoiled the occasion for us!" So she replied: "By Him who sent him with the truth, he [i.e., the Prophet ﷺ] never saw any food made of sieved out grains from the time he was sent as a Prophet until he died."

(*Al-Maṭālib al-ʿĀliyah*: 3159)

306

عَنْ عَائِشَةَ رَضِيَ اللهُ عَنْهَا، قَالَتْ: «سَمِعْتُ رَسُولَ اللَّهِ صَلَّى اللهُ عَلَيْهِ وَآلِهِ وَسَلَّمَ وَهُو يَخْطُبُ النَّاسَ يَقُولُ: مَنْ حَفِظَ مَا بَيْنَ لَحْيَيْهِ وَحَفِظَ مَا بَيْنَ رِجْلَيْهِ فَهُو فِي الْجَنَّةِ».

(المطالب العالية:٣٢٣٧)

‘Ā’ishah ﵁ related that she heard the Messenger of Allah ﷺ say while delivering a sermon: “Whoever protects what is between his jaws [the tongue] and what is between his legs [the private parts] shall enter Paradise.”

(*Al-Maṭālib al-‘Āliyah*: 3237)

307

عَنْ عَائِشَةَ رَضِيَ اللهُ عَنْهَا، قَالَتْ: «قَالَ رَسُولُ اللَّهِ صَلَّى اللهُ عَلَيْهِ وَسَلَّمَ: مَنْ سَرَّهُ أَنْ يَسْبِقَ الدَّائِبَ الْمُجْتَهِدَ، فَلْيَكُفَّ عَنِ الذُّنُوبِ».

(المطالب العالية:٨٤٢٣)

ʿĀ'ishah ﷺ related that the Messenger of Allah ﷺ said: "Whoever feels happy over outdoing those who continuously make an effort [in acts of worship] let him desist from committing sins."

(*Al-Maṭālib al-ʿĀliyah*: 3248)

308

عَنْ عَائِشَةَ رَضِيَ اللهُ عَنْهَا، قَالَتْ: «سَلُوا اللَّهَ عَزَّ وَجَلَّ كُلَّ شَيْءٍ حَتَّى الشِّسْعَ، فَإِنَّ اللَّهَ إِنْ لَمْ يُيَسِّرْهُ لَمْ يَتَيَسَّرْ».

(المطالب العالية :٨٥٣٣)

‘Ā’ishah رضي الله عنها said: “Ask Allah, glorified and exalted is He, for everything even if it be a shoelace, for if Allah does not facilitate it, it would not be facilitated.”

(*Al-Maṭālib al-‘Āliyah*: 3358)

309

عَنْ عَائِشَةَ، قَالَتْ: «قَالَ رَسُولُ اللَّهِ صَلَّى اللهُ عَلَيْهِ وَسَلَّمَ : «مَنْ تَكَلَّمَ فِي الْقَدَرِ بِشَيْءٍ سُئِلَ عَنْهُ يَوْمَ الْقِيَامَةِ».

(المطالب العالية:٢٩٤٤)

'Ā'ishah ﷺ related that the Messenger of Allah ﷺ said: "Whoever speaks about Destiny [according to his own surmise] shall be held answerable on the Day of Judgement."

(*Al-Maṭālib al-'Āliyah*: 2944)

310

عَن أبي بُرْدَ قَالَ: «أَتَيْتُ عَائِشَةَ رَضِيَ اللهُ عَنْهَا، فَقَالَتْ: قَالَ رَسُولُ اللَّهِ صَلَّى اللهُ عَلَيْهِ وَسَلَّمَ: الطَّيْرُ يَجْرِي بِقَدَرٍ، وَكَانَ صَلَّى اللهُ عَلَيْهِ وَسَلَّمَ يُعْجِبُهُ الْفَأْلُ الْحَسَنُ».

(المطالب العالية:٢٩٥٥)

Abū Burdah related that ʿĀ'ishah ﷺ related to him when he went to see her that the Messenger of Allah ﷺ said: "Misfortune is preordained." And "he ﷺ used to like good omens."

(*Al-Maṭālib al-ʿĀliyah*: 2955)

311

عَنْ شَهْرِ بْنِ حَوْشَبٍ، قَالَ: «إِنَّ رَجُلا قَالَ لِعَائِشَةَ: إِنَّ أَحَدَنَا يُحَدِّثُ نَفْسَهُ بِشَيْءٍ لَوْ تَكَلَّمَ بِهِ ذَهَبَتْ آخِرَتُهُ، وَلَوْ ظَهَرَ عَلَيْهِ لَقُتِلَ». قَالَ: «فَكَبَّرَتْ رَضِيَ اللهُ عَنْهَا ثَلاثًا، ثُمَّ قَالَتْ: سُئِلَ عَنْهَا رَسُولُ اللَّهِ صَلَّى اللهُ عَلَيْهِ وَسَلَّمَ، فَكَبَّرَ ثَلاثًا، ثُمَّ قَالَ: إِنَّمَا يُخْتَبَرُ الْمُؤْمِنُ».

(المطالب العالية:٣٠٠٣)

Shahr ibn Ḥawshab related that a man said to ʿĀ'ishah ﵂: "Sometimes some thoughts cross the mind of one of us but if he were to express them, it would ruin the Hereafter for him, and if others would find out about them, he would be beheaded." Upon hearing this, ʿĀ'ishah ﵂ pronounced, '*Allāhu Akbar* (Allah is great)' thrice and then added: "The Messenger of Allah ﷺ was asked the same question and he said '*Allāhu Akbar*' thrice and then said: 'Only the believer is tested.'"

(*Al-Maṭālib al-ʿĀliyah*: 3003)

312

عَنْ عَائِشَةَ رَضِيَ اللهُ عَنْهَا أَنَّ رَسُولَ اللَّهِ صَلَّى اللهُ عَلَيْهِ وَسَلَّمَ قَالَ: «إِذَا دَخَلَ عَلَيْكِ صَبِيُّ جَارِكِ، فَضَعِي فِي يَدِهِ شَيْئًا فَإِنَّهُ يَجُرُّ الْمَوَدَّ».

(المطالب العالية:٩٣٧٢)

ʿĀ'ishah ﷺ related that the Messenger of Allah ﷺ said: "When your neighbour's child enters your home, put something in his hand [as a gift] for this enhances affection [between neighbours]."

(*Al-Maṭālib al-ʿĀliyah*: 2739)

313

عَنْ عَائِشَةَ، قَالَتْ: «قُلْتُ: يَا رَسُولَ اللَّهِ، بِأَيِّ شَيْءٍ يَتَفَاضَلُ النَّاسُ فِي الدُّنْيَا؟» قَالَ صَلَّى اللهُ عَلَيْهِ وَسَلَّمَ: «بِالْعَقْلِ». قُلْتُ: «فَفِي الآخِرَ؟» قَالَ صَلَّى اللهُ عَلَيْهِ وَسَلَّمَ: «بِالْعَقْلِ». قَالَتْ: «قُلْتُ: إِنَّمَا يُجْزَوْنَ بِأَعْمَالِهِمْ!» قَالَ صَلَّى اللهُ عَلَيْهِ وَسَلَّمَ: «وَهَلْ عَمِلُوا إِلا بِقَدْرِ مَا أَعْطَاهُمُ اللهُ تَعَالَى مِنَ الْعَقْلِ؟ فَبِقَدْرِ مَا أُعْطُوا مِنَ الْعَقْلِ كَانَتْ أَعْمَالُهُمْ وَبِقَدْرِ مَا عَمِلُوا يُجْزَوْنَ».

(المطالب العالية:٢٧٦٨)

ʿĀ'ishah ﷺ related that she asked: "O Messenger of Allah, what is the thing that makes some people better than others in this world?" The Messenger of Allah ﷺ replied: "It is the intellect." I then asked him: "What is the thing that makes some people better than others in the life to come?" He said: "It is the intellect." I said: "But people are requited according to their deeds." The Messenger of Allah ﷺ explained: "Are not their deeds according to the measure of intellect that Allah the Most High has given them? Their deeds are according to the measure of intellect they have been given, and they are requited according to their deeds."

(*Al-Maṭālib al-ʿĀliyah*: 2768)

314

عَنْ عَائِشَةَ رَضِيَ اللهُ عَنْهَا، قَالَتْ: «مَرَّ رَسُولُ اللَّهِ صَلَّى اللهُ عَلَيْهِ وَسَلَّمَ بِأَرْضٍ يُقَالُ لَهَا غَبَرَةٌ فَقَالَ: هِيَ خَضِرَةٌ.

(المطالب العالية:٢٨٠٣)

ʿĀʾishah ﵂ related that once the Messenger of Allah ﷺ passed by a place called Ghabarah [dusty patch], so he renamed it as Khaḍirah [green patch].

(*Al-Maṭālib al-ʿĀliyah*: 2803)

315

عَنْ سَعِيدٍ بْنِ المُسَيَّبِ قَالَ: «قَالَتْ عَائِشَةُ رَضِيَ اللهُ عَنْهَا: رَأَيْتُ ثَلَاثَةَ أَقْمَارٍ سَقَطْنَ فِي حُجْرَتِي، فَسَأَلْتُ أَبَا بَكْرٍ رَضِيَ اللهُ عَنْهُ فقال: يَاعَائِشَةَ، إِنْ صَدَقَتْ رُؤْيَاكِ يُدْفَنُ فِي بَيْتِكِ خَيْرُ أَهْلِ الأَرْضِ ثَلَاثَةٌ. فَلَمَّا قُبِضَ رَسُولُ اللهِ صَلَّى اللهُ عَلَيْهِ وَسَلَّمَ وَدُفِنَ قَالَ لِي أَبُو بَكْرٍ رَضِيَ اللهُ عَنْهُ: يَاعَائِشَةَ هَذَا خَيْرُ أَقْمَارِكِ وهُوَ أَحَدُهَا».

(المطالب العالية:٢٨٤٨)

Sāʿīḍ ībn āl-Mūṣāyyīb related that ʿĀ'ishah ﷺ said: "I saw [in my dream] three moons falling into my room and so I asked Abū Bakr ﷺ [her father] about its interpretation. He answered: 'O ʿĀ'ishah, if your dream comes true, the three most outstanding people on earth will be buried in your room.' When the Messenger of Allah ﷺ died and was buried, Abū Bakr ﷺ said to me: 'O ʿĀ'ishah, this is the first and best of your three moons.'"

(*Al-Maṭālib al-ʿĀliyah*: 2848)

316

عَنْ عَائِشَةَ رَضِيَ اللهُ عَنْهَا قَالَتْ: «سُئِلَ رَسُولُ اللَّهِ صَلَّى اللهُ عَلَيْهِ وَسَلَّمَ عَنِ الشِّعْرِ، فَقَالَ: هُو كَلاَمٌ فَحَسَنُهُ حَسَنٌ وَقُبْحُهُ قَبِيحٌ».

(المطالب العالية:٢٦٠٣)

ʿĀʾishah ﷺ related that the Messenger of Allah ﷺ was asked about poetry, so he said: "Poetry is mere speech, that which is good of it is good, and that which is odious of it is odious."

(*Al-Maṭālib al-ʿĀliyah*: 2603)

317

عَنْ مَرْيَمِ بِنْتِ طَارِقٍ قَالَتْ: «دَخَلْتُ على عَائِشَةَ رَضِيَ اللهُ عَنْهَا .... فَذَكَرَتِ الحَدِيثَ، قَالَتْ: «وَقَدْ قَالَتْ اِمْرَأَةٌ لِعَائِشَةَ أُمِّ المُؤْمِنِينَ رَضِيَ اللهُ عَنْهَا: يَا أُمَّ الْمُؤْمِنِينَ! إِنَّ كَرِيِّي يَتَنَاوَلُ سَاقِي، فَأَعْرَضَتْ عائشةُ عَنْهَا بِوَجْهِهَا، وَقَالَتْ: أَخْرِجِيهَا، فَأُخْرِجَتِ المرأةُ عَنْهَا، ثُمَّ أَقْبَلَتْ عَائِشَةُ عَلَى النِّسَاءِ فَقَالَتْ: يَا نِسَاءَ الْمُؤْمِنِينَ! مَا يَمْنَعُ الْمَرْأَةَ إِذَا أَصَابَتِ الذَّنْبَ فَسُتِرَ عَلَيْهَا أَنْ تَسْتُرَ مَا سَتَرَ اللَّهُ عزَّ وَجَلَّ، وَلَا تُبْدِي لِلنَّاسِ، فَإِنَّ النَّاسَ يُعَيِّرُونَ وَلَا يُغَيِّرُونَ، وَإِنَّ اللهَ يُغَيِّرُ وَلَا يُعَيِّرُ».

(المطالب العالية :٩٠٦٢)

Maryam bint Ṭāriq related that once she visited ʻĀ'ishah ﵂ and there a woman said to ʻĀ'ishah ﵂: "O Mother of the Believers, the person from whom I hire a mount fondles my shank." Upon hearing this, she turned her face away and directed that the woman be thrown out. After she was driven out, she turned to the other women and said: "O wives of the believers, what prevents a woman who commits a sin from concealing what Allah has concealed and not divulge it to others? For verily, people reproach but do not change one, whereas Allah changes one and does not reproach."

(*Al-Maṭālib al-ʿĀliyah*: 2609)

318

عَنْ عَائِشَةَ رَضِيَ اللهُ عَنْهَا أَنّ رَسُولَ اللّهِ صَلَّى اللهُ عَلَيْهِ وَسَلَّمَ قَالَ لَهَا: «يَاعَائِشَةُ، إِنَّ الْفُحْشَ لَوْ كَانَ رَجُلًا لَكَانَ رَجُلَ سُوءٍ».

(المطالب العالية:٢٦٢٤)

ʿĀ'ishah ﷺ related that the Messenger of Allah ﷺ said to her: "O ʿĀ'ishah, indeed if obscenity were a man, he would be an evil man."

(*Al-Maṭālib al-ʿĀliyah*: 2624)

319

عَنْ أُمِّ عَلْقَمَةَ، مَوْلاَ عَائِشَةَ، قَالَتْ: «أَتَيْتُ عَائِشَةَ رَضِيَ اللهُ عَنْهَا بِغُلاَمٍ صَبِيٍّ تَدْعُو لَهُ، فَرَفَعُوا وِسَادَ كَانَ عَلَيْهَا الصَّبِيُّ، فَرَأَتْ عَائِشَةُ تَحْتَهَا مُوسَى، فَقَالَتْ: مَا هذِهِ؟ قَالَتْ: نَجْعَلُهَا مِنَ الْجِنِّ وَالْفَزَعِ. قَالَ: فَأَخَذَتْهَا عَائِشَةُ رَضِيَ اللهُ عَنْهَا فَرَمَتْ بِهَا وَقَالَتْ: إِنَّ رَسُولَ اللَّهِ صَلَّى اللهُ عَلَيْهِ وَسَلَّمَ كَانَ يُبْغِضُ الطِّيَرَ وَيَكْرَهُهَا».

(المطالب العالية :٦٩٤٢)

Umm ʿAlqamah, ʿĀ'ishah's slave girl, said: "One day I brought ʿĀ'ishah ﵂ a baby boy so that she may pray for him. When they removed the cushion on which the baby was placed, ʿĀ'ishah ﵂ noticed a razor underneath it. Upon enquiring about it, a woman said: 'We use it to ward off jinn and evil spirits.' ʿĀ'ishah ﵂ threw away the razor and said: 'The Messenger of Allah ﷺ loathed bad omens.'"

(*Al-Maṭālib al-ʿĀliyah*: 2496)

320

عَنْ عَائِشَةَ رَضِيَ اللهُ عَنْهَا، قَالَتْ: «قَالَ رَسُولُ اللَّهِ صَلَّى اللهُ عَلَيْهِ وَسَلَّمَ: أَنَا وَكَافِلُ الْيَتِيمِ فِي الْجَنَّةِ كَهَاتَيْنِ، وَجَمَعَ بَيْنَ السَّبَّابَةِ وَالْوُسْطَى، وَالسَّاعِي عَلَى الْيَتِيمِ وَالأَرْمَلَةِ وَالْمِسْكِينِ كَالْمُجَاهِدِ فِي سَبِيلِ اللَّهِ وَالصَّائِمِ الْقَائِمِ لاَ يَفْتُرُ»

(المطالب العالية:٢٥٦٥)

ʿĀ'ishah ﷺ related that the Messenger of Allah ﷺ said: "I and the guardian of the orphan will be like this - and he joined his index and middle fingers together - in Paradise. And the person who takes care of the needs of orphans, widows, and the needy is like the one who fights for the sake of Allah or like the person who constantly fasts and stands to pray at night."

(*Al-Maṭālib al-ʿĀliyah*: 2565)

321

عَنْ عَائِشَةَ، قَالَتْ: «أَتَيْتُ النَّبِيَّ صَلَّى اللهُ عَلَيْهِ وَسَلَّمَ بِابْنِ الزُّبَيْرِ فَحَنَّكَهُ بِتَمْرٍ وَقَالَ: هَذَا عَبْدُ اللَّهِ وَأَنْتِ أُمُّ عَبْدِ اللَّهِ».

(المطالب العالية :٦٠٣٢)

‘Ā’ishah رضي الله عنها said: “I took al-Zubayr’s baby son to the Prophet ﷺ and he chewed a date and ran it through the baby’s tongue (*taḥnīk*) and then he said: ‘This is ‘Abdullāh and you are Umm ‘Abdullāh.’”

(*Al-Maṭālib al-‘Āliyah*: 2306)

322

عَنْ عَائِشَةَ رَضِيَ اللهُ عَنْهَا، قَالَتْ: «قَالَ رَسُولُ اللَّهِ صَلَّى اللهُ عَلَيْهِ وَسَلَّمَ لِرَجُلٍ: كَمْ فِي بَيْتِكَ مِنْ بَرَكَةٍ؟» يَعْنِي: الشَّاءَ.

(المطالب العالية :٢٣٦٨)

'Āishah ﷺ related that the Messenger of Allah ﷺ asked a man: "How many blessings do you have at home?" By blessings he was referring to sheep.

(*Al-Maṭālib al-'Āliyah*: 2368)

323

عَنْ عَائِشَةَ رَضِيَ اللهُ عَنْهَا، قَالَتْ: «كَانَ رَسُولُ اللَّهِ صَلَّى اللهُ عَلَيْهِ وَسَلَّمَ يَأْكُلُ قَائِمًا وَقَاعِدًا».

(المطالب العالية :٢٤٠٤)

ʿĀʾishah ﷺ said: "The Messenger of Allah ﷺ used to eat both while standing and sitting."

(*Al-Maṭālib al-ʿĀliyah*: 2404)

324

عَنْ عَائِشَةَ رَضِيَ اللهُ عَنْهَا أَنَّ النَّبِيَّ صَلَّى اللهُ عَلَيْهِ وَسَلَّمَ كَانَ إِذَا أَرَادَ أَنْ يَأْكُلَ غَسَلَ يَدَيْهِ.

(المطالب العالية:٢٤٠٦)

ʿĀ'ishah ﵂ related that whenever the Prophet ﷺ wanted to eat, he washed his hands.

(*Al-Maṭālib al-ʿĀliyah*: 2406)

325

عَنْ أَبِي سَلَمَةَ قَالَ: «سَمِعْتُ عَائِشَةَ رَضِيَ اللهُ عَنْهَا تَقُولُ وَذُكِرَ عِنْدَهَا الزَّيْتُ: «كَانَ رَسُولُ اللَّهِ صَلَّى اللهُ عَلَيْهِ وَسَلَّمَ يَأْمُرُ أَنْ يُؤْكَلَ وَيُدَّهَنَ بِهِ، وَيَقُولُ: إِنَّهَا مِنْ شَجَرٍ مُبَارَكَةٍ».

(المطالب العالية :٢٤١٧)

Abu Salamah related that he heard 'Ā'ishah ﵂, upon the mention of olive oil in her presence, say: "The Messenger of Allah ﷺ used to enjoin eating it and rubbing oneself with it, saying: 'It is from a blessed tree.'"

(*Al-Maṭālib al-'Āliyah*: 2417)

326

عَنْ عَائِشَةَ رَضِيَ اللهُ عَنْهَا، قَالَتْ: «لَعَنَ رَسُولُ اللَّهِ صَلَّى اللهُ عَلَيْهِ وَسَلَّمَ الرَّاشِيَ وَالْمُرْتَشِيَ».

(المطالب العالية :٢١٨٦)

ʿĀ'ishah ﷺ said: "The Messenger of Allah ﷺ cursed the person who bribes others as well as the person who takes bribes."

(*Al-Maṭālib al-ʿĀliyah*: 2186)

327

عَنْ أُمِّ الْمُغِيرَ، مَوْلَاةِ الأَنْصَارِ، قَالَتْ: «سَأَلْتُ عَائِشَةَ رَضِيَ اللهُ عَنْهَا عَنِ الْحَرِيرِ، يلْبَسُهُ النِّسَاءُ؟ قَالَتْ: كُنَّا نُكْسَى عَلَى عَهْدِ رَسُولِ اللَّهِ صَلَّى اللهُ عَلَيْهِ وَسَلَّمَ ثِيَابًا يُقَالُ لَهَا السِّيَرَاءُ».

(المطالب العالية :٢٢٣٩)

Umm al-Mughīrah, a client woman of the Anṣār, related that she asked ʿĀ'ishah ﷺ if women can wear silk and she replied: "In the time of the Messenger of Allah ﷺ we used to wear clothes called al-Siyarā' [they were made of silk]."

(*Al-Maṭālib al-ʿĀliyah*: 2239)

328

عَنْ عَائِشَةَ قَالَتْ: «كَانَ رَسُولُ اللهِ ﷺ لَا يَزِيدُهُ ذَا شَرَفٍ عِنْدَهُ وَلَا يُنْقِصُهُ إِلَّا التَّقْوَى».

(المعجم الأوسط للطبراني:٦٢٣٧)

ʿĀ'ishah ﵂ said: "The Messenger of Allah ﷺ did not treat people of nobility more favourably than others nor did he treat anyone less favourably unless it be because of [lack of] Godfearingness."

(*Al-Muʿjam al-Awsaṭ* of al-Ṭabarānī: 7326)

329

عَنْ عَائِشَةَ رَضِيَ اللهُ عَنْهَا، قَالَتْ: «قَالَ رَسُولُ اللَّهِ صَلَّى اللهُ عَلَيْهِ وَسَلَّمَ: مَنْ قُتِلَ كَانَ كَفَّارَ لِكُلِّ ذَنْبٍ دُونَ الشِّرْكِ».

(ااطاا.، العالية :٠٥٩١)

ʿĀ'ishah ﵂ related that the Messenger of Allah ﷺ said: "When a person is killed, his killing would serve as an expiation for all his sin except associating others with Allah."

(*Al-Maṭālib al-ʿĀliyah*: 1950)

330

عَنِ ابْنِ أَبِي مُلَيْكَةَ أَنَّ عَائِشَةَ رَضِيَ اللهُ عَنْهَا كَانَتْ إِذَا سُئِلَتْ عَنِ الْمُتْعَةِ قَالَتْ: «بَيْنِي وَبَيْنَهُمْ كِتَابُ اللَّهِ، قَالَ اللَّهُ عَزَّ وَجَلَّ: {وَالَّذِينَ هُمْ لِفُرُوجِهِمْ حَافِظُونَ إِلَّا عَلَى أَزْوَاجِهِمْ أَوْ مَا مَلَكَتْ أَيْمَانُهُمْ فَإِنَّهُمْ غَيْرُ مَلُومِينَ} [المؤمنون: 6-5] ، فَمَنِ ابْتَغَى غَيْرَ مَا زَوَّجَهُ اللَّهُ عَزَّ وَجَلَّ أَوْ مَا مَلَكَهُ فَقَدْ عَدَا».

(المطالب العالية :١٧٢٢)

Ibn Abī Mulaykah related that whenever ʿĀ'ishah ﵂ was asked about temporary marriage (*mut'ah*) she would reply: "The Book of Allah stands as a judge between me and them. Allah, glorified and exalted is He, says: {Those who abstain from sex, except with their wives, or those whom their right hands possess. For in this case, they are free from any blame}." [*al-Mu'minūn* 23: 5–6], and so, whoever seeks sexual relations with anyone other than his wives or slave girls has transgressed."

(*Al-Maṭālib al-ʿĀliyah*: 1722)

331

عن عَائِشَةَ رَضِيَ اللهُ عَنْهَا قَالَتْ: «لَا أُحِلُّ مُسْكِرًا وَإِنْ كَانَ خُبْزًا أَوْ كَانَتْ مَاءً».

(المطالب العالية :١٨٢٨)

ʿĀʾishah ﵂ said: "I do not declare any intoxicant to be lawful, even if it was bread or water."

(*Al-Maṭālib al-ʿĀliyah*: 1828)

332

عَنْ عَائِشَةَ رَضِيَ اللهُ عَنْهَا، قَالَتْ: «قَالَ رَسُولُ اللَّهِ صَلَّى اللهُ عَلَيْهِ وَسَلَّمَ: «الْعِبَادُ عِبَادُ اللَّهِ وَالْبِلادُ بِلادُ اللَّهِ وَلَيْسَ لِعِرْقٍ ظَالِمٍ حَقٌّ».

(المطالب العالية:١٥٠٥)

ʿĀ'ishah ﷺ related that the Messenger of Allah ﷺ said: "All the servants are Allah's servants and all the land is His, and no one has a right over someone's else land just because he has planted something on it."

(*Al-Maṭālib al-ʿĀliyah*: 1505)

333

عَنْ عَائِشَةَ أَنّ النَّبِيَّ صَلَّى اللهُ عَلَيْهِ وَسَلَّمَ مَرَّ بِقَوْمٍ يُلَقِّحُونَ فَقَالَ: «لَوْ لَمْ تَفْعَلُوا لَصَلُحَ». قَالَتْ: «فَخَرَجَ شِيصًا، فَمَرَّ بِهِمْ، فَقَالَ:مَا لِنَخْلِكُمْ؟»

قَالُوا: «قُلْتَ كَذَا وَكَذَا». قَالَ: «أَنْتُمْ أَعْلَمُ بِأَمْرِ دُنْيَاكُمْ».

((صحيح مسلم:٦١٢٨

ʿĀ'ishah ﷺ related that the Prophet ﷺ passed by some peoples who were engaged in grafting their trees and he remarked: "It will come good if you did not do that." [So they did as he said] but the result was poor quality dates. The Prophet ﷺ happened to pass by them again and asked them: "What happened to your palm trees?" They said: "You said such-and-such' [you told us not to graft them]. The Prophet ﷺ replied: "You know better than me your worldly matters."

(*Ṣaḥīḥ Muslim*: 6128)

334

عَنْ عَائِشَةَ رَضِيَ اللهُ عَنْهَا قَالَتْ: «إِنَّ النَّبِيَّ صَلَّى اللهُ عَلَيْهِ وَسَلَّمَ قَالَ: «إِنَّ اللَّهَ تَبَارَكَ وَتَعَالَى يُحِبُّ إِذَا عَمِلَ أَحَدُكُمْ عَمَلًا أَنْ يُتْقِنَهُ».

(المطالب العالية :١٣٤٤)

ʿĀʾishah ﵄ related that the Prophet ﷺ said: "Indeed, Allah loves, when one of you does a job, that he does well."

(*Al-Maṭālib al-ʿĀliyah*: 1344)

335

عَنْ عَائِشَةَ أَنَّهُ بَلَغَهَا أَنَّ ابْنَ عُمَرَ يُحَدِّثُ عَنْ أَبِيهِ عُمَرَ بْنِ الْخَطَّابِ أَنَّ رَسُولَ اللَّهِ صَلَّى اللهُ عَلَيْهِ وَسَلَّمَ قَالَ: «الْمَيِّتُ يُعَذَّبُ بِبُكَاءِ أَهْلِهِ عَلَيْهِ»، فَقَالَتْ: «يَرْحَمُ اللهُ عُمَرَ وَابْنَ عُمَرَ فَوَاللَّهِ مَا هُمَا بِكَاذِبَيْنِ وَلَا مُكَذَّبَيْنِ وَلَا مُتَزَيِّدَيْنِ، إِنَّمَا قَالَ ذَلِكَ رَسُولُ اللَّهِ صَلَّى اللهُ عَلَيْهِ وَسَلَّمَ فِي رَجُلٍ مِنَ الْيَهُودِ وَمَرَّ بِأَهْلِهِ وَهُمْ يَبْكُونَ عَلَيْهِ فَقَالَ: إِنَّهُمْ لَيَبْكُونَ عَلَيْهِ وَإِنَّ اللَّهَ عَزَّ وَجَلَّ لَيُعَذِّبُهُ فِي قَبْرِهِ».

(مسند أحمد :٦٣١٩)

It was related to 'Ā'ishah ﷺ that Ibn 'Umar ﷺ reports from his father 'Umar ibn al-Khaṭṭāb that the Messenger of Allah said: "A deceased person is chastised because of the crying of his family over him." So she said: "May Allah have mercy on 'Umar and his son 'Abdullāh; by Allah, they are not liars nor are they of those that one cries lie to what they say. However, the Messenger of Allah ﷺ said that regarding a Jewish man who died and he saw his family crying over him when he passed by them, and so he remarked: 'They are crying over him while Allah, glorified and exalted is He, is chastising him in his grave.'"

(*Musnad Aḥmad*: 6319)

336

عَنْ أَبِي عُبَيْدَ بْنِ عَبْدِ اللَّهِ قَالَ: «قُلْتُ لِعَائِشَةَ مَا الْكَوْثَرُ؟ قَالَتْ: نَهْرٌ أُعْطِيَهُ النَّبِيُّ صَلَّى اللهُ عَلَيْهِ وَسَلَّمَ فِي بُطْنَانِ الْجَنَّةِ». قَالَ: «قُلْتُ: وَمَا بُطْنَانُ الْجَنَّةِ؟» قَالَتْ: «وَسَطُهَا، حَافَّتَاهُ دُرٌّ مُجَوَّفٌ».

(مسند أحمد :٦٣١٣)

Abū ʻUbaydah ibn ʻAbdullāh related that he asked ʻĀ'ishah ﵂: "What is al-Kawthar?" She replied: "It is a river that the Prophet ﷺ is given in the *Buṭnān* of Paradise." Again he asked her: "What is the *Buṭnān* of Paradise?" She said: "It is its middlemost part and there are pearls around it."

(*Musnad Aḥmad*: 6313)

337

عَنْ عَائِشَةَ أَنّ النَّبِيَّ صَلَّى اللهُ عَلَيْهِ وَسَلَّمَ قَالَ: «النِّكَاحُ من سُنَّتِي فمَنْ لمْ يَعْمَلْ بِسُنَّتِي فَليسَ مِنِّي وتَزَوَّجُوا فَإِنِّي مُكَاثِرٌ بِكُمُ الأُمَمَ، ومَنْ كَانَ ذَا طَوْلٍ فَلْيَنْكِحْ وَمَنْ لمْ يَجِدْ فَعَلَيْهِ بِالصِّيامِ فَإِنَّ الصَّوْمَ لَهُ وِجَاءٌ».

(سنن ابن ماجه:١٨٤٦)

Āʾishah ﷺ related that the Prophet ﷺ said: "Getting married is part of my practice and whoever does not follow my practice is not of me; do marry, for I will show off your great number to the other communities [on the Day of Judgement]. Whoever has the means, let him marry; and whoever does not, let him fast for fasting is a protection for him."

(*Sunan Ibn Mājah*: 1846)

338

عَنْ عَائِشَةَ أَنَّهُ ذُكِرَ لَهَا أَنَّ نَاسًا يَقْرَؤُونَ الْقُرْآنَ فِي اللَّيْلَةِ مَرَّةً أَوْ مَرَّتَيْنِ، فَقَالَتْ: «أُولَئِكَ قَرَؤُوا وَلَمْ يَقْرَؤُوا. كُنْتُ أَقُومُ مَعَ رَسُولِ اللَّهِ صَلَّى اللَّهُ عَلَيْهِ وَسَلَّمَ لَيْلَةَ التَّمَامِ، فَكَانَ يَقْرَأُ سُورَ الْبَقَرَةِ وَآلِ عِمْرَانَ وَالنِّسَاءِ فَلَا يَمُرُّ بِآيَةٍ فِيهَا تَخَوُّفٌ إِلَّا دَعَا اللَّهَ عَزَّ وَجَلَّ وَاسْتَعَاذَ، وَلَا يَمُرُّ بِآيَةٍ فِيهَا اسْتِبْشَارٌ إِلَّا دَعَا اللَّهَ عَزَّ وَجَلَّ وَرَغِبَ إِلَيْهِ».

(مسند أحمد:٩٠٦٤٢)

It was mentioned to ʿĀ'ishah ﵂ that some people recite the entire Qur'ān once or twice in one single night, and so she said: "Such people do recite [the Qur'ān] but it is as if they do not recite it. I used to stand to pray along with the Messenger of Allah ﷺ the whole night and he would recite *Sūrah al-Baqarah* and Sūrah *Āl ʿImrān* and *Sūrah al-Nisā'* but he never recited a verse in which there is prompting of fear except that he supplicated Allah, glorified and exalted is He, and sought refuge in Him, and he never recited a verse in which there is good to be hopeful about except that he supplicated Allah, glorified and exalted is He, and asked for it."

(*Musnad Aḥmad*, 24609)

339

عن عَائِشَةَ قَالَتْ: «قَالَ رَسُولُ اللهِ عَلَى المِنْبَرِ وَالنَّاسُ حَوْلَهُ: أَيُّها النَّاسُ، اسْتَحْيُوا مِنَ اللهِ حَقَّ الحَيَاءِ»، فَقَالَ رَجُلٌ: «يَا رَسُولَ اللهِ، إِنَّا لَنَسْتَحِي مِنَ اللهِ تَعَالَى». فَقَالَ: «مَنْ كَانَ مِنْكُمْ مُسْتَحْيِيًا فَلَا يَبِيتَنَّ لَيْلَةً إِلَّا وَأَجَلُهُ بَيْنَ عَيْنَيْهِ وَلْيَحْفَظِ البَطْنَ وَمَا حَوَى وَالرَّأْسَ وَمَا حَوَى وَلْيَذْكُرِ المَوْتَ وَالبِلَى وَلْيَتْرُكْ زِينَةَ الدُّنْيَا».

(المعجم الأوسط للطبراني:٧٣٠٤)

ʿĀʾishah ﷺ related that, one day while standing on the minbar surrounded by people, the Messenger of Allah ﷺ said: "O people, be truly diffident vis-à-vis Allah!" A man said: "O Messenger of Allah, we are diffident vis-à-vis Allah the Most High." The Prophet ﷺ replied: "If one of you is really diffident vis-à-vis Allah, then let him not spend a night without remembering the limited time he has in this world, let him protect his belly and what he consumes, and let him protect his head and the thoughts that cross it, and let him remember death and the disintegration of the body [in the grave], and let him leave the bedazzlement of this world."

(*Al-Muʿjam al-Awsaṭ* of al-Ṭabarānī: 7304)

340

عن عَائِشَةَ قالت: «قَالَ رَسُولُ اللهِ ﷺ: تَخَيَّرُوا لِنُطَفِكُمْ وَانْكِحُوا الأَكْفَاءَ وَأَنْكِحُوا إِلَيْهِمْ».

(سنن ابن ماجه:١٩٦٨)

ʿĀ'ishah ﵂ related that the Messenger of Allah ﷺ said: "Choose well the woman you want to be the mother of your children; marry those who are socially compatible with you, and give your daughters to the same as brides."

(*Sunan Ibn Mājah*: 1968)

341

سُئِلَتْ عَائِشَةَ: «بِأَيِّ شَيْءٍ كَانَ يُوتِرُ رَسُولُ اللَّهِ صَلَّى اللهُ عَلَيْهِ وَسَلَّمَ». قَالَتْ: «كَانَ يَقْرَأُ فِي الرَّكْعَةِ الأُولَى بِـ {سَبِّحِ اسْمَ رَبِّكَ الأَعْلَى} وَفِي الثَّانِيَةِ {قُلْ يَا أَيُّهَا الْكَافِرُونَ} وَفِي الثَّالِثَةِ {قُلْ هُوَ اللَّهُ أَحَدٌ} وَالْمُعَوِّذَتَيْنِ».

(سنن ابن ماجة :١١٧٣)

ʿĀ'ishah ﵂ was asked: "Which parts of the Qur'ān did the Prophet ﷺ recite in his *witr* prayer?" She replied: "*Sūrah al-Aʿlā* in the first unit, *Sūrah al-Kāfirūn* in the second, and *Sūrah al-Ikhlāṣ* in the third."

(*Sunan Ibn Mājah* 1173)

342

عَنْ يَزِيدِ بْنِ أَبِي حَبِيبٍ قَالَ: «قَالَتْ عَائِشَةُ: «كَانَ رَسُولُ اللَّهِ صَلَّى اللهُ عَلَيْهِ وَسَلَّمَ إِذَا تَكَلَّمَ تَكَلَّمَ نَزْرًا وَأَنْتُمْ تَنْثُرُونَ الكَلَامَ نَثْرًا».

(مسند إسحاق بن راهويه:١٦٧٩)

Yazīd ibn Abī Ḥabīb related that ʿĀ'ishah ﵂ said: "The Messenger of Allah ﷺ spoke in a focused and precise manner whereas you people talk in a haphazard way."

(*Musnad Isḥāq ibn Rāhawayh*: 1679)

343

عَنْ عَبْدِ اللَّهِ بْنِ أَبِي قَيْسٍ، قَالَ: «سَأَلْتُ عَائِشَةَ: كَيْفَ كَانَتْ قِرَاءَةُ رَسُولِ اللَّهِ صَلَّى اللهُ عَلَيْهِ وَسَلَّمَ بِاللَّيْلِ يَجْهَرُ أَمْ يُسِرُّ؟» قَالَتْ: «كُلُّ ذَلِكَ قَدْ كَانَ يَفْعَلُ رُبَّمَا جَهَرَ، وَرُبَّمَا أَسَرَّ».

(مسند إسحاق بن راهويه :١٦٧٧)

ʿAbdullāh ibn Abī Qays related that he asked ʿĀ'ishah ﵂: "How was the recitation of the Messenger of Allah ﷺ in his prayer at night: was it a silent or loud recitation?" She said: "He did both: sometimes he recited aloud and sometimes silently."

(*Musnad Isḥāq ibn Rāhawayh*: 1677)

344

عَنْ عَبْدِ اللَّهِ بْنِ أَبِي قَيْسٍ قَالَ: «سَمِعْتُ عَائِشَةَ تَقُولُ: إِنْ كَانَتْ إِحْدَانَا لَتَحْرُمُ عَلَيْهَا الصَّلَاةُ فَيَأْمُرُهَا رَسُولُ اللَّهِ صَلَّى اللهُ عَلَيْهِ وَسَلَّمَ أَنْ تَسْدِلَ إِزَارَهَا ثُمَّ تَدْخُلُ مَعَهُ فِي اللِّحَافِ».

(مسند إسحاق بن راهويه :١٦٧٤)

ʿAbdullāh ibn Abī Qays related that he heard ʿĀ'ishah ﷺ say: "Indeed, it happened that one of us [the Prophet's wives] were in a state of menstruation and the Messenger of Allah ﷺ would direct her to cover her lower part of the body and then share a blanket with him."

(*Musnad Isḥāq ibn Rāhawayh*: 1674)

345

عَنْ عَبْدِ اللَّهِ بْنِ أَبِي قَيْسٍ، قَالَ: "سَأَلْتُ عَائِشَةَ: بِكَمْ كَانَ رَسُولُ اللَّهِ صَلَّى اللَّهُ عَلَيْهِ وَسَلَّمَ يُوتِرُ؟» فَقَالَتْ: «بِأَرْبَعٍ وَثَلَاثٍ، وَبِسِتٍ وَثَلَاثٍ، وَثَمَانٍ وَثَلَاثٍ، وَعَشْرٍ وَثَلَاثٍ، وَلَمْ يَكُنْ يُوتِرُ بِأَكْثَرَ مِنْ ثَلَاثَ عَشْرَ وَلَا أَنْقَصَ مِنْ سَبْعٍ، وَكَانَ لَا يَدَعُ رَكْعَتَيْ الفَجْرِ».

(مسند إسحاق بن راهويه :١٦٦٧)

'Abdullāh ibn Qays related that he asked 'Ā'ishah ﵂ about the number of units that the Messenger of Allah ﷺ offered in his night prayers, so she said: "four and three, and six and three, and eight and three, and 10 and three. He never prayed more than 13 units nor less than seven, and he never missed the two units of Fajr."

(*Musnad Isḥāq ibn Rāhawayh*: 1667)

346

عَنْ خَالِدِ بْنِ مَعْدَانٍ عَنْ عَائِشَةَ قَالَتْ: «كَانَ رَسُولُ اللَّهِ صَلَّى اللهُ عَلَيْهِ وَسَلَّمَ يَتَحَرَّى صِيَامَ الاِثْنَيْنِ وَالخَمِيسِ».

(مسند إسحاق بن راهويه :١٦٦٥)

Khālid ibn Maʿdān related that ʿĀ'ishah ﵂ said: "The Messenger of Allah ﷺ made it a point to fast Mondays and Thursdays."

(*Musnad Isḥāq ibn Rāhawayh*: 1665)

347

عَنْ أَبِي إِسْحَاقَ قَالَ: «سُئِلَ ابْنُ عُمَرَ: اعْتَمَرَ رَسُولُ اللَّهِ صَلَّى اللَّهُ عَلَيْهِ وَسَلَّمَ ؟» فقال: «لا». فَبَلَغَ ذَلِكَ أُمَّ الْمُؤْمِنِينَ فَقَالَتْ: «يَرْحَمِ اللهُ أَبَا عَبْدِ الرَّحْمَنِ، لَقَدْ عَلِمَ أَنّ رَسُولَ اللَّهِ صَلَّى اللَّهُ عَلَيْهِ وَسَلَّمَ اعْتَمَرَ أَرْبَعًا، إِحْدَاهُنَّ فِي حَجَّةِ الوَدَاعِ».

(مسند إسحاق بن راهويه :١٦٥٢)

Abū Isḥāq related that Ibn ʿUmar ﵄ was asked whether the Messenger of Allah ﷺ had performed *ʿumrah* and he replied in the negative. When ʿĀ'ishah ﵄ learnt this, she said: "May Allah have mercy on Abū ʿAbd al-Raḥmān [the agnomen of Ibn ʿUmar ﵄]! He well knows that the Messenger of Allah ﷺ did perform *ʿumrah* four times, one of which was at his Farewell *Ḥajj*."

(*Musnad Isḥāq ibn Rāhawayh*: 1652)

348

عَنِ الشَّعْبِي أَنَّ عَائِشَةَ قَالَتْ لِابْنِ أبي السَّائِبِ وَكَانَ قَاصًّا: «اجْتَنِبْ السَّجْعَ مِنَ الدُّعَاءِ فَإِنِّي عَهِدْتُ رَسُولَ اللَّهِ صَلَّى اللَّهُ عَلَيْهِ وَسَلَّمَ وَأَصْحَابَهُ وَكَانُوا لَا يَفْعَلُونَ ذَلِكَ».

(مسند إسحاق بن راهويه :١٦٣٤)

Al-Sha'bī related that 'Ā'ishah ﵂ said to Ibn Abī al-Sā'ib, who was a storyteller: "Shun using rhyming in your supplications for the Messenger of Allah ﷺ and his Companions did not do that."

(*Musnad Isḥāq ibn Rāhawayh*: 1634)

349

عَنْ عَائِشَةَ أَنَّهَا قَالَتْ: «يَا رَسُولَ اللهِ، إِنَّ ابْنَ جَدْعَانَ - وَكَانَ ابْنَ عَمِّهَا - كَانَ يُقْرِي الضَّيْفَ وَيَصِلُ الرَّحِمَ وَيَفُكُّ العَانِي فِي الجَاهِلِيَّةِ فَهَلْ يَنْفَعُهُ ذَلِكَ؟» فَقَالَ: «لَا، إِنَّهُ لَمْ يَقُلْ يَوْمًا: رَبِّ اغْفِرْ لِي خَطِيئَتِي يَوْمَ الدِّينِ».

(مسند إسحاق بن راهويه :١٣٦١)

One day ʿĀ'ishah ﵂ said to the Prophet ﷺ: "O Messenger of Allah, Ibn Jadʿān – a cousin of hers – used to receive and honour guests, maintain ties of kinship and free captives in the pre-Islamic period, would all that benefit him?" The Prophet ﷺ replied: "No! For he never said: O my Lord, forgive my sins on the Day of Judgement."

(*Musnad Isḥāq ibn Rāhawayh*: 1631)

350

عَنْ عَائِشَةَ قَالَتْ: قَالَ لِي أَبِي: «أَلَا أُعَلِّمُكِ دُعَاءً عَلَّمَنِيهِ رَسُولُ اللَّهِ صَلَّى اللهُ عَلَيْهِ وَسَلَّمَ ، وَكَانَ عِيسَى يُعَلِّمُهُ الْحَوَارِيِّينَ، لَوْ كَانَ عَلَيْكِ دَيْنٌ مِثْلُ أُحُدٍ قُلْتِيهِ لَقَضَاهُ اللهُ عَنْكِ».قَالَتْ: «قُلْتُ:بَلَى»، قَالَ: «قُولِي:اللَّهُمَّ فَارِجَ الْهَمِّ وَكَاشِفَ الْكَرْبِ مُجِيبَ دَعْوَ الْمُضْطَرِّ رَحْمَنَ الدُّنْيَا وَالْآخِرَ، أَنْتَ رَحْمَانِي فَارْحَمْنِي رَحْمَةً تُغْنِينِي بِهَا عَمَّنْ سِوَاكَ».

(مُسْنَد البَزَّار: ٦/٦٨)

'Āishah ﷺ said: "One day my father [Abū Bakr al-Ṣiddīq ﷺ] said to me: 'Shall I not teach you a supplication that the Messenger of Allah ﷺ taught me? Prophet 'Īsā ﷺ too used to teach it to his disciples. Through this supplication Allah will repay your debts even if they were as huge as the Mount of Uḥud.' I said: 'Please do.' He said: 'Say: O Allah, Reliever of distress, Remover of anxiety, Answerer of the call of the one in duress, Most Merciful in this world and the next, You are One who has most mercy on me, so have mercy on me in a way that makes me need no one besides You.'"

(*Musnad al-Bazzār*: 6: 86)

351

عَنْ عَائِشَةَ، قَالَتْ: «جَاءَ سَائِلٌ إِلَى رَسُولِ اللَّهِ صَلَّى اللهُ عَلَيْهِ وَسَلَّمَ وَفِي الْبَيْتِ ضَبٌّ فَقَالَ رَسُولُ اللَّهِ صَلَّى اللهُ عَلَيْهِ وَسَلَّمَ : إِنَّا لَا نُطْعِمُهُ مِمَّا لَا نَأْكُلُ».

(مسند إسحاق بن راهويه :١٢٦١)

ʿĀ'ishah ﵂ said: "One day a beggar came to the Messenger of Allah ﷺ when we did not have at home anything but a lizard, so the Messenger of Allah ﷺ said: 'We do not give him to eat what we do not eat ourselves.'"

(*Musnad Isḥāq ibn Rāhawayh*: 1621)

352

عَنْ عَائِشَةَ قَالَتْ سَمِعْتُ رَسُولَ اللَّهِ صَلَّى اللهُ عَلَيْهِ وَسَلَّمَ يَقُولُ: «مَنْ صَلَّى صَلَاةً لَمْ يَقْرَأْ فِيهَا بِأُمِّ الْقُرْآنِ فَهِيَ خِدَاجٌ».

(مسند أحمد:٢٥٠٩٩)

ʿĀ'ishah ﵂ related that she heard the Messenger of Allah ﷺ say: "Whoever does not recite the Mother of the Book [*Sūrah al-Fātiḥah*] in his prayer, his prayer is defective."

(*Musnad Aḥmad*: 25099)

353

عَنْ أُمِّ الدَّرْدَاءِ أَنَهَا قَالَتْ: «سَأَلْتُ عَائِشَةَ عَمَّنْ دَخَلَ الْجَنَّةَ مِمَّنْ قَرَأَ الْقُرْآنَ: مَا فَضْلُهُ عَلَى مَنْ لَمْ يَقْرَأْهُ؟» فَقَالَتْ عَائِشَةَ: «إِنَّ عَدَدَ دَرَجِ الْجَنَةِ بِعَدَدِ آيِ الْقُرْآنِ، فَمَنْ دَخَلَ الْجَنَّةَ مِمَّنْ قَرَأَ الْقُرْآنَ فَلَيْسَ فَوْقَهُ أَحَدٌ».

(المُصَنَّفُ لِابْنِ أَبِي شَيْبَةَ:٣٠٥٧٢)

Umm al-Dardā' ﵂ related that she asked 'Ā'ishah ﵂: "The one who enters Paradise and is amongst the reciters of the Qur'ān, does he have any merit over the one who does not recite it?" She replied: "The number of ranks in Paradise are by the number of the verses of the Qur'ān; there is no one higher in rank than the one who enters Paradise and is amongst the reciters of the Qur'ān."

(*Al-Muṣannaf* of Ibn Abī Shabah: 30572)

354

عَنْ عَائِشَةَ، قَالَتْ: قَالَ رَسُولُ اللَّهِ صَلَّى اللهُ عَلَيْهِ وَسَلَّمَ: «مَنْ قَرَأَ الْقُرْآنَ فَأَعْرَبَهُ كَانَتْ لَهُ عِنْدَ اللَّهِ دَعْوَةٌ مُسْتَجَابَةٌ، إِنْ شَاءَ عَجَّلَهَا لَهُ فِي الدُّنْيَا، وَإِنْ شَاءَ ذَخَرَهَا لَهُ فِي الْآخِرَةِ».

(حلية الأولياء: ٦/٣٤٩)

'Āishah ﷺ related that the Messenger of Allah ﷺ said: "The one who recites the Qur'ān in a correct grammatical manner has, because of this, an answered supplication with Allah; if He wills, He brings it to be for him in this world; and if he wills, he defers it for him until the Hereafter."

(*Ḥilyat al-Awliyā'*: 6: 349)

355

عَنْ عَائِشَةَ قَالَتْ سَمِعْتُ رَسُولَ اللَّهِ صَلَّى اللهُ عَلَيْهِ وَسَلَّمَ يَقُولُ: «إِنَّ أَوَّلَ مَا يُكْفَأُ - قَالَ زَيْدٌ: يَعْنِي الْإِسْلَامَ - كَمَا يُكْفَأُ الْإِنَاءُ كَفْيَ الْخَمْرِ». فَقِيلَ: «فَكَيْفَ يَا رَسُولَ اللَّهِ وَقَدْ بَيَّنَ اللهُ فِيهَا مَا بَيَّنَ». قَالَ رَسُولُ اللَّهِ صَلَّى اللهُ عَلَيْهِ وَسَلَّمَ: «يُسَمُّونَهَا بِغَيْرِ اسْمِهَا فَيَسْتَحِلُّونَهَا».

(سنن الدارمى:٢٠٠٨)

ʿĀ'ishah ﵂ related that she heard the Messenger of Allah ﷺ say: "Indeed, the first thing to be reversed in it – i.e., in Islam – is the consumption of wine." Someone retorted: "How is that, O Messenger of Allah, when Allah has already stated its legal status?" The Messenger of Allah ﷺ said: "They will call it by a different name."

(*Sunan al-Dārimī*: 2008)

356

عَنْ عَائِشَةَ أَنَّ رَسُولَ اللَّهِ صَلَّى اللهُ عَلَيْهِ وَسَلَّمَ لَمَّا فَرَغَ مِنَ الْأَحْزَابِ دَخَلَ الْمُغْتَسَلَ فَاغْتَسَلَ، فَأَتَاهُ جِبْرِيلُ عَلَيْهِ السَّلَامُ قَالَتْ: «فَرَأَيْتُهُ مِنْ خَلَلِ الْبَيْتِ قَدْ عَصَبَ رَأْسَهُ الْغُبَارُ، فَقَالَ: يَا مُحَمَّدُ وَضَعْتُمْ سِلَاحَكُمْ؟ قَالَ جِبْرِيلُ: مَا أَلْقَيْنَا السِّلَاحَ بَعْدُ انْهَدْ إِلَى بَنِي قُرَيْظَةَ».

(مسند أحمد: ٩٠٣٤)

ʿĀ'ishah ﷺ related that when the Messenger of Allah ﷺ returned from the battle of the Battlements (*al-Aḥzāb*), he went to the lavatory and had a bath. Then Jibrīl ﷺ came to him. ʿĀ'ishah ﷺ said: "I saw him through the cracks of the room, and his head was covered with dust. He said: 'O Muḥammad, have you laid down your arms? As for us, we have not done so yet; proceed to Banū Qurayẓah.'"

(*Musnad Aḥmad*: 9036)

357

عَنْ أَبِي هُرَيْرَ قَالَ: «مَنْ أَدْرَكَتْهُ الصَّلَاةِ جُنُبًا لَمْ يَصُمْ». قَالَ فَذَكَرْتُ ذَلِكَ لِعَائِشَةَ فَقَالَتْ: «إِنَّهُ لَا يَقُولُ شَيْئًا قَدْ كَانَ رَسُولُ اللَّهِ صَلَّى اللهُ عَلَيْهِ وَسَلَّمَ يُصْبِحُ فِينَا جُنُبًا ثُمَّ يَقُومُ فَيَغْتَسِلُ فَيَأْتِيهِ بِلَالٌ فَيُؤْذِنُهُ بِالصَّلَاةِ فَيَخْرُجُ فَيُصَلِّي بِالنَّاسِ وَالْمَاءُ يَنْحَدِرُ فِي جِلْدِهِ ثُمَّ يَظَلُّ يَوْمَهُ ذَلِكَ صَائِمًا».

(مسند أحمد: ٢٨٢٤)

It is related that Abū Hurayrah ﵁ said: “Whoever finds himself in a state of major ritual impurity (*junub*) upon the arrival of the time of prayer, his should not fast.” When this view was reported to ‘Ā’ishah ﵂, she said: “What he is saying is of no consequence. The Messenger of Allah ﷺ used to get up in the morning in a state of major ritual impurity, perform a purificatory bath (*ghusl*) and then go out and lead people in prayer while water was still dripping from him, and then he would continue fasting that day.”

(*Musnad Aḥmad*: 2826)

358

عَنْ عَائِشَةَ قَالَتْ: «لَمَّا نَزَلَ عُذْرِي مِنْ السَّمَاءِ جَاءَنِي النَّبِيُّ صَلَّى اللهُ عَلَيْهِ وَسَلَّمَ فَأَخْبَرَنِي بِذَلِكِ، فَقُلْتُ: نَحْمَدُ اللَّهَ عَزَّ وَجَلَّ لَا نَحْمَدُكَ».

(مسند أحمد)

ʿĀ'ishah ﷺ said: "When my innocence [regarding the slander I was exposed to] came down from heaven, the Prophet ﷺ came to inform me about it, and I said: 'We praise Allah, glorified and exalted is He, not you.'"

(*Musnad Aḥmad*)

359

عَنْ عَائِشَةَ زَوْجِ النَّبِيِّ صَلَّى اللهُ عَلَيْهِ وَسَلَّمَ قَالَتْ: «مَرَّتْ بِرَسُولِ اللَّهِ صَلَّى اللهُ عَلَيْهِ وَسَلَّمَ الْحَوْلَاءُ بِنْتُ تُوَيْتٍ فَقِيلَ لَهُ: يَا رَسُولَ اللَّهِ إِنَّهَا تُصَلِّي بِاللَّيْلِ صَلَاةً كَثِيرَةً فَإِذَا غَلَبَهَا النَّوْمُ ارْتَبَطَتْ بِحَبْلٍ فَتَعَلَّقَتْ بِهِ. فَقَالَ رَسُولُ اللَّهِ صَلَّى اللهُ عَلَيْهِ وَسَلَّمَ: فَلْتُصَلِّ مَا قَوِيَتْ عَلَى الصَّلَاةِ فَإِذَا نَعَسَتْ فَلْتَنَمْ».

(مسند أحمد: ٦٢١٩)

‘Ā’ishah رضي الله عنها said: “Once al-Ḥawlā’ bint Tuwayt رضي الله عنها passed by the Messenger of Allah ﷺ, so it was said to him: ‘O Messenger of Allah, this woman prays throughout the night and when sleep overtakes her, she binds herself with a rope so that she remains standing.’ The Messenger of Allah ﷺ said: ‘Let her pray as long as she is able to do so but when slumber overtakes her, let her go to sleep.’”

(*Musnad Aḥmad*: 9126)

360

عَنْ عَائِشَةَ قَالَتْ قَالَ لِي رَسُولُ اللَّهِ صَلَّى اللهُ عَلَيْهِ وَسَلَّمَ: «يَا عَائِشَةُ إِنْ كُنْتِ أَلْمَمْتِ بِذَنْبٍ فَاسْتَغْفِرِي اللَّهَ فَإِنَّ التَّوْبَةَ مِنْ الذَّنْبِ النَّدَمُ وَالِاسْتِغْفَارُ».

(مسند أحمد:٦١٩١)

ʿĀ'ishah ﵂ related that [at the time of the slander campaign against her] the Messenger of Allah ﷺ said to her: "O ʿĀ'ishah, if you committed a sin, then seek forgiveness from Allah, for repentance from sin requires one's regret over the sin committed and seeking forgiveness [from Allah]."

(*Musnad Aḥmad*: 1916)

361

عَنْ عَائِشَةَ، قَالَتْ: «قَالَ رَسُولُ اللَّهِ صَلَّى اللهُ عَلَيْهِ وَسَلَّمَ: إِذَا أَكَلَ أَحَدُكُمْ طَعَامًا فَلْيَقُلْ: بِسْمِ اللَّهِ، فَإِنْ نَسِيَ فِي أَوَّلِهِ فَلْيَقُلْ: بِسْمِ اللَّهِ فِي أَوَّلِهِ وَآخِرِهِ».

(سنن والترمذى:٨٥٨١، سنن أبي داود:٧٦٧٣)

ʿĀ'ishah ﵂ related that the Messenger of Allah ﷺ said: "When one of you starts eating, let him say: 'In the name of Allah, Most Compassionate, Most Merciful (*bismillāh al-Raḥmān al-Raḥīm*).' If he forgets to say this at the beginning, then let him say: 'In the name of Allah, Most Compassionate, Most Merciful, at its beginning and at its end (*bismillāh fī awwalihi wa ākhirihi*.)

(*Sunan al-Tirmidhī*: 1858, *Sunan Abī Dāwūd*: 3767)

362

عَنْ عَائِشَةَ أَنَّ رَسُولَ اللَّهِ صَلَّى اللهُ عَلَيْهِ وَسَلَّمَ دَخَلَ عَلَيَّ بَيْتِي فِي إِزَارٍ وَرِدَاءٍ فَاسْتَقْبَلَ الْقِبْلَةَ وَبَسَطَ يَدَهُ ثُمَّ قَالَ: اللَّهُمَّ إِنَّمَا أَنَا بَشَرٌ فَأَيُّ عَبْدٍ مِنْ عِبَادِكَ شَتَمْتُ أَوْ آذَيْتُ فَلَا تُعَاقِبْنِي فِيهِ».

(مسند أحمد:٦١٤٦)

ʿĀ'ishah ﵁ related that one day the Messenger of Allah ﷺ came to my apartment wearing an upper and lower garment, then he turned towards the *qiblah*, raised his hands and said: "O Allah, I am only a human being, so if I have ever hit or hurt any of Your servants, do not punish me for it."

(*Musnad Aḥmad*: 6416)

363

عَنْ عَائِشَةَ قَالَتْ: «كَانَ رَسُولُ اللَّهِ صَلَّى اللهُ عَلَيْهِ وَسَلَّمَ إِذَا فَاتَهُ الْقِيَامُ مِنْ اللَّيْلِ غَلَبَتْهُ عَيْنَاهُ بِنَوْمٍ أَوْ وَجَعٍ صَلَّى ثِنْتَيْ عَشْرَ رَكْعَةً مِنْ النَّهَارِ».

(مسند أحمد:٦١٣٦)

ʿĀ'ishah ﵂ said: "When the Messenger of Allah ﷺ missed his prayer at night due to his illness or overwhelming sleep, he prayed twelve units of prayer the following day [in the daytime]."

(*Musnad Aḥmad*: 6316)

364

عَنْ عَائِشَةَ قَالَتْ :«كان رَسُولُ اللهِ صَلَّى اللهُ عَلَيْهِ وَسَلَّمَ إِذَا أَخَذَ أَهْلَهُ الوَعْكُ، أَمَرَ بِالحَسَاءِ فَصُنِعَ، ثُمَّ أَمَرَهُمْ فَحَسَوا مِنْهُ، وَكَانَ يَقُولُ: إِنَّهُ لَيَرْتُو فُؤَادَ الحَزِينِ وَيَسْرُو عَنْ فُؤَادِ السَّقِيمِ، كَمَا تَسْرُو إِحْدَاكُنَّ الوَسَخَ بِالمَاءِ عَنْ وَجْهِهَا».

(مسند أحمد:٤٠٢١)

Ā'ishah ﵂ said: "Whenever any family member of the Messenger of Allah ﷺ became unwell, he ordered that broth be made and then he made them eat from it. He used to say: 'It fortifies the heart of a grieving person and removes his worries like a woman washes her face to clear dirt.'"

(*Musnad Aḥmad*: 1204)

365

عَنْ عَائِشَةَ أَنَّ رَسُولَ اللَّهِ صَلَّى اللهُ عَلَيْهِ وَسَلَّمَ كَانَ يَنَامُ أَوَّلَ اللَّيْلِ وَيُحْيِي آخِرَهُ.

(مسند أحمد:٦٠٧٤)

ʿĀ'ishah ﷺ related that the Messenger of Allah ﷺ used to sleep in the first part of the night and wake up to pray in the last part of it.

(*Musnad Aḥmad*: 4706)

Index